the escape artist

Center Point
Large Print

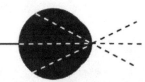

**This Large Print Book carries the
Seal of Approval of N.A.V.H.**

the escape artist

HELEN FREMONT

CENTER POINT LARGE PRINT
THORNDIKE, MAINE

This Center Point Large Print edition
is published in the year 2020 by arrangement with
Gallery Books, a division of Simon & Schuster, Inc.

The text of this Large Print edition is unabridged.
In other aspects, this book may vary
from the original edition.
Printed in the United States of America
on permanent paper.
Set in 16-point Times New Roman type.

ISBN: 978-1-64358-592-5

The Library of Congress has cataloged this record under
Library of Congress Control Number: 2020931015

For Donna

author's note

This memoir, as well as its predecessor, *After Long Silence*, attempts to make sense of the secrets that underlie the family in which I grew up. In both books, I have changed many names, locations, and other identifying details to provide a measure of privacy to my family and others, and to underscore that this is my story. I have been careful in making changes to select settings that are consistent with the actual events described. Because different events are considered in this volume, readers of both works will notice that I have changed the geographic setting and other details from those provided in my first volume to better maintain this consistency with the actual events described in this book.

This book also considers aspects of my relationship with my sister and our personal difficulties that did not appear in my first book. Some events recounted had already occurred; some had not. I turn to them now because I have come to understand the extent to which they inform my story.

I have relied on my journals and memories spanning decades in setting out what I have come to remember, believe, and understand about my life. Like all personal narratives, mine is inherently subjective. However intertwined my life is with the lives of others, I can only speak my own truth; I recognize that their memories may vary from mine, no matter how many experiences we share and how much I love them.

predeceased

The light started to seep into the foothills of the Berkshires, the outline of trees barely visible against the dark sky. February 2002: I was driving the Mass Pike to Schenectady to meet with an estate lawyer. My dog, who had come along for support, sat in the back seat with his tongue hanging out, filling my rearview mirror with his blocky golden head.

I'd grown up in a town near Schenectady and had driven this road hundreds of times, with its old-fashioned tollbooths and Pilgrims' hats on green signs. My mother had taken me and my older sister, Lara, to Jiminy Peak on this road when I was barely old enough to hold a ski pole in a mittened fist. She'd taken us to the Clark Art Institute to gape at giant paintings of satyrs and nymphs. Later she'd driven me to Williamstown to see Bertolt Brecht's *Mother Courage* and *Arturo Ui*, and other plays my father refused to see because they were about war and suffering, and he had already seen too much war and suffering. Later still, I'd driven the Mass Pike to college and law school in Boston. The road to the Atlantic Ocean always returned home to Schenectady, like a fishing line cast out and reeled back in, over and over.

The last time I had driven this road was in November—three months before—to attend my father's funeral. It had seemed, at the time, a transformative reunion. My mother, sister, and I had spent hours talking, crying, laughing, and catching up, and in my little ballroom of wishful thinking, I believed we had regained our footing. But now, heading to the lawyer's office, I had trouble figuring out what had really happened.

Just six weeks after Dad's funeral—the letter arrived on Christmas Eve—I found out that I had been disowned by my family. My father had signed a last-minute codicil to his will, declaring me to have "predeceased" him. I'd responded like a dead person: I took to my grave. I made no attempt to contact my mother or sister, and they made no attempt to contact me.

For more than forty years, our family had been closer than fused. My parents and Lara were my cell structure and membrane, my very identity. Yet so much had been hidden from me—shadows and illusions that I'd never understood. I'd spent most of my life trying to decipher the mystery of my family, and I was still at a loss. Perhaps loss was precisely the point of our story.

When I was growing up, my mother said that our family was held together by the great glue of suffering. World War II had shattered my parents, and they had emerged from the charred remains of Europe with pieces missing. Around these holes they had built our family of four. We loved each other like starved people: we always wanted more.

A Sad and Difficult Time for All of Us

On the day I found out I was disowned, I woke before dawn as usual, slipped quietly out of bed, and stepped over my dog who lay on his side like a toppled Sphinx. I pulled on my gym shorts and T-shirt, laced up my sneakers, zipped up my parka, and went down the three flights of stairs. The streets were empty as I walked to the Y. It was the day before Christmas and the students who often made my building feel like a frat house were gone. Boston was between storms, so the sidewalks were clear, and the wind didn't hit me till I crossed Huntington Avenue. It was too early for traffic, a nice time to be out in the city, a little before 5 a.m.

I was forty-four years old and feeling optimistic: there was good reason to think that the three-year rift in my family was starting to heal. In 1999, I had published a memoir revealing my family's true identity and history. The book's unexpected success proved catastrophic for my mother, and her distress, of course, wreaked havoc for the rest of us. But now, over the past six weeks since the funeral, my mother had started writing to me again, handwritten letters telling me how she was managing now that Dad had died, and hoping that we could repair our relationship. And I wrote her too, telling her about my own grief, and that I loved her, and that I was so relieved to have her back. It was not the first time my mother had cut me off, but it had been the longest and most searing of our separations, and I felt grateful and relieved and lucky and sad all at the same time. At eighty-six, my father had been suffering from Parkinson's for a dozen years. Although he and I had always been close, Mom's refusal to speak to me had meant I was not permitted to see him for the last years of his life when he lived at home with her.

During those three years, my older sister and I had also not spoken, and the longer I had been cast off from my parents, the closer she had grown to them. And so, although I felt the enormity of my loss of my father, and although I didn't know whether my sister and I could mend our relationship, I felt heartened that my mother was finally emerging from her silent rage, and we could begin to be friends again. She was, I thought, starting to soften; she was letting in a little light and warmth through the cracks that my father's death had opened in her, and I wanted to stand in that sunshine and drink in all the warmth I could. I wanted to beam it back to her tenfold; I wanted her to know how much she meant to me.

When I got home from the gym, I took the dog out and picked up the mail. Among the bills, I saw a fat business-size envelope from my mother, addressed in her familiar European handwriting. I looked forward to her letters. But when I opened the envelope, I found a typed cover letter on legal letterhead from a lawyer. The letter, addressed to my mother, began, *As you know . . .* and went on to say something about signing my father's will. I pushed it aside and turned to a ten-page stapled document, a photocopy of my father's last will and testament. I'd never seen this before, and with growing unease, I turned the pages. The paper felt stiff and kept buckling in my hands— it had been folded into thirds, and now seemed to want to fold itself up again. It was a standard form will, and although I had trouble taking any of it in, I recognized my name here and there, together with my sister Lara's and my mother's, sprinkled among the numbered paragraphs of legalese.

I didn't want to read this document; it seemed a violation of my father's privacy somehow, and I was disturbed by this cold, impersonal evidence of his death. But I forced myself to skim a few pages, and I saw that everything in my father's estate was to be distributed through a family trust equally to my sister and me; my mother was the executor, my sister and I were trustees, and various distributions were to be made . . . *equally to my children Lara and Helen* . . . and *in equal shares to Lara and Helen* . . . and so on. The will was signed and dated October 1998.

And then I came to the last page, a single sheet not stapled to anything. The word *CODICIL* was written at the top in bold letters, and as my eyes trailed down the page, I saw my name in capital letters, repeated in a series of paragraphs that stated: *Delete HELEN FREMONT from each paragraph, and replace her with* . . . The final sentence read: *For the purposes of this my Last Will and Testament, my daughter, HELEN FREMONT, and her issue, if any, shall be deemed to have predeceased me.*

And there, at the bottom of this piece of paper that removed me from his life, was my father's shaky, Parkinsonian signature. He could barely hold a pen by then; my mother must have helped him. It was dated July 2001, soon after he'd suffered a near-fatal collapse and four months before his death. My mother had now sent me these documents with her own attached hand-written note, saying simply, *It is a sad and difficult time for all of us.*

Because of the new names of Lara's partner and, improbably, of her swim coach that "replaced" Helen in the codicil, I felt sure that my sister had been complicit. She was now declared my parents' only daughter.

It would take me a long time to understand how my sister could have participated in this. I have no doubt that she did so out of a sense of loyalty to my parents. Our family was built on lies to protect one another from what we believed to be more painful truths. In the end, we got tangled up in our own fictions. Our stories had sharp edges; I was sliced off.

part one

Sisters are a setup. Shot from the same cannon, you're sent on a blind date for the rest of your lives.

My sister, Lara, and I had a script we were supposed to follow. My mother and her sister, Zosia, had written it, and they were our role models, which is pretty scary when you consider what they'd been through. During the war, Zosia had saved my mother's life. Or maybe it was the other way around. The stories were twisted and my mother and aunt were bound together in ways that Lara and I didn't begin to understand, but we did our best to follow for most of our lives. Although Zosia lived in Italy and we lived in upstate New York, Mom and Zosia's love was formidable, the stuff of legend, built on a mythic past. One day, they told us, my sister and I would have what they had.

But unlike our mother and aunt, Lara and I didn't have any real wars to test our bond; we had to make up our own. From our earliest years, we liked to go to extremes with each other. We tested our limits, pushed ourselves and each other a little further, a little harder, to see how much we could take. To prove how much we loved each other. Usually these tests of strength took place in the wilderness, far from the comforts and complications of our everyday lives.

In 1990, when I was thirty-three and Lara was thirty-six, we went ski mountaineering in the remote Battle Range of British Columbia. A helicopter dropped us off on a mountain ridge above a wall of ice. The pilot would come back for our group of ten a week later, weather permitting.

Forty feet of snow had fallen in the last three months, and they'd had to dig down to find the entrance to the hut we would use as our base. We hustled our gear inside and went back out for avalanche practice. We were going to learn how to save each other's lives. After clipping on our skis, Lara and I followed our guide into an unannounced blizzard. The storm had come out of nowhere, and we weren't going far—just far enough to feel like an avalanche was possible. Then we began the drill, making an imaginary grid in the snow and finding the buried "victim" using our transceivers. The guide timed us. It was hard to see in the swirling snow, and we struggled against the wind, holding the transceivers in front of us as we walked back and forth in the deep powder trying to locate the signal. We weren't very good at search and rescue, and I could see that the real purpose of the drill was to teach us that we would never survive an avalanche. The guide had come through a few, but despite our years of exercising poor judgment in the mountains, Lara and I had never tripped one.

It was Lara who had talked me into this trip, and I was a little anxious about skinning up a few thousand vertical feet each day. The next morning under clear skies we trekked single-file up a steep ravine, skirting a series of heart-stopping crevasses—freakish blue gashes in the snow that dropped hundreds of yards into darkness. Sweat poured from our faces. Not a sound—just the whistle and whip of the wind, the huff of our breathing, and the hushed swish of our skis moving through deep powder, like giant silencers on our feet.

I liked to follow behind Lara, and imagined that our legs were connected by the same body. When she pushed her right leg forward, mine slid forward automatically, as if invisible strings attached my ski boot to hers. I could sink into her rhythm without using any of my own energy; I could siphon off her. You can really lose yourself like this. Your *self* actually disappears. Your body is there, a huffing, puffing, pounding machine that slides along with your sister's. But your mind stretches out, and your spirit soars, and there is nothing that binds you to the earth. A giddy feeling of floating high above the thousands of miles of mountains around you, and for a moment you feel as if you have touched God, that you dwell in the bodiless land of the spirit, whether it's the wind on your cheek or the blue in the sky or the sharp knives of the peaks in the distance, surrounded by emptiness and snow and the simplest of elements. It's a kind of rapture, a sort of passionate love affair with the universe.

This was the heady bond Lara and I had shared since childhood. You have to climb to the end of the earth because the middle of your life is too weighed down by trinkets of the mundane, the alarm clock with its rigid hands, the same twelve numbers arranged in the same circle, the same wheels that carry you to this street or that; to this desk or that; to this bed or that. I had found my true north. It was the world away from everything. Lara had brought me here, above the trees, above life. It was as cool and creamy and thrilling as death itself.

Back then, there was no doubt that if an avalanche had come for my sister, I'd have leapt in front of it and pushed her to safety.

But that was a long time ago.

one

Lara and I grew up outside Schenectady, near the snow belt of upstate New York. Winter moved in for good by November and didn't really start to lose interest until well into April. Summers were short, crisp, and businesslike, so brief as to seem a false memory. By mid-August, you could already feel the air changing, sharpening its teeth. In October, the ground frosted and hardened. Winter storms swooped down from the northwest with a thrilling blast of cold air that you had to bite into, just to breathe.

While our father saw patients at his office and made hospital rounds, our mother cleaned the house and everything in it. And I spent my earliest years stumbling after Lara, who seemed to be in constant motion—flying down the hills behind our house on a sled or a cart, running through the woods, and leaping off the ledges of my mother's rock garden.

It was obvious to anyone that she owned me. Like most big sisters and mob bosses, she ordered me around, insisted on my participation in her schemes, and, if I balked, she could use brute force to get me to comply. Through her, I absorbed galaxies of information—about climbing trees and Indian wrestling, stick fighting, rock throwing, berry picking, and igloo building. Most importantly, I learned that resistance was pointless.

We were allies: we both loved adventure and action, tests of strength and courage.

We were enemies: we hated each other. I was half her size and a crybaby; she could throw me to the ground with one hand while eating an ice cream cone with the other.

Home Movies, 1956–61

The movies begin in Italy in 1956, before I was born: two-year-old Lara and Mom and her older sister, Auntie Zosia, are walking through the gardens at the Villa d'Este in Tivoli, outside Rome, where Auntie and Uncle live. Mom is walking briskly—short dark hair, very trim; she cuts a smart figure. Auntie Zosia is a curvy redhead, with high cheekbones and an alluring, mysterious face. And there's Uncle Giulio, daintier than the women, a small gem. He smiles sweetly at my father, who holds the movie camera. An authentic Italian count, Uncle is conspicuously beautiful, slim and sophisticated in his tailored linen slacks, yellow polo shirt, and sporty ascot.

Now Dad must have given Mom the movie camera, because here he is, striding toward us: freakishly tall compared to the rest of them, athletic. His hair is striking—white with a single dark stripe down the middle, combed straight back off his forehead like an exotic animal. He towers over the world, his legs crazy long, his chest and shoulders broad, his waist trim. He looks like some bizarre exaggeration of the ideal male body.

Trailing behind is my cousin Renzo, a gangly thirteen-year-old, dark and handsome with hooded eyes and a bored look on his face. Thirty-five years later, Lara and I would realize that things were not always as we'd been told. Renzo looks more like my mother than like anyone else in these movies, and he certainly doesn't look like Giulio. For my mother, identity was slippery, and history was a vast game board on which the pieces could be moved, exchanged, and transformed at will. My mother's survival of the war had depended on such sleights of hand and shifts in identity. For the rest of her life she would continue to rely on the stories she told to stay alive, long after the need for lies was apparent.

My father focuses the camera on Lara now. Here she's running toward him, stumbling about, exploring everything. She's curious, fearless, a live wire. She wears a little white dress over her diaper.

Cut back to my mother, who looks severe and unhappy. She barely glances at my father.

In the next scene, it's the summer of 1957, and there I am, hidden from view inside my mother's giant belly. She sits, very pregnant, on a lawn chair in Evans Mills outside the clapboard house with peeling paint that my parents rented as their first home and medical office. Despite her belly, she looks hollowed out, cold, devoured.

Suddenly it's Christmas 1957, and it's all Lara, all the time. My father cannot get enough of her. She's opening presents, pure delight. And now a quick glimpse of me in the crib—holding on to the bars, stunned and wide-eyed, which is how I look in the movies for the next several years. A blob with big dark eyes, sort of in a daze, trying to make sense of all these characters.

And now my parents are working outside the rakish brick house they bought near Schenectady six months after I was born. The house was a full-fledged member of our family, and it had its own problems. Built on a hill, surrounded by woods, it was all sharp angles and soaring ceilings. The whole thing was made of mistakes. Its walls, inside and out, were a patchwork of partially exploded bricks, scarred by the kiln but not completely destroyed, and we liked them for their character. As a child I often had bruises in the shape of those bricks, whenever my sister shoved me against them. Even the floors were made of brick, shellacked and bumpy on our bare feet.

Then there was all that glass: an entire wall of giant floor-to-ceiling glass slabs running the length of the loft-style living room. If you leaned with all your weight and some of your father's, you could slide one slab past the other along an extended track, and open the living room onto the screened-in porch.

I loved the house for its soaring self-confidence and the explosion of sky-splitting light, the way the land and woods seemed to be part of our living room. It had great flair, despite all its broken-brick bones. Everyone else I knew lived in ordinary homes with the rectilinear promise of solidity, propriety, and order. Our house, like our family, was dangerous and unpredictable, a wild adventure.

Here in our home movies, my parents are hauling rocks and building the slate steps from the driveway up the steep hill to the front door. And there's Mom in a green surgeon's cap, raking leaves in the fall, and in winter she's out there shoveling paths through two feet of snow up those slate steps and around the house. Then it's spring again, and she's lugging boulders and heaving the earth like a steam shovel.

Together with my father, she pummeled the wilderness into lush hills of honeysuckle and pachysandra. This was where they put all the parts of themselves that they couldn't put into words. All of their losses and betrayals and grief and rage went into the ground and rocks and trees around us. And unlike my sister and me, the house and grounds accepted everything they did without question or objection, and reflected back the best of them.

In all these home movies, there isn't an ounce of play in either of my parents. They have work to do, hard, knuckle-breaking work, and there is a sense of great productivity and drive.

By 1959 they've already turned the house into a jewel of lawns and gardens in the middle of a forest. The isolation is striking. You could run through those woods, but you would not find another human being for what seemed like miles. In fact, there were a couple of houses some distance away, but they were hidden, childless, equally isolated.

That nowhere-ness of home. The sense of being apart from the rest of the world. No relatives or extended family, just us. And I was on my own planet, apart somehow from this family.

After I was born in 1957, my mother and aunt set up a schedule so that the two sisters could be together as often as finances allowed. Like the Summer Olympics, we went to visit Zosia every four years. On an alternating schedule, Zosia came to visit us in Schenectady. Renzo, already a teenager by then, was off in the parallel universe of girls and motorcycles.

Zosia and Mom would spend their days in Schenectady cooking and baking and inviting friends for dinner and bridge, and going for walks, and always talking, talking, talking in Italian. Once, Uncle Giulio came along with Zosia, and nearly froze to death because the Schenectady summers were so cold. Another year, Renzo—already an engineer—came and built Lara and me a superb underground fort in a field behind our house. But the main event was always my mother and aunt, who immersed themselves in a bubbling stream of Italian.

The two sisters endured the years between their summers together by writing letters to each other every day. When the mail arrived each afternoon, Mom made herself a ritual cup of tea and settled down to read Zosia's letter. She typed her response on a blue aerogram, licked and folded down the flaps, and left it for my father to post the next morning. Lara and I learned not to disturb her during her reading and writing of Zosia's letters. Even Dad must have realized by then that my mother's heart belonged to her sister, and not to him.

Aside from this daily communion between the two sisters, my family was on its own in the New World—free of context, as far as Lara or I could tell. My father had no surviving relatives.

Whatever possessions my family had once owned had been lost or destroyed in the war. There were no existing photographs of my parents until after the war, when my father's hair was already white and my mother was sharp-angled and serious. As a child, I had trouble believing that my parents had ever actually been children, since no evidence supported this. I knew that my father had spent six years as a prisoner in Siberia during the war, but aside from that, my parents wouldn't talk about the past, and everyone who'd known them was dead. In my mind, they had always been adults and always would be—hardworking, long-suffering, and serious. I was determined never to let adulthood happen to me, and by and large, I succeeded.

When my parents moved to our brick house outside Schenectady in the late 1950s, my father developed a small circle of doctor friends who worked at the local hospital. Their wives took turns hosting dinner parties followed by a couple of tables of bridge. Every few months when it was my mother's turn, she dutifully followed the elaborate recipes of Julia Child, set the dining room table, and made sure the bar was stocked with sherry and vermouth. By the time my father came home from work and changed into his navy-blue suit, my mother had already zipped herself into one of her Italian dresses, combed and shaped her eyebrows, and glossed her lips red. Lara and I stared, amazed at the transformation.

Around the house, Mom wore no-nonsense slacks for her daily housecleaning rampages. Armed with scouring pads, rags, and cleaning solutions, she was a veritable cleaning dynamo—furiously dusting, vacuuming, and mopping up after us. She washed the windows inside and out, scrubbed the toilets, tubs, and sinks, and vacuumed not only the dog hair from the carpets but also the dog himself. The surfaces of our house sparkled, especially when she was upset or anxious or angry. "Cleaning is my outlet," she said. The worse things got at home, the better our house looked. The minute you put something down—a book, a sweater, a pair of glasses—it was swept up, dusted under, and dispatched to your room.

But she had a number of elegant dresses from her years in Rome, when clothes had been bartered and tailor-made in a perpetual recycling of prewar garments. In 1946, she'd married my father on her lunch break in Rome wearing a wool business suit that had been made out of one of Uncle's black Fascist uniforms. Her shoes, too, were Italian, and every Sunday, when she dressed to take us to St. Pius, our local Catholic church, she looked stylish and sophisticated.

When she stood next to my father in her

Florentine high heels, my mother's head, with its defiant waves of thick, dark hair, barely grazed my father's armpit. You could fit three of her into his chest alone. My father's shoulders rose like a mountain range above her. His head, too, was large and majestic, with a chiseled nose, ice-blue eyes, and white hair combed straight back. While my mother was quick, lithe, and impossible to catch, my father was tall, powerful, and impossible to move.

But their attachment was more intellectual than physical. They liked each other's minds, and they were closely matched in the areas of self-confidence and stubbornness. I never saw them kiss or hold hands; they rarely touched each other with affection.

When their guests arrived, it sounded like a home invasion—women screeching their hellos, heels clattering on the brick floor, pots and pans banging in the kitchen. In the safety of the television room, Lara and I hunkered down with the dog, listening to the adult voices rising and falling like boats on the ocean, here a crescendo of chatter and laughter, there the tinkling of ice in cocktail glasses, now the booming laughter of one of the men, and above it all my mother's animated voice, lively, bright, filled with theater.

Careful to keep quiet, Lara taught me various kung fu moves that she invented on the spot. We practiced in the hallway, flying through the air, folding ourselves into pretzels. In her Wrangler jeans and Fruit of the Loom T-shirt, she looked like a loose-limbed boy with wild brown hair. We had matching short haircuts, but mine was darker and more obedient.

At some point after the guests had been fed and tamed and seated at their bridge tables, Lara and I would be trotted out to say hello to them. Then we disappeared into the kitchen, stunned by the mess that adults could make: stacks of dirty dishes, decapitated hors d'oeuvres, and a scattered graveyard of cigarette butts stained with garish pink lipstick. It was the Lebanese lady who smoked. She took only a few puffs from each cigarette, then stubbed it out and lit another. Her lips were everywhere.

By morning, my mother had already scrubbed everything clean. The bridge tables had been folded up and rolled back into their boxes; pots and pans glistened like cairns of stainless steel rising from the dish rack.

My mother acquitted herself of such social obligations quite well, offering genuine warmth to her friends without burdening them with too much intimacy. Later I came to understand that my mother did not have close friends on purpose. She was a chameleon, effortlessly blending in everywhere, attuned to everyone, but trusting no one. Whenever I saw her with others, I marveled at her complete fluency in the world, the ease with which she displayed her many colors. She dazzled me.

My father was less adept at social skills. His idea of conversation was cornering one or two people at a party and telling them the intricate details of something he had just read about— cold fusion, perhaps, or gravitational collapse. He could never read the glazed-over faces of his victims, who were too polite to extricate themselves.

His most successful relationships were his chess friendships. He had become something of a chess champion in the Gulag, where playing chess was punishable by death, so he had developed a lightning-quick technique that he still deployed. While his opponents contemplated their next move, my father would busy himself by cracking open and eating all the nuts in the bowl on the table, or getting up and stretching his legs. The second his opponent had completed his move, Dad would pounce, snatching his own chess piece and slamming it down on another square, leaving his opponent once again to study the board and ponder the possibilities.

Of my parents, Mom was the one you wanted to be with. She was strict, but warmer, more patient. Dad, on the other hand, waited for no one and accepted no excuses. His word, he always told Lara and me, was *iron,* and whenever he said this, he made a powerful fist with his right hand. He had a sharp wit and a sly sense of humor, but his bitterness ate into everything he did. While he was in Siberia, fellow prisoners had broken his left elbow while trying to steal his clothes. Years later, surgeons in Italy removed the calcified joint and sewed him back together, but he never recovered full use of his arm. My father tried not to speak of his years as a prisoner, but he acted like a man who had lived with beasts. He wolfed his meals in seconds, and nothing my mother said or did could get him to slow down. "I can't," he'd say helplessly. "It's food."

He kept ferociously busy, saw patients day and night, built rock ledges behind the house, planted bushes, mulched trees, chopped wood. One year he bought a thousand evergreens and planted them across the grounds, along the driveway, all over the lawn. He was a colossus of efficient, if furious, energy. At night, his shrieking nightmares jolted us awake. The next morning my mother would dismiss them with a weary shrug, saying, "The Gulag again," as if genocide were just one more annoyance that kept intruding into our lives.

We never knew when an image or a sound or a fight between my sister and me would trip the invisible wire, and my father would blurt out a horrifying incident from the camps, or my mother would cry, "I should have died with my parents! Don't you understand? We shouldn't be alive!" My sister and I would freeze—the whole planet froze—as we watched our parents being stolen from us by the past.

These moments would never be spoken of afterward. Our family circled them with a thick layer of silence, around which my sister and I tiptoed, magically thinking that if we were careful, we could avoid sparking another explosion.

Through such experiences Lara and I laid down the framework of our own story. We absorbed their secrets and turned them into our own drama. Maybe it wasn't an exact translation of our parents' war, but it was the best we could do with what we had. To Mom and Dad's unspoken past we added our own hunger, the rapacity of children who have everything and still want more—love, attention, adoration. Lara and I fought each other as if battling for the last scrap of oxygen in the house, as if there were room in our parents' hearts for only one child.

By the time I was in second grade, I decided that Lara's usefulness as an older sister had expired. She had become baggage. Her socks sagged at different heights. She buttoned her blouses right up to her chin, and wore braces on her buck teeth. She was flat-footed, with long narrow feet that didn't seem to match her solid body. Even the clothes my mother sewed for us looked all wrong on her—her legs were too long and her waist too wide. She had no friends. She got straight As. In class, she was obedient, polite, and brilliant. And she had a gift for math and music and science, and she later learned Russian—all the skills and talents my father had—ensuring a lifelong competition between them.

Although her teachers loved her, her classmates at Glenwood Elementary School laughed at her for her geeky height, her chipmunk cheeks and weird hair. Every day she ran home in tears. "Why are they so mean to me?" she cried to my mother.

I was exactly the opposite. Perhaps I had learned something from watching her, or perhaps I was just plain lucky, but from the moment I set foot in school, I began my conquest of friends. Although I wore Lara's hand-me-down clothes, I wore them at a raffish angle and thought I looked cool. I had no time for Lara now. Without so much as a backward glance, I shucked my sister like an old T-shirt, and courted my classmates. Lara watched this parade of little kids in and out of our house, and saw me laughing and goofing off with Jill and Pam and Lori and Freddie, and it made her want to break my smile over her knee.

One day I came home from second grade to find Lara writhing on the floor in the doorway to the kitchen. She was screaming that she would never go back to school again. Her eyes had a wild look to them, and her teeth were clenched. When she saw me standing in the entranceway, she shouted, "I hate you!" and started hissing. Her hair, thick and tangled, flared from her head. On the other side of my sister, a safe distance away, my mother tried to reason with her. Mom glanced up at me. "Helen," she said in her most ordinary voice. "How was school?"

I decided to take her cue and pretend Lara wasn't there. "Can I get a glass of milk?" I asked.

"Of course," Mom said.

I tried to step over Lara, but she emitted a snarl, then a gurgling sound deep in her throat. Her eyes widened, and for a moment it seemed she would leap from the floor and sink her teeth into my leg. I backed off. At ten, she was already bigger and stronger than my mother.

"She won't let me in," I said.

My mother considered this. "Lara, let her into the kitchen."

"Make me!" Lara shouted. "You make me!" She planted her foot against the doorjamb for leverage.

My mother looked disappointed.

"Mom," I pleaded.

"I'll get you a glass of milk," she said. She took a step toward the refrigerator, but Lara kicked at Mom's ankles. My mother backed away. "All right, never mind, Helen." Mom was not in the mood to fight. "Change your clothes. You can have a glass of milk later."

My father came home from the office two hours later. By then my mother and sister were murmuring softly in each other's arms in Lara's bedroom. I watched them from the hallway, jealous. I heard the quiet of my father's entrance, the way the air shifted around his body. He always entered the house as if on a stealth mission—ears pricked, eyes alert, every muscle tensed. He and I were hooked up to the same radar. He seemed to weigh the valence of electrons in each room. I met him at the top of the stairs. He cocked his head.

"They're in Lara's room," I said.

I steered a wide berth around my sister after that. It took nothing to set her off. She would slam me against the brick wall if she happened to pass me in the hallway. An elbow to the jaw, a knee in my ribs. I quickly learned to fight back: whenever I was safely out of reach, I would snicker and call her a weirdo, or laugh at her for being such a creep. I delighted in seeing her face turn red, even though I already knew I was toast. Because that was my trump card; Lara could beat the living crap out of me, but I knew she feared being different, freakish. I did my best to remind her of it every chance I got. And so we went to war.

My parents couldn't do much about this. We fought offstage, while my mother was cleaning the house or writing her sister, and my father was at the office or the hospital. Our fights did not compare to the more pressing concerns of earning a living and running a household. In the annals of competitive suffering, Lara and I knew from an early age that we were lucky to be irrelevant. But on the scorecard of our daily lives as children, we wanted to matter.

And of course we did matter very much to our parents, as long as we did our jobs as blue-chip children and straight-A students.

"My life is over," Mom often told us. "My life ended in the war. You are all that matter."

We were small shoots now, perhaps, but with care and feeding and sunlight, with green vegetables and vitamins and snowsuits in winter and sunblock in summer, with French lessons and piano lessons and ballet lessons and swim lessons, we would grow strong and cultured and smart, and we would redeem all that had been taken from her, restore reason in the world.

And, oh my, the love. Our parents loved Lara and me with such a ferocity, it was hard to remain standing in the face of it. They loved us with cyclone force. They loved the arms right out of our sockets. My friends were loved with the casual American ease of prairie love, of cows grazing in a fenced-in field. My sister and

I were loved with the blazing heat of immigrant love. The scorched-earth love of a people hunted down, displaced, and resettled countless times before clawing their way to the topsoil of upstate New York.

Overlooking our increasingly frequent fights, Mom seemed gratified to see how closely Lara and I mirrored our mother and aunt. "You're just like me," Mom always told me. "You were an easy child." I opened my mouth and words came to me. I closed my eyes and sleep embraced me. I went to school and children played with me. For Lara, nothing came easily. She was in constant battle with herself and the world. "Lara is so much like Zosia," Mom would say. "Always in motion, always restless." She assured me that Lara and I would be closer than anyone else in the world. Sisters shared each other's secrets and saved each other's lives. It sounded good. But by the time I was in the second grade, I started to think I had the wrong sister for that. I brought this up with my mother. "I don't think Lara is right for me," I said. Mom smiled. "Just wait. You'll see when you get older."

But with time, things only got worse. Night would fall, and Lara's eyes snapped open with the certainty of danger. Enemies filled her room, hid in her closet, slipped between the sheets of her bed, stole behind the radiator, leaked under the windowsill. If she closed her eyes, they would spring out to get her.

The voices began as whispers, then grew louder, she would tell me years later. Everything buzzed. Her bed began to move. She leapt from it and stared at it—but of course, now it was still. The curtains fluttered. She lifted one corner and traced the pattern of movement across the fabric, a wave on the beach. So elusive, the shadows. The creatures had no shape or form, but only a function—to hurt her, to laugh at her, to twist her into knots.

While Lara was fighting her demons in her bedroom, my father was back in Siberia, and my mother was having her own nightmares of being taken by the "police" from her home, as she would tell us in the morning. I knew nothing of this at the time, but now I wonder if Lara's voices were coming to her through the walls of our parents' unspoken memories.

When she was eleven, Lara finally went crazy in a way that perhaps our whole family had been waiting for. Every night after our mother had turned out our lights and retreated to the living room, Lara would start.

I could hear her get out of bed and flick the light switch in her room on and off rapidly, dozens, maybe hundreds of times. My room shared a wall with hers, and I could hear the sharp *click-clack-click-clack,* like a rapid-fire machine gun. I'd hear her snapping the curtains back and forth along their runners the length of the room: *Zhiiiiing! Zhiiiiing! Zhiiiiing!* Then back to the light switch—*click-clack-click-clack.* Then a muffled rummaging sound, when she must have dropped to the floor and scanned under her bed. Then the curtains sang again. Now she was rustling in her closet, sweeping the skirts and blouses back and forth on their hangers.

I didn't understand what she was doing, and I didn't care. As far as I could tell, most of the things Lara did were intended to irritate me, and I wasn't about to give her the satisfaction. Out of vengeance, I fell asleep.

But her rituals got even longer and more elaborate. I would wake in the middle of the night to the sound of my sister's drapes flying across their runners. I would listen for what would come next. Midnight, one o'clock, two. The rest of the house was dead, and only Lara's room was alive with sound. Her Concerto for Lights and Drapes.

It never occurred to me to tell my parents about this. One night, though, I tiptoed down the hall to the bathroom. Lights blazed in my sister's room, and I could hear the murmur of my parents' voices. Just as I walked past the door, I heard my mother say, "psychologist," and the door to Lara's room swung shut. The hairs stood up on my neck.

Lara's gone psycho, I thought with a chill.

Like those wide-eyed freaks in the horror movie reruns on TV, arms outstretched, lurching robotically. All of a sudden, I realized that stuff like that didn't just happen to people on TV; it was happening to *my sister.*

The implications were terrifying. If such a condition could strike Lara, it was only a matter of time before I too succumbed. She'd given me everything—measles, chicken pox, mumps—and I'd catch this from her too. I hovered outside Lara's closed door, transfixed by the seam of light glowing under it. I could not make out my parents' words, just their hushed mumbling voices.

After that night, Lara skulked around the house under a dark cloud of dread. I was careful not to get too close to her, but I studied her for signs of craziness. Her hair had always been thick and unruly, and now it looked even worse. She had dark hollows under her eyes, and her fingernails were picked to bloody stumps. When she caught me looking at her, she bared her teeth and growled wolfishly. My parents spoke Polish all the time now in hushed tones.

A few days later, my mother carried the skinny fold-up cot from the basement and set it up in Lara's room. Mom assured my father it would only be for a night or two, but it turned out to be three nights and then four, then a week, then two weeks, and then we just pretended it was normal that my mother slept in Lara's room.

. . .

Soon after she moved into Lara's room, my mother told me that Lara was going to start seeing a psychologist who would help her feel better. "You cannot mention a word of this," she said in a low voice.

I nodded. Mom looked hardened, like metal.

"I want you to take a vow," she said. "You must promise never to say a word about this to anyone."

"Okay," I said.

"This is a private matter," she said. "A family matter."

I knew what that meant. Our family had many things we were not allowed to speak of. We didn't speak about my parents' war, or about their parents, or about anything that had happened Before.

When I went to school the following morning, the secret of my sister's illness weighed on me. I saw my eight-year-old classmates as if from a great distance, and I felt a strange gap open up between us. They were still my friends, but suddenly they seemed so young and free. They were unaware of the enormity of danger in the world, and although I myself didn't understand what that danger was, I knew that our family had it, that it was in our house. A deep, unspeakable line separated me from everyone outside my family.

45

two

I was in the kitchen one afternoon after grade school when my father came home to take Lara to the psychologist. "Make me!" she shouted, throwing herself to the floor. "Go ahead, make me!" My father grabbed her by the wrist. Lara kicked and clawed and spat at him as he dragged her to his car and planted her in the front seat. He had a hard time of it. My father had been a world-class athlete before the war, and although he seemed to rise above everyone in the state of New York, he really only had the use of his good arm. Lara, however, seemed to have a dozen arms. He finally got her in the car and gunned it down the driveway.

An hour and a half later, he brought her home. Lara burst into the kitchen shouting that she hated the psychologist, and she hated my parents, and most of all she hated me. As if the idea had just occurred to her, she lunged and knocked me to the floor. My mother had been cooking dinner, and the kitchen smelled of mashed potatoes, which I hated, and I remember a splotch of potato on the green linoleum. It was my father who pulled her off me, and while Lara was screaming that she would kill me, my father hustled me out to his car. Even before I'd closed the passenger door, he had started the engine. I was still sniffling, rubbing my elbow where I'd hit the linoleum. "Fasten your seat belt," he ordered. I understood that my crying was grating on his nerves, so I clicked in and shut up.

He turned onto Natchaug Road. "Are you hungry?" he asked. I shook my head.

"Let's get a hot dog," he said. We drove to a fast-food place near his office, and he gulped his down in two bites.

"I hate her guts," I said.

My father looked at me sternly. "Don't say that."

"Well, it's true."

He said nothing. We drove through the seedier part of State Street to his office, where he let me hang out in one of his exam rooms while he did his bookkeeping. Neat jars of sterile gauze and long Q-tips, bottles of ammonia and medicines gleamed on the Formica counters. In his kitchen he had beakers and test tubes and a centrifuge and an autoclave so he could do his own lab work and minor surgery. He even had his own X-ray equipment down the hall, a monster of a machine that filled the entire room, and a separate little glassed-in booth where my father worked the controls like the Wizard of Oz. He was a family doctor, and his patients were mostly immigrants and working-class people who came to him because he didn't charge much, he worked around the clock, and he cut his patients some slack if they couldn't pay him right away.

Being with my father made me feel safe (he was big) and proud (he was successful), but he was not my mother, whose warmth we all craved. When I was younger, I used to crawl into her lap while she was reading on her chaise longue, and she would absentmindedly stroke my hair and tuck it behind my ear. But after a moment she would tell me to find something to do with myself and I would climb down and go to my room, feeling that I had gotten something precious—a small package of warmth from the one I adored.

My father, by contrast, was all sharp edges and modern efficiency, like a chrome-framed chair to my mother's chaise longue. When he finally drove me home late that night, I could hear my mother in my sister's room, murmuring over and over that she loved her, she forgave her, it wasn't her fault at all.

My jealousy caught flame and heated my face as I crawled into bed. I kicked off the covers, hating my sister for taking my mother away from me. I wanted Lara out of the house; I wanted her dead. The feeling was mutual; we were exactly alike in that regard.

• • •

In the all-or-nothing language of childhood memories, by the time I was eight years old, I saw Lara as two separate identities—sometimes she was my beloved big sister, and other times she was a wild animal, unpredictable and vicious. But of course the reality was much more complicated. The Lara who helped me herringbone up a ski slope when I was five, who calmed my fears and planted her poles in the snow to prevent me from slipping downhill, was the same Lara who taught me to eat lemons (rind and all) to gross out the babysitters my parents hired when they went out to the movies; the same Lara who taught me how to swallow the giant penicillin pills Dad prescribed for my ear infection. (She demonstrated by using M&M's.) And it was the same Lara who later taught me to dribble a basketball, switching hands as we ran through an obstacle course of sneakers she'd thrown down on the driveway. My sister and I had always been teammates, coconspirators. But something happened in 1965 that changed our relationship— it was then that my sister seemed capable of turning suddenly into this other Lara, a terrifying creature whom I could neither recognize nor reason with. Decades later, when we tried to talk about those times, our feelings were still too brittle, and in order to preserve our adult bond, she and I inevitably switched to safer topics. To this day, I think, both of us preserve within us the inconsolable core of an injured child, each certain of our own innocence—convinced that it was the other who caused such irreparable damage, the other who deserved whatever justifiable rage we unleashed on each other.

But maybe Lara and I were just set up by history—the war, the secrets, the silence. Or perhaps we were set up by the perfect sisterhood of Mom and Zosia. Sometimes Lara and I felt that we could never fulfill their expectations; sometimes we felt we weren't even supposed to be alive. More than once our mother told us that surviving the war had been her biggest mistake.

History Lesson

From the time Lara and I were little kids until we went to college, my mother had told us bits and pieces of her life before we were born—partial truths, incomplete stories that didn't always fit together. She, Dad, and Zosia were the only ones from their city in eastern Poland who had survived the war, she said. Although they were Catholic—or so they said—their parents, friends, and entire community had been killed by bombs.

Zosia, seven years older than Mom, had left Poland before the war. Zosia had gone to graduate school in Italy in the 1930s, fallen in love, and eventually married my uncle Giulio, an Italian count and high-level lawyer in Mussolini's government.

Mom, in the meantime, had remained in Poland during the war and stayed alive through her wits, enormous luck, and a daring born of desperation. She told us that after her parents were killed in 1942, she escaped the Nazis by cutting her hair short, dressing as an Italian soldier, and marching out of Poland with the Italian Army. She had grown very close to an Italian officer named Luigi, who helped her escape. "He risked his life for me," Mom told us. "I was trying to reach Zosia in Rome, and without Luigi, I would never have gotten out of Poland." Mom was arrested at the Italian border and presumed to be a spy, but with Zosia's and Giulio's help, she was miraculously saved from the firing squad and imprisoned in a camp instead. Afterward she lived in Rome with her sister, her brother-in-law, and their baby, Renzo. Mom got a job as a translator with the American Red Cross and married my father after the war; finally, in 1950, she and Dad emigrated to the States.

In 1953, the postwar relief services sent my parents to Evans Mills, a tiny outpost in upstate New York not far from the Canadian border, where my father replaced the country doctor who had just died. It was there that my thirty-five-year-old mother became pregnant with Lara and fell into an all-consuming depression. In the emptiness of Evans Mills, separated from her sister and nephew by an ocean, the sheer weight of Mom's losses crushed her.

My father, on the other hand, was on fire to build his new life and start a family. Nearly forty years old, he'd lost half his twenties and thirties to the war. Imprisoned for six years in forced labor camps in Siberia, he'd miraculously escaped in 1946 and made his way back to his hometown. There he learned that everyone had been killed except his sweetheart—my mother—who, he was told, had escaped to Italy to live with her sister. He spent the next several months walking across Europe by night as a fugitive until he reached Rome, found my mother, and married her in November 1946, ten years to the day after they'd first met.

Within months, he had learned Italian and passed his Italian medical boards. But jobs were scarce in postwar Rome, and my mother, now a translator for the new government, was the sole supporter of her sister's family. The only work my refugee father could find was at a tuberculosis sanitarium in the Italian Alps. So for three years in the late 1940s, the newlyweds were once again separated. They saw each other once a month, when my mother made the long journey north to spend a weekend with Dad. Often (to my father's consternation) she brought along her five-year-old nephew, Renzo, who could not bear to be separated from her.

It wasn't until 1950 that my parents were finally allowed entry to the United States. My mother immediately got a job at an import-export firm in New York City, while my father worked as a resident at Mount Sinai Hospital. It took him another two years to gather sufficient evidence of his medical credentials to be allowed to sit for the New York State medical boards. (His first medical diploma, the Polish one, was in the hands of the Russian police; his second, the Italian license, was unacceptable in America.) Finally, after passing his medical boards in America, he was hungry for the happiness—or at least the freedom and productivity—for which he had struggled for so long. Instead, in 1954, at the age of thirty-nine, he found himself starting a medical practice in an impoverished town a few hours from Schenectady, while his baby screamed in the other room and his wife stared at the ceiling of her bedroom, sunk in a state of despair so profound she could not rise from bed.

My mother later told me that in Evans Mills, after a brief stint as my father's receptionist and bookkeeper, she told him that she would never again have anything to do with his medical practice. "I couldn't stand him telling me what to do," she told me. "I was a women's libber before the word was even invented." Headstrong as my father was, it turned out Mom was even more so. "That's when I laid down the rules of our marriage," she told me. "I told Dad he could have sole authority over his medical practice, and I would have sole authority over the household and the children. I wouldn't interfere with his business, and he wouldn't interfere with mine."

By the end of my father's first year as a struggling self-employed physician, my parents had managed to save a few hundred dollars by scrimping on their own food and necessities. It still wasn't enough to cover the cost of a plane ticket for my mother to visit her sister, so instead, my mother bought the newest American invention—a washing machine—and shipped it to Zosia in Italy, where no one had heard of such a thing. Two years later, in 1956, my mother could finally afford the round-trip airfare for herself, my father, and Lara. This was the trip to Rome that my father captured with his first movie camera.

It wasn't until Lara and I were in our thirties that we tried to find out more about our family history. Lara sent letters to various international organizations, and one day in 1992 she received a packet of documents from a rabbi in Israel. *Jackpot,* he wrote. He enclosed pages of testimony from survivors describing how each of our relatives had been shot or gassed or starved in ghettos and camps by Germans, Ukrainians, and Poles during the war. Lara and I were stunned to discover that we were not Catholic but Jewish, and our parents were Holocaust survivors with huge families—dozens and dozens of aunts and uncles and cousins we'd never even heard of—all of whom were Jews, and all of whom had been killed.

Ironically, just as Mom and Zosia had been bound together by their lifelong vow of secrecy, Lara and I now forged our bond as the younger pair of sisters determined to discover what the older pair were hiding. Over the next few months, we interviewed hundreds of survivors and historians and rabbis and shrinks and anybody else who could shed light on our family.

At first we kept our research a secret from our parents, who, by then, were in their mid-seventies. But in May 1992 Lara and I sat down with them and told them about our discovery, and as anticipated, they didn't want to talk about it. Or at least, not at first. Two months later they finally acknowledged that we were Jewish and told us more about how they had survived. The revelation was a watershed in our family; we began to dismantle the walls between us and see each other in a new light. Lara and I finally began to understand the unspoken forces that had been acting on us all our lives.

But throughout our childhood and into our thirties, before we learned the truth of our past, Lara and my parents and I seemed locked in a script of madness from which we were helpless to escape.

1965

A few weeks after Lara started seeing a psychologist, my mother told me they'd made an appointment for me to see the psychologist too.

"Why me?" I asked.

"Well, the doctor felt that he should do some tests on you too."

"But I'm fine," I said.

"Of course you're fine!" My mother smiled unconvincingly. "Dr. Johnson just wants to learn as much as he can about our family," she said. "So that he can help Lara."

"What if he thinks I'm crazy?"

"No one's crazy," my mother said. "How could you say such a thing?"

"Well, Lara's . . . um . . ."

My mother's face turned fierce. "Don't ever use that word!" she said. "Where did you hear that?"

I shrugged.

"We're trying to help her," my mother said in a kinder voice. "Don't you want to help?"

Lara wanted to maim me, and "help" wasn't exactly what I wanted to offer her in return.

"She's sick, darling. We all have to help her."

My mother drove me downtown to Dr. Johnson's office and sat in the waiting room while I went into his office. He had a round, moist face with thick caterpillar eyebrows above horn-rimmed glasses. His hair was slicked back with Brylcreem. I tried not to look at him because he was definitely creepy.

"Have a seat." He smiled nervously, running one hand over a pad of lined paper on his desk. "I just want you to relax." He picked up a pen and put it down.

"Now, to start with, I'm going to show you some pictures, and I want you to tell me the first thing that pops into your head. Okay?"

I nodded. My heart was pounding so hard I was afraid he could hear it.

He pulled out a stack of white boards with black splotches all over them. He held one out on the desk for me. "Now, just look at this, and tell me what you see."

I knew exactly what I saw. "A monster," I said.

He nodded. "Uh-huh." He placed the board facedown and scribbled something on his pad. "Okay," he said. He held up another picture. This time the monster was even bigger and scarier.

"A monster," I said.

One of his giant eyebrows shot up. "Mm-hmm." Again he wrote something on his notepad.

When he held up the third card, the monster was practically leaping off the board at me. I bit my lip. This was not looking good. I figured three monsters in a row meant I was certainly very disturbed, possibly crazy. "A house," I said.

His lips twitched as if he might speak, but then he clamped his mouth shut. I was afraid he might be on to me. "A house," he finally said.

I began sweating. The monster had an enormous hairy head and sharp ears. Its mouth was open, and it seemed to know I was lying.

"Can you show me the house?"

"Right there," I said vaguely, pointing to the picture.

"Where? What do you see?"

"Um, here's a door," I said, pointing to a part of the monster that was clearly a foot and not a door. "And, um, here are the windows."

"Okay," Dr. Johnson said. He laid the card facedown and wrote on his pad before holding up the fourth card.

I couldn't believe he was showing me another monster. No one saw so many monsters. They would lock me up for sure.

"It's an Easter basket," I said.

He must have shown me a dozen cards, and every one of them was a different-shaped monster. I told him I saw a sunny day, a boat

58

on a lake, a tree with songbirds, a friendly dog romping in a meadow, anything to sound happy and well-adjusted.

Finally it was over. He got up and opened the door to the waiting room where my mother was reading her latest *New Yorker* magazine. She stood and smiled at the doctor, who said he'd call her later.

She thanked him and we walked out. My scalp felt tingly and my mouth was dry. My mother took me home. I never heard about Dr. Johnson again; Lara stopped seeing him too, and in all the years since then, we've never talked about him. I wonder sometimes what Lara saw in those Rorschach images, and I wonder what I would see in them today. I never found out how I did on the test. At the time, I was afraid Dr. Johnson would pronounce me unfit to be my parents' child and I would be taken away. I didn't dare ask my mother; I just waited to see what would happen next.

What happened next was family therapy, but that's not what it was called. We called it Taking Lara to the Hoffman Children and Family Center, where we were all going to help her get better. We were all ferociously unhappy, and incurable, of course, but the psychiatrists kept working on us with their trowels, trying to make us grow up properly in the garden of mental health.

My father directed all of this. I have no idea how he shopped for our shrink or how he found the Hoffman Center. Mainly, I think, he wanted to send my mother and sister to therapy, but he didn't trust them to do it right; he needed to be there to get the record straight. And they said I had to be there too, which bothered me. I hadn't done anything wrong, why did I have to go? "You're part of the family," my mother explained. At the age of eight, I bit down hard on that nut of indisputable fact, and did as I was told.

Every Friday afternoon my mother picked me up from Glenwood Elementary School. I had been granted a weekly early release for "dental" reasons, my mother told me in a hushed tone. *Under no circumstances,* she said, was I to divulge the real reason for my absence from the third grade on Friday afternoons. To my amazement, my teacher, a fierce woman with flaming orange hair, never so much as batted an eye at my dental excuse. No one in Glenwood Elementary School went to therapy, I was quite certain.

My mother always dressed up for our Hoffman Center appointments. She wore one of her tailored Italian dresses from the forties. She'd also combed her eyebrows, powdered her cheeks, and applied her Cherry Blossom lipstick. I wore whatever my sister had outgrown: the boxy jumpers my mother had sewn, Lara's old button-down blouses, her pathetic socks. I carried my books and baseball glove under my arm and climbed into the back seat of my mother's Dodge Dart.

We drove to St. Mary's, a private girls' school where my parents had enrolled Lara in the seventh grade, to protect her from the cruelty of public school kids. Now she trudged out from the stone building in her navy-blue uniform, plaid book bag thrown over her shoulder like a sack of bones. She flopped onto the front seat and brooded the whole ride downtown.

Schenectady was a hardscrabble town back then. Ragged apartment buildings leaned against one another, windows boarded up, doors hanging off hinges. People sat on the front stoops with empty eyes, smoking and drinking from bottles in paper bags. I stared out the window of our car as my mother steered us through the broken streets. I was shocked by this other world, dark and dismal and foreign. Surely these people needed help more than we did?

My mother parked behind my father's blue Chrysler New Yorker at the Hoffman Center. Entering the building seemed to drain the color from our cheeks and the strength from our bodies. My father, in his usual gray business suit, was already pacing slowly up and down the waiting room, staring at the drab carpet as if measuring the weight of each footfall. My parents exchanged a few words in Polish.

When the door swung open, we traipsed in, heads bowed. The social worker, Miss Jameson, tall and pear-shaped, with hips that looked pneumatic, closed the door behind us. Mom and Lara sat together on a little couch in the middle of the dimly lit room, and the rest of us sat in chairs around them. Our psychiatrist, Dr. Grokle, was a shriveled woman with dark whiskers. She sat calmly in a wingback chair, her long black-and-gray hair wound up in a frizzy beehive. It wobbled slightly when she turned from my father to my mother and Lara, and it looked a little sinister, as if it might be concealing something.

At first I thought family therapy might work to my benefit: I was hoping that a professional psychiatrist would remove my sister from our house and lock her up somewhere. My mother, of course, would sooner drink lighter fluid than lose Lara to an institution, so I did not voice my hopes to her. Between my father and me, I sensed an illicit understanding, but once when I mentioned that I wished Lara were gone, he said nothing. No one ever asked me my opinion in family therapy.

My father started each session by recounting the family's transgressions of the past week. He had memorized the entire chronology of misery—our mopiness, our disrespect, our bickering, our violent outbursts, our personal failures. Nothing got past him. Sometimes he consulted his notes scribbled on blue-lined paper from Woolworth's.

But most of the time he could recite the entire week's melodrama from memory. I was usually missing from my father's list of psychological crimes, which I attributed to my deceptively angelic character. He focused primarily on Lara, whose outbursts were our ignition switch, and on my mother, who couldn't hit the brakes. Mom and Lara must have felt like a car wreck, to hear their behavior reduced to my father's score pad. Although we knew it was coming, his recital still felt like a fresh crash every week.

"Now," my father said at the beginning of one session, crossing his legs so that one of his size-twelve shoes dangled just above the other. "Last Friday night, Lara picked a fight with Helen. When Maria intervened, Lara started fighting with her. This went on till after midnight. Lara would not take a Valium. And Maria would not put her foot down; she would not send Lara to her room. I had to be the one to—"

"That's not true!" Lara said. She burst into tears. My mother leaned over and stroked Lara's shoulder. My father glanced at the shrink, his eyebrows raised as if to say, *See what I mean?*

Dr. Grokle maintained her look of quiet concern.

"He hates me!" Lara said. Her face was red and contorted, like one of those twisted gourds at Halloween.

My mother leaned closer to Lara, the two

of them in a huddle. "He doesn't hate you, darling—"

"He hates me!" Lara said. "He doesn't understand!"

"What doesn't he understand?" Dr. Grokle's voice was so quiet that no one paid any attention to her.

"I love you," my father said haughtily. "But I will not tolerate your manipulative behavior."

"All right, Kovik," my mother said. "That's enough."

"I am simply stating the facts," my father said. "I am a realist."

"You don't even know what's going on!" Lara said.

"I know what I see."

"Kovik, let her speak."

"He's a bully!" Lara said. "I hate him!"

My father sat straight in his gray suit, dwarfing the chair.

"What is it that you hate?" the shrink said to Lara in a gentle voice.

"You have to admit that you refused to practice the piano Monday night," my father said.

"I had a stomachache!"

"And you refused to practice the piano on Wednesday."

"That's not true!"

"She did practice on Wednesday," my mother said.

"Not for the entire half hour," my father corrected. "She barely started the Chopin before storming off—"

"That's because you yell at me every time I make the slightest mistake!" Tears streaked Lara's face.

"I never yell," my father said. "But we are paying for your lessons, and you're just wasting it! If you don't play the piano, that's fine—no more lessons! But as long as you want private lessons, you have to practice."

"Kovik, let her speak."

"Why do you always defend her?" my father said. He turned to Dr. Grokle. "She always takes Lara's side. This is a typical pattern. I try to point out a problem, but Maria always undermines me. Instead of supporting me, she caves in to Lara. And Lara takes advantage of it. She—"

"You don't know a thing!" Lara said.

My mother passed Lara a tissue. Tissues were free at the Hoffman Children and Family Center. You could have as many as you wanted.

To my dismay, no one paid any attention to me. Sitting in my chair next to the social worker, feet dangling, I could have been on Mars, for all they knew. Even more disturbing, no one seemed to think that my life was in danger. My father's reports to Dr. Grokle mentioned Lara's attacks on me as if they were mere pretexts for a larger battle—as if I were simply the lure that Lara used to get at my mother, and therefore irrelevant.

I didn't dare speak of my own terror, because I was ashamed of it. My parents always told me that I was overreacting when I tried to tell them about Lara's assaults, and I hated myself for being such a chickenshit. I knew that whatever Lara did to me was nothing compared to what the Russians had done to my father in the war.

Dr. Grokle was a complete disappointment to me, with her furrowed brow and high-rise hair. And Miss Jameson, in a candy-colored dress, just scribbled notes on a steno pad balanced on her eye-popping thighs. I realized that these two experts were never going to figure out how to send Lara anywhere.

So I kept my mouth shut. My life was directly linked to the outcome of these sessions—who would win and who would lose at therapy, and by how much. I simply hoped that whoever won would be good to me. In my experience, you never got what you wanted by asking for it. You were better off waiting to see what you were going to get, and then figuring out how to deal with it.

Recently I gave a reading at a college. In the women's room, notices were posted on the walls. The questions were simple and direct: *Do you feel safe in your home? Have you ever been struck by someone you live with? Are you afraid that you may be hurt by someone in your home?*

You were supposed to call a confidential hotline if you answered yes to any of the questions. You were not supposed to tolerate living in fear. This was considered domestic abuse, and there were agencies to help you. The idea seemed so strange to me. If I had seen such a sign in my school, would I have called for help? Of course not. Like most kids, I would never have admitted to anyone what happened in our home. Speaking out would be a deadly betrayal of my parents. Besides, they were all-powerful: if they could do nothing, then there was nothing to be done.

It was always dark when we got out of therapy. The four of us marched into the cold night in stony silence. My mother and father consulted briefly about dinner before climbing into their separate cars. Sometimes we went to the cafeteria at Macy's for dinner, but usually we went to Sears. The food was not as good at Sears, but my father was the store doctor, and we got a 10 percent discount.

Lara always rode with my mother, but I went with my father because I felt sorry for him; no one would ever choose my father's company over my mother's. He was too stiff and awkward, too painfully needy. As we drove through the city streets after those exhausting sessions, neither of us could think of anything to say.

My father's despair was like an animate being riding between us. I always wanted to make him feel better, but the pressure was too great and I remained silent.

Occasionally, as we sat at a traffic light, he might ask, "Tell me how you are. How is school?" By this, I took him to mean, *Are you happy? Am I a good father?* I would reply that I was happy and doing well. He always accepted this information at face value, with great relief.

As we glided north, I would mull over what had gone on in the session. My parents and Lara always tore into each other, and then my parents assured Lara they loved her, and then they'd all rip each other apart some more. Mom and Dad kept batting the word *love* back and forth like a shuttlecock in a game of badminton. I, for one, was ready to concede the point.

But I learned not to say this. If I so much as expressed doubt as to whether I loved my sister, my mother would come down on me like rain. "Don't ever say that!" she would snap. "Lara is your sister. Of course you love her!"

Her fury always alarmed me. "It's just that—"

"She's your sister!" my mother said.

I could see I wasn't going to win this. I kept my angry love to myself.

My father and I parked outside the shopping mall and went into the Sears cafeteria, where we waited for Lara and my mother, who was a dangerously cautious driver. The cafeteria was empty; no one else in the world ate dinner there. We'd never gone there before we started family therapy, and three years later, after we finally quit therapy, we never again ate at Sears.

I stayed close to my mother as we slid the plastic trays along the steel rails and selected our food. We sat at a table in the far corner lit by orbs of orange lights that hung like giant insects from the ceiling. The whole place was creepy and dark, and even our food had a radioactive orange glow to it.

We ate in silence. Lara brooded through dinner, picking at her food and looking away. I pushed the meat around my plate until it looked tired and beat-up. Then I dug into my chocolate cake. My father, as always, had engulfed his entire meal before the rest of us had even unfolded our paper napkins. He sat nervously across from us, jiggling one leg under the table, causing his body to tremble as if an electric current were running through him. He had the patience of a fruit fly. We were all nursing our wounds, replaying the awful things that had been said in the session. We were stung by the injustice of our roles as father, mother, daughter, sister. None of us saw any escape, and this realization was so depressing and infuriating, we sat in our chairs and ate until we could leave.

We didn't fight till we got home. Then the dam burst. Even before our jackets were off, we lost our heads and were swept up in the torrent of our rage. Sometimes Lara jumped me, sometimes she ransacked my room; sometimes she threw herself on the floor in the doorway to the kitchen, and kicked and clawed at anyone who tried to get past her. My parents fought with each other about how to handle Lara—my mother insisting on patience, and my father on discipline—and I shrieked bloody murder whenever Lara came near me.

But the thing about Lara was that she could also be really, really fun. You just never knew when. "Let's pig-pile Mom," she whispered to me one Sunday morning later that fall, her green eyes sparkling with excitement. As usual, my father had gotten up at six, and now, at eight, he was still at the hospital doing rounds. My mother was the sleepyhead of the family, and Lara and I tiptoed into my parents' dark bedroom. Mom was crashed on her side of the bed as always, lying on her belly like a little kid, arms flung up on either side of her head. You couldn't see her face for the cloud of thick brown hair, roots graying between monthly visits to the beauty parlor.

Lara and I drew closer, suppressing giggles—completely unnecessary, since Mom's relationship with sleep was passionate and exclusive.

70

"Now!" Lara whispered, and we jumped onto the bed, shouting, "Pig pile! Pig pile!"

A groan emerged from somewhere under my mother's hair. Her voice came as if from a deep cave. "Oh, let me sleep."

Lara and I set to tickling her.

"Ohhhhh," Mom said louder, a note of sorrow and sleepy joy in her voice. "Give me five minutes. Just five more minutes."

Lara laughed. "Come on, you lazy bum! Get up!"

My mother curled into a ball. "I'm a lazy bum," she said pleadingly. "Let me sleep."

But in my mother's Eastern European accent, it came out "la-*zee* bum," which sent Lara and me into peals of laughter.

"She's a la-*zee* bum!" Lara crowed. I chimed in, and we chanted, "A la-*zee* bum with a potbel-*lee!*"

"What?" my mother said. "A what?"

"A potbelly!" I said. "A potbel-*leee!*"

My mother laughed. Her stomach was flat as a pastry board. There wasn't an ounce of unnecessary flesh on her.

"I'm a la-*zeee* bum with a potbel-*leee,*" she agreed, pleading.

We tugged on her arms now, and got her to sit up. We poked at her belly. "Look at the potbel-*lee,*" Lara said.

My mother puffed her belly out so it would

look round. Then she grabbed me suddenly and flopped back on the bed, pulling me down with her. In an instant, Lara and I were tickling her again, but Mom had come to life, and she tickled us back, and the three of us rolled around on the bed, a mother with her two cubs, our delight in each other as natural and easy as the sun streaming through the trees behind the pulled curtains.

I don't know how or why these windows of joy opened and closed in our lives. They seemed to come without warning, like sudden changes in the weather. No one ever came up with a diagnosis for Lara. There was plenty of mother-blaming going around in the sixties, and in our double sessions at the Hoffman Center, my father and the shrink seemed to think that Mom's depression during her pregnancy with Lara had caused the problem. The way I understood it, my mother's unhappiness had surrounded Lara when she was still in Mom's womb. It seeped into Lara's body through her skin, so Lara "caught" a mental illness, the way you caught a cold. By the time I came along, my mother was in a better mood, so I came out okay.

I don't remember my mother ever being depressed. She possessed a colossal history and big emotions compacted into a body the size of a small vacuum cleaner. She had enormous energy, she sucked everyone into her vortex, and she was virulently anti-dirt. You could not tire her out. She had been through everything—the war, the ghetto, camps, prison, poverty, humiliation, as well as bridge parties, garden clubs, the Women's Auxiliary. And she tended the grounds and raised the children and got a graduate degree and taught German and sewed the drapes and still had time to read world literature. My mother was a giant. At five foot three and 110 pounds, she had the confidence of a world leader and an even more amazing ability to bluff. She figured that if she was still alive, the world was a very stupid place, and it was not hard to outwit it.

Over the following weeks, our fights got worse. Lara started going on eating binges and tore through the kitchen, devouring boxes of crackers and cookies. My mother followed her. "Please, Lara," she begged. "Talk to me." Mom seemed to be as dependent on these fights as my sister— as if she needed to prove her devotion to Lara over and over. Sometimes my mother would fall to her knees and sob that she should have died with her parents, and Lara would start crying and they would hug and console each other for hours. I didn't understand it at the time, but I think that my mother was fairly drowning in grief and rage; the weight of her secrets and losses was almost too much for her to bear. And Lara had always been the sensitive one in our family. She and my mother seemed to be acting out a drama of love and war and loss and death.

One time Lara grabbed a carving knife and backed my mother out of the kitchen, before ransacking the cabinets for flour and sugar to make a batch of cookies. Mom marched back in and stunned Lara by pouring half a gallon of milk down the sink. For Mom, throwing away food was like slashing open a vein; it was as if the milk going down the drain were her own blood.

"You want to bake cookies?" my mother shouted. "You want to eat more?" She slammed the empty carton down on the counter. "There. No more milk. No cookies. No baking."

Lara stared at Mom in horror. "I'm sorry, Mommy," she said. "I'm sorry!"

I cowered just outside the door. I pictured the police coming afterward to photograph the bodies and wipe up the blood and gather the bloody knife and milk carton and chocolate chips as evidence, and I would be able to testify for Mom. I would be able to tell someone what had happened to our family.

My father lived at his office during most of these fights. He could not break the grip Lara had on Mom, nor Mom on Lara. He could not compete with Mom in his own house. And so he paced up and down the world outside, fuming over his lack of access. In his office late at night, he wrote in his journal, transcribing his arguments with my mother, his frustrations with my sister, his discussions with the shrink. Hundreds of pages of meticulous record-keeping of how our family had gone so wrong. Years later, he would show them to me when I was home from college. "These will be for you," he told me. "I am writing them for you so you will have them after I die. Then you will understand."

It was so like my father to offer intimacy after he was dead, as if life were no time for explanations or understandings. I felt special being the daughter he trusted, but I knew it wasn't enough. He needed what he'd never had—a happy childhood, the love of his life, the years the Soviets had stolen from him. And all those journals that he'd written for me, that he put in boxes with my name on them—all of his journals now belong to my sister.

three

I work in the public defender office in Boston. From the minute I started in 1985, I knew I belonged here—everyone is committed to equal rights and justice, and more to the point, we all have a huge problem with authority. We revel in tripping up cops on the witness stand, and crow about our victories over the state's attorneys with a glee that could be considered . . . well, undignified.

When I was growing up, both my parents ruled my world, but it was my father who had always represented unassailable authority. Dad was a man of principle. He was a man of honor. He was a man of his word. He had impressed upon us that these were rare commodities, and he had all of them. He always obeyed the law, but he was also quick to point out that the law was often misapplied, misinterpreted, and even mistaken. Lawyers, he said, were slippery opportunists who capitalized on other people's misfortunes. He was not particularly thrilled when I became a lawyer, and he was even more disappointed when I chose a field of law in which I made no money at all.

"But I'm fighting for human rights and justice," I told him. Americans already had human rights, he said. Just look at the Soviet Union for comparison. What I was really doing as a public defender, he scoffed, was obstructing justice. My father's moral compass was flawless—of this he was certain.

It was his certainty that was most annoying, more so than his morals. He was not a particularly pious man, but his confidence was almost too much to bear. He was always right, and this seemed unfair. My sister and I were eager to find him wrong on something, but it never happened—at least, not until much later.

Like my colleagues, I felt at home on the side of the lowly and despised, crusading for civil rights. I took everything personally. But the adrenaline rush of trial work—the whiplash of highs and lows—got to me. When I lost, my guilt at having failed my clients was overwhelming. I couldn't bear to see them handcuffed and led off to prison. I thought of my father, sentenced to ten years of hard labor without the right to defend himself. It was complicated—he was at once authoritarian and ruthless, a force against whom I fought, and also a man who had been unjustly condemned, a man I wanted to rescue.

"Daddy's little defender," he used to call me when I was little, because I stood up for him in family fights. Despite his size and strength, he didn't hold much power in our household. It was my mother and sister who called the shots. I sided with him so he wouldn't be outnumbered.

Given his disdain for lawyers, it's ironic that in the final months of his life, my father relied on a lawyer to create a legal instrument—a codicil to his will—to disown me. And it's also ironic that in order to find out what had happened, I had to hire a lawyer myself. Through my attorney I learned of my mother's role in seeking out the lawyer who wrote the codicil for both of them. It was Mom—and perhaps Lara—who drove my father to the lawyer's office four months before his death, and who helped him hold the pen to sign the codicil. My parents' final words to me were executed by law. The man they'd hired to eliminate me shared my profession.

1966

Lara felt great sensitivity to animals, and grieved for weeks when one of our pet turtles or mice died. I recovered from such losses within the twenty minutes it took my mother to drive us to the pet store to get a new one. But I had an unseemly devotion to things—*my* things—and I kept everything I owned in a pristine, OCD state of unblemished perfection. I worshipped my collection of shiny Matchbox cars that I took out to play with (indoors only) and returned to their special carrying case, fitting each car into its corresponding numbered compartment. And I was devoted to my collection of little souvenirs from various trips—a small wooden skier from Vermont, a miniature seal from Canada, and so on. I dusted them every Saturday and replaced them in precisely the same configuration on the display shelf my father had built for me. My prize possession was a diary my parents had given me in 1965. I wrote in it every day, and carefully hid it in a box in my desk drawer. I recorded various important facts about my life, like what we did in gym class that day, or what the weather was like. And with the knowledge that I was committing a subversive act, I wrote about how much I hated Lara. Writing was dangerous, and my diary reflected the fact that I lived in the country of Big Sister. Discovery meant certain death.

When I was eight, I begged my parents for a lock for my bedroom door. I would be able to lock myself in my room, I explained, so that Lara couldn't get me. And I would be able to leave my room without worrying about Lara wrecking my things in my absence. To my surprise, my father agreed and went to Sears, purchased a doorknob and lock, and installed it in my door. He kept one key for himself and gave me the other.

From then on, I always locked my door whenever I stepped out—even for a moment—when I walked to the bathroom, or to the kitchen, or to ask my mother a question. It drove Lara crazy, because she had always counted on being able to jump me in my room, or to get at my diary, or to ransack my belongings when I was out. As long as I was vigilant, I could keep the contents of my room safe from her. I carried the key in the front pocket of my jeans, and miraculously, Lara never succeeded in getting it away from me. I was prepared to die for that key.

On Easter Sunday 1966, we were invited by the Palowskis to an afternoon cocktail party. Unlike my parents, who typically observed the Easter holiday by cleaning the house and eating matzos, the Palowskis were real Polish Catholics who had fled Kraków to escape the Communists. That morning, Lara refused to get out of bed. My mother sat at her bedside, pleading with her to get dressed and come with us. Mom pushed a strand of Lara's hair behind her ear, and Lara swatted it away. My father strode down the hallway in his dark-blue suit and polished shoes. "We'll leave her here," he said. "It's time to go." This is what the experts at the Hoffman Children and Family Center had told us to do when Lara refused to participate in family outings. She was almost twelve, capable of making her own decisions and staying home if she chose not to go. Lara hated being left alone, but wouldn't budge from bed. "It's all right, darling," my mother assured her as we left. "We'll be home in a few hours."

The Palowskis' house sat on a hill like an exotic gem on green velvet. It had a grand entrance and powder-blue Oriental carpets in the living room. I went out to the yard with the children of other guests, all of us painfully overdressed in Easter outfits, ruling out the possibility of any real fun. The grown-ups drank cocktails and laughed and spoke in Polish. After a few hours, my parents called for me. We put on our coats and walked down to the car, my patent-leather shoes clacking on the asphalt and my mother's high heels making little bird-pecking sounds. We drove home in silence.

As usual, my father slowed the car to a crawl as we approached our driveway so that we could admire the grounds. I could see him mentally comparing his work to that of the Palowskis' professional landscapers. The blue spruce and fir trees he had planted years before were already taller than I was, and the forsythia bushes were starting to burst open.

It was eerily quiet when we came in the house. There was no sign of Lara. My mother went to the closet to hang up her coat. I went to my room to take off my stupid dress, but for some reason my key wouldn't fit in the door. I looked closer and saw that nails had been hammered into the keyhole. From her bedroom, I could hear the low rumble of Lara's laughter.

The assault felt visceral, as if she had hammered nails into my own flesh. I let out a scream. The sound was terrible, but I couldn't stop. My father and mother came running. When they saw the doorknob, they rolled their eyes. "Oh, Helen, it's nothing," my mother said. "Nothing happened." They were tired and battle-weary, and they wanted to take off their formal clothes and relax and get a look at the Sunday *Times*, and maybe have a cup of tea and unwind. They did not want to deal with what they always dealt with: their children fighting childish wars.

My father went down to his workbench in the basement and returned with a hammer and pliers and a screwdriver. He set to work and yanked and pulled and twisted and banged. Eventually he was able to remove the ruined knob and open the door.

What lay before me was even more devastating. It looked as if a bomb had exploded: everything I owned had been flung across the room. Matchbox cars, games, figurines, socks, underwear—all ripped apart and scattered. My clothes had been clawed from their hangers and shelves and tossed in all directions. The desk drawers were yanked open, shredded papers and pens and books everywhere. And on the upended desk chair, my diary—torn open, pages fluttering.

It took a moment for me to grasp what had happened. My windows had been pried open with a screwdriver, and the screen had been removed from the frame. My sister had come in through the windows. I began shrieking with new horror. It was the end, I thought. I could not live here anymore. I wanted her dead; I wanted her sent away, locked up, thrown out.

My father spent the rest of the day repairing my window, replacing the screen, and removing the nails from the doorknob. The key still worked, after a fashion. I locked myself in my room and sat on my bed, rocking and crying and folding my clothes. I would never be the same, I thought. Nothing would ever be the same.

But I was wrong. Everything was exactly, precisely the same. As always, my father left for his evening office hours at four forty-five, right after our fifteen-minute dinner. For the next several months, as soon as his blue Chrysler slipped down the driveway, my sister would begin. She waited until I emerged from my room, and knocked me into the wall as I tried to reach the bathroom. She threatened to kill me and called me a crybaby if I made a sound.

Over time I learned not to react. I learned that to cry was to play into her hands, to give her what she most wanted: proof of my terror. I began to learn that my best defense was passive resistance. The pretense of unruffled composure. She could bang me around, she could knock me down, but

I swallowed my fear and presented only a calm, bland exterior. This drove her nuts, of course, and I liked that. I sensed my power. Sometimes I even whistled a tune, to really drive her over the edge. Then she had to go to even greater lengths to get a rise out of me. She was training me to ignore pain, and I was learning, but I was also keeping score.

How did we manage to keep this up day after day? There were no broken bones, no trips to the emergency room. We trafficked in terror and shame, strictly small-time stuff. I remember thinking, *This is how I learn to hurt someone. I can do it all by myself, without lifting a hand. I can go numb*—and this numbness was my sharpest sword of all.

I practiced on Lara, and she practiced on me, and we maximized our tolerance for inflicting and receiving pain. And every few weeks, between bouts of murderous rage, like some sort of diabolical interval training, we played well together, swimming at the local pool, playing basketball, collecting stamps, and inspecting insects.

Our parents stayed out of it as much as possible. They knew, of course, that sibling rivalry was to be expected, and my mother had an uncanny ability to see only what she wanted to see. And so I learned how to fight at home. I learned how to hate, and how to do harm. Sometimes, after

84

long hours of combat, after my mother and sister had collapsed in tears in each other's arms, I went outside and stood on the lawn, staring up at the stars. Everything dark, silent, mysterious. I wanted to strike the match that would explode the sky.

four

In the weeks following the receipt of my father's will in the mail, I tried to follow the path of my daily life as best I could: I went to the gym; walked the dog; walked my wife, Donna, to the health-care center where she worked, and then took the T to my office downtown. I could do almost everything but sleep. At night I padded around our apartment and wrote in my journal, recording everything I knew about my family, trying to make sense of my father's last words in his codicil.

Donna had known my family back when all of us had been close; she had watched our implosion over the years. Now, as I moved restlessly around our apartment, I was careful not to wake her. But I could hear her voice in my ear, a warm, slow-rolling Alabama accent that made you feel that all would be well. She was tall and lithe, with honking red toenails and dark almond eyes that tilted slightly on her thin face. When I'd first met her eight years earlier in my backyard—the neighbors had set us up!—her eyes had been so strangely beautiful, I'd run inside and changed my T-shirt, as if that might improve my chances.

It did. Two months later I moved into her apartment, and two years after that we exchanged rings. It wasn't yet legal, but we knew not to expect much of the law, and therefore we were not disappointed.

That winter of 2002, Donna was still recovering from ten months of chemotherapy after a recurrence of cancer. We had been through a hard year. She had managed to sidestep a literal death sentence just as I was dealt a figurative one.

I was nine when my parents started talking about divorce during our Children and Family sessions, and they went on talking about it at home behind closed doors, when they thought Lara and I weren't listening. Of course, Lara and I were always, *always* listening, especially when they spoke in Polish, a language neither of us understood. All the dangerous, important discussions between our parents were in Polish, and Lara and I translated them into our worst fears.

Lara's worst fear was that they'd send her to a mental institution. My worst fear was that they would not.

I didn't really understand what divorce was. I had classmates whose parents had died, but none who had divorced. This was back in the days before divorce spread through the suburbs like color TVs.

It was my father who first brought it up one

Friday night at the Hoffman Children and Family Center that spring of 1966. He was sitting with one knee over the other in the chair across from me, his maroon striped tie slightly askew under his dark suit jacket. He sounded very business-like. "After we get a divorce, I could move into my office."

A divorce sounded like something that you bought, like a coffin in which you put your dis-carded marriage. As I understood it, once my parents went out and got one, Dad would visit us from across town, which made sense, because he mostly worked all the time anyway.

My mother didn't say anything, but sat very rigid, her back straight and knees together, her mouth a thin line. I stole a glance at Lara, who looked bug-eyed. For once she wasn't even picking at her fingers; she was barely breathing.

Dr. Grokle also sat motionless, but her beehive of hair quivered. It was my father who could no longer live with us, he said icily, because he was a realist and my mother was not. Mom, I could tell, was angry—she didn't say a word, but stared at him as if he were a stack of dirty dishes. I said nothing, believing that things were more likely to go away if I ignored them.

Now I wonder. What if my father had a girl-friend? Or perhaps he wanted a girlfriend, but felt constrained by the vows of marriage? "My word is like iron," he used to say proudly. He would not break his word for all the nooky in the world.

But perhaps he would break his marriage for just one big, buxom blonde. Decades later, Lara reminded me that Miss Jameson, the social worker at the Hoffman Center, mysteriously disappeared from our therapy sessions at some point in the midsixties, and was never spoken of again. "She was hitting on Dad," Lara told me. "She kept calling the house. That's why we got an unlisted number, remember? Mom went apeshit over it."

Dad and Mom were always fighting over the correct use of a word, or the proper translation of a phrase from Latin or German or Italian into English. They ran for the dictionary and gloated when they got the expression right. But what came between them was far more treacherous than grammar or syntax. Mom depended on the illusion of a happy family, and could not admit that ours was broken. She would never have agreed to divorce. My father, on the other hand, could not tolerate pretense.

Lara's problems were the field on which they fought, but their troubles went deeper. There was something about my mother's all-consuming bond with her older sister that my father resented. He complained that my mother's attention was never on him; instead she lavished her love on

Zosia and Renzo in Italy. "It's not normal," he said. I don't think it ever occurred to him that Mom and Zosia might be keeping a secret from him. He only knew that, despite appearances, he was left out of his own marriage. Divorce would be more honest.

They didn't get divorced.

Something shifted the fall after I turned eleven and Lara was fourteen—at first it seemed that Lara had simply gone on a diet and lost weight, but then it turned out that she'd more or less stopped eating. We had been on a two-year reprieve from family therapy for good behavior, but now we went back. Anorexia was sort of a parole violation.

At dinner now, Lara would cautiously tap at her food with the tines of her fork, as if a green bean might suddenly leap from the plate and strangle her. She slowly pushed a piece of steak to the left of her plate, then to the right. She turned it ninety degrees. She lifted her glass of water and took a few sips, then returned it to the counter and stared at it, exhausted by the effort.

My mother started cooking special meals for her: steamed vegetables, tiny portions of New York sirloin, lettuce with vinegar, fish with lemon. Lara ate less and less and grew tiny before our eyes. My mother became desperate. My father threatened hospitalization. Dr. Grokle at the Hoffman Center continued to bob her beehive at us.

None of this concerned me too much. What rocked my world was that Lara was no longer a physical threat to me. As I grew taller and stronger, she grew thinner, more frail, twig-like. For the first time in my life, I felt completely safe.

But within a month or two, Lara had risen to a new kind of power over our family—by disappearing before our eyes. I didn't see what the big deal was. Let her starve herself, I thought—at least she didn't bother me anymore. To my surprise, it looked like anorexia might actually get her hospitalized. Even Dr. Grokle started talking about it. Only my mother held out.

"Please, Lara, you have to eat," Mom begged at every meal. Please, darling. Try."

Lara would slouch so low over the counter you couldn't see her plate for her hair.

"I'm too fat!" More of a moan than words.

My father, sitting next to me at the opposite end of the counter, had just finished my potatoes and pork chop for me. I was not a big eater in those days, and my father was always hungry. When my mother wasn't looking, I'd broom my leftovers onto his plate. He hoovered them up before anyone noticed. Sometimes I wondered whether he even realized that the food had come from my plate.

"But you're skin and bones, darling! Look at yourself! Do you know how many times I've had to take in your school uniform? It's hanging off of you."

"Well, I'm not hungry," Lara said. "You can't make me eat when I'm not hungry."

"Oh yes we can," my father said in a low voice.

Lara leaped up, sending her chair crashing to the floor. "No you can't!" she shouted. "You can't make me do anything!"

"They'll do it at the hospital," he said coolly. "If you don't eat, they'll insert a food tube and force the food directly into your stomach."

"Oh, you'd like that, wouldn't you? You'd love to see—"

"Lara, please—" My mother held out her arms, but Lara swatted them away.

"Get away from me!" she shouted. "Why do you hate me so much?"

"We don't—"

"Leave me *alone!*" She ran to her bedroom and slammed the door.

At the time I had no sympathy for Lara, and even less curiosity about what she might be going through. Looking back now, it occurs to me that she was given an impossible role as my older sister—everything was riding on her. All of my parents' losses—their broken hopes and dreams, the heartbreak of our murdered grandparents— landed on Lara's shoulders. There was no way she could repair the past, and the weight of our parents' needs must have been crushing. Perhaps Lara fought against the burden, thrashing and kicking and bucking them in the only way she could—with her body. I was luckier: I came after her, and while she commanded everyone's attention, I was able to slip by relatively unnoticed. At least for a while, until I grew old enough to engage in the battle with our family's past as a full-fledged participant.

Hospitalization was my father's ace in the hole. Even my mother knew she couldn't keep Lara at home if she didn't eat. Deadlines were set, weigh-ins established, calories counted. Cheating, broken promises, threats to call the police. New bargains, new deadlines, more fights. Lara ate enough to stay out of the hospital, and we settled into a sort of detente. Time slipped by, and Lara got better, apparently all by herself. By the time she was seventeen, Lara was feeling good enough to switch from the safety of St. Mary's to the raucous regional public high school for her senior year.

I didn't realize it at the time, but I was learning from a master. Years later, when I was in college, I would follow in Lara's dangerous footsteps and engage in my own food wars. But back in 1969, when I was twelve, food was my friend. The bigger I grew, the safer I felt around Lara. Our mutual hatred was alive and well, but now our skirmishes became more strategic.

"Helen is going out with boys," she told Mom when I was thirteen.

This was a stroke of genius on Lara's part, because Mom considered my interest in boys evidence of my lack of allegiance to our household. At the time, I would rather have been almost anywhere than attached to the flypaper of my family. And it was this apparent desire of mine to escape from home that most angered my mother. To her, family was sacrosanct and friends were suspect. Boys—the entire gender—were just plain off-limits.

"You are not to date," my mother informed me.

"I'm not *dating* anyone," I lied. "I hang out with my friends. We go to parties." This was true. I didn't mention that we also paired off and necked with the lights out.

"All right, no more parties then," my mother said. "Weekends are for family." To Mom, I was worse than crazy or violent like Lara: I was *disloyal*.

Lara had never had a boyfriend in her life, and her standards were even more Victorian than my mother's. I couldn't fight both of them. And to be honest, it wasn't that much of a sacrifice—I didn't really care that much about boys or partying to begin with. I just wanted to be loved by everyone.

During the fall of 1971, Lara was applying to colleges, and brochures were spread across the dining room table—Williams, Amherst, Middlebury, Smith. All those glossy scenes of swirling autumn leaves, students tossing Frisbees and reading books under giant oak trees. My mother had done her homework, and I could see the excitement growing in her eyes. College, I realized, was where I needed to focus my energy. I tagged along with Mom and Lara on their tours of prospective schools all over New England. As we strolled across the leafy campus of Wellesley College, I recognized immediately what my mother's eyes said: they said, *I want.* She wanted the luxury of time and books and immersion in the world of academia. I decided to give her Wellesley. She'd worked hard to make college material of me, and she deserved to have me go to the college of her choice.

I began amassing my credentials. I threw myself into the student government, the school newspaper, varsity sports. I performed in a talent show at the old-age home. I was aiming high—for the beam in my mother's eye. Even my dad started noticing me—I had finally risen to his line of vision. This was wealth. I would soar into the stratosphere for my parents.

I asked my teachers for extra-credit assignments in addition to my schoolwork, in order to inch my grades higher. Now I was spending all my time reading, studying, brownnosing, ass-kissing, teacher-petting, and good-girling. My teachers loved me because their jobs were hard and I was easy. I wanted to please. I followed directions, and only rebelled in the privacy of my own mind, when no one was looking.

Mainly I wanted to prove to my parents how capable I was; I wanted them to beam with pride. I considered that my job description: Perfect Child.

Looking at my photos from that freshman year of high school, I see I was relatively dark-skinned, with long dark hair and brown eyes. I liked myself, or thought I did, and I had a self-confidence that I did not deserve, perhaps, but I believed I would go places and do things that other people would not do. It would take decades to realize that my young confidence covered for a sense of terrifying responsibility to excel, and a life-threatening fear of failure.

My ninth-grade physics teacher, a John Belushi look-alike with muttonchop sideburns and a wreck of rumpled clothes, was the only one who saw this as a problem. One day after class, Mr. Moskowitz grabbed me by a few strands of my hair and said, "C'mere." I thought he was joking (he had a malicious sense of humor that was usually pretty funny), but this hurt, and I had to bend sideways and tilt my head toward him as he pulled me down the hall. Students gaped as we passed by. When we reached the cafeteria, he sat me at a table across from him. My scalp was burning.

"You've got to stop this," he said.

"What?" I still thought this was some kind of joke, but I couldn't figure it out.

"Just cut the bullshit."

"What are you talking about?"

"All this extra credit, all this trying to get into college. You're fourteen! Cut the crap! You're missing out on your own life."

I was stung. I suddenly hated Mr. Moskowitz.

"I am living my life," I snapped.

In retrospect, it's strange that Mr. Moskowitz, the most unlikely person on the planet, had me *nailed.* He just didn't know the half of it, or how to help. Of course, no one could have helped me then; my need to impress my parents trumped my own interests, whatever they were.

The spring of my freshman year, through no fault of my own, a senior named Kevin Flanagan took an interest in me. My sister happened to be in the same homeroom as Kevin, now that she was in the public school system. Lara immediately reported to my mother that Kevin was a thug who smoked dope and mouthed off in class.

This was only partly true. He did smoke dope and mouth off in class, but he was also a voracious reader, passionate about history, philosophy, and ethics. And he was tall and broad-shouldered, with a head of free-flying rust-colored hair, a tanned face from working outdoors, and something like a beard-in-progress. Despite our four-year age difference, Kevin and I were in the same elective French class, where we learned to speak French with a Brooklyn accent like our teacher. One day Kevin approached me after class, introduced himself, and told me he made leather belts and wallets; would I like one? He pointed to his own belt as evidence of his craftsmanship, and I felt a little funny staring at his hips. He was long-waisted and trim, and his faded jeans rode low on his hips. He pulled his wallet from his back pocket, and handed it to me so I could admire how smooth the leather was, how fine the stitching.

"I'll show you how I make them," he offered.

My mother, with her firm grip on the choke collar of my social life, dropped me off at Kevin's house for the sole purpose of letting me watch Kevin stitch two pieces of leather together. Upon completion of this task, Kevin's father drove me home.

Over the next few weeks, I bought a wallet from Kevin that I didn't need, a belt, and a sort of purse that looked more like a saddlebag, sturdy enough to withstand a stampede of horses. My mother examined and scoffed at each purchase, making it clear that I could throw away my babysitting money however I wished, but I was certainly not going to see Kevin Flanagan for anything other than arm's-length financial transactions.

My sister left for college in the fall of 1972. A mini-flotilla of two long-finned Chryslers filled to the brim with clothes, stereo, and the members of our nuclear family moved solemnly east across the state line to Smith, an ivy-whiskered institution of Gothic sobriety. My father, whose finger was always on the safety lock of his wallet, broke out in a sweat when he saw the manicured lawns of Lara's new campus. He was a provider *par excellence*, and proud of it, but he had grown up in abject poverty, and never felt comfortable with wealth.

By sundown we had transferred the contents of both cars into her dorm room, and left the old green Chrysler with Lara. She stood at the curb, tearfully waving good-bye to us as we receded into darkness. Stretched out in the back seat, I could barely contain my excitement at having gotten rid of my older sister in this perfectly legitimate way. I spent the ride dreaming of my freedom from Lara's surveillance: the escapades I would lead, the days I would spend with my friends in her absence.

I had not yet stumbled upon the addictive quality of misery as Lara had. Every Friday she would drive the hour and a half from college directly to her shrink's office in Schenectady. From there, she drove home to unleash her first downpour, and our family fell into the familiar pattern. It was like getting Lara's Doom in concentrate: a full week's misery condensed to fit a weekend. By midday Sunday, the anxiety in the household had ratcheted up; we were all waiting to see whether she would manage to return to college in time for Monday classes. We tiptoed around her, afraid to start another fight, while she sat slumped over the kitchen counter, anger rising from her like chlorine gas. Sometimes she would leave Sunday afternoon; sometimes she would wander back to bed and not emerge till dinnertime. Sometimes she would leave Sunday night, and sometimes, when our nerves were about to snap, she would brood through the night and not drive back to college until Monday morning.

In the meantime, Kevin Flanagan had enrolled in a nearby college, where his father was chair of the Physics Department. ("He's not a *real* doctor," my mother sniffed, offended that anyone with a mere PhD could appropriate the title of "doctor.") I was fifteen now, and my mother grudgingly agreed to let me play tennis with Kevin on the asphalt courts behind his school. Kevin and I were both sufficiently athletic, competitive, and inept at tennis to keep this interesting.

As my mother feared, I actually liked Kevin. He was much more worldly than I, yet he seemed genuinely interested in what I thought about things like the war in Vietnam and the role of students in overthrowing the government. (I was against war, I said. I didn't know much about overthrowing anything.)

In those days, Mom monitored me closely and allowed daytime activities, as long as I didn't *date*. She defined *dating* in the old-fashioned sense of the word, where the boy comes to the house, picks up the girl, and takes her out to the movies or the basketball game or the school dance. These common uses of boys were *verboten* in my family, or at least for me. So instead, on warm Saturday afternoons, Kevin and I went bicycling on deserted country roads, surrounded by endless fields of wildflowers and woods and wilderness. When the sun grew too hot, we leaned our bikes against a tree and walked into the woods and settled on a grassy knoll and kissed. We were surprisingly restrained, and never lost our heads or clothes or any of the other things we had to lose.

We also kissed in the basement of his house. His parents were upstairs; they'd invited me for dinner. Kevin leaned over me and kissed me full on the mouth and I kissed him back, hard, and we stood there, kissing with necks of steel, pressing against each other like contestants in the World's

Strongest Kissing Competition. Then we went upstairs and had dinner with his parents, and his father drove me home.

For me, kissing was a life skill one ought to acquire, like grammar or long division. It never had any effect on me physically. I never stopped to wonder about this.

Some weeks later, while we were once again standing in his basement and kissing (a bit less strenuously), Kevin ventured to touch my breast, so softly, through the cotton of my T-shirt and the polyester padding of my AA-cup bra. I brushed his hand away. "Come on, Kevin. Cut it out." For some reason, alarm signals went off in my head. Kissing was one thing—I used my mouth in public all the time, for talking, for eating; it was right out there for all the world to see. But no one had ever touched my breasts before; they were a part of my body that were, to my mind, an unpleasant encumbrance, twin bumps that I preferred not to think about. His touching them was a reminder of the danger that lay within me that my mother was so afraid of.

Kevin seemed hurt but said nothing, and we continued kissing, like *nice* people.

I'm not sure what Kevin was thinking at the time. I suspect he was actually falling in love, or something like it; he was a hopeless romantic, and he was going to get hurt. Or maybe my intransigence was exactly what made the relationship safe for him. Years later we would talk about our natural affinity for disappointment. Both of us were used to making do with whatever we got—a little attention, some affection, some love.

It was after that evening of the Bra Touch that I started to panic. I was clearly doing something illegal behind my mother's back—something my sister would never have dreamed of doing. Lara would have been as outraged as Mom, and would have ratted me out in an instant. I couldn't bear to enter this treacherous uncharted territory of boys against my mother's wishes.

And I knew this meant something was wrong with me. After all, my classmates had boyfriends in plain view, in front of their siblings and parents, as if it were the most natural thing in the world. There was no way I could do that. Maybe I could fudge certain details that Mom didn't really care about, but I absolutely could not break the law of family loyalty. Between Kevin and my mother, there was really no contest. I would choose Mom. I would choose my family.

So I called Kevin in tears. "I have to see you," I said. "I have to tell you something. You're going to hate me, but we need to talk."

It was a chilly Sunday afternoon in late April. I got my mother to give me a ride to his house. Wringing my hands, I walked with him up and down the hills where he lived. "I can't have a romantic relationship with you," I told him. "I want to, and I've tried, but I know my mother is against it, and I just can't make myself go against her wishes. It's driving me crazy."

Kevin murmured reassuring words and tried to calm me down. Why was he being so nice?

"This is my own problem," I said, choking back tears. "If I were you, I'd be really angry, and really hurt."

But Kevin looked incredibly sweet and concerned. "It's okay, Helen," he kept saying.

"You won't want to see me again," I continued, my tears flowing freely now. "And you shouldn't. You should just move on, find a normal girl who will love you and be a proper girlfriend."

To my amazement, he told me it didn't matter. It mattered more to him that we continue our friendship, even if it remained platonic.

I was stunned. This fairly blew me away. It had never occurred to me that Kevin would want to be friends if we couldn't be more than that.

So there it was. At fifteen, I was still too much my mother's daughter to be Kevin's girlfriend. In fact, I was too much my mother's daughter to be *myself.*

five

The summer I turned sixteen, Mom, Lara, and I flew to Rome to stay with Zosia and Uncle in their apartment in the city. Uncle spent his days puttering around his bedroom, which doubled as his office. Stacks of books and papers rose from floor to ceiling: legal documents, genealogical charts, books of heraldry, history, Nostradamus, astronomy, and law. We sneaked a peek now and then when he opened the door a crack, but no one—not even Zosia—ever set foot in it. Zosia's bedroom was as small and tidy as Uncle's was big and unwieldy. Mom, Lara, and I slept in the majestic living room on narrow cots that we folded up each morning before tiptoeing out of the apartment at dawn.

Mom marched Lara and me all over the city. She knew and loved Rome as a native, and blossomed into a new person here, as if she'd stepped into another version of herself, one with color and joy. Her exhilaration was contagious, and Lara and I fell under her spell. This was the city where she and Zosia had reinvented themselves, where they had begun their lives together after Mom had escaped the Nazis in Poland.

Here was the grand Teatro dell' Opera, and here the catacombs of Sant'Agnese, my mother told us, where she'd taken groups of American GIs from the Red Cross Rest Center during the war. And here, the rusticated palazzo of the Ministero dell'Agricoltura where she'd worked as a translator after the war, before handing her job off to Zosia and emigrating to the States with Dad. Lara and I followed her everywhere, enthralled. She introduced us to her Italian friends, who told us stories about how she had bartered for food on the black market; how she'd helped them smuggle cigarettes out of the Red Cross Center.

Years later, my mother would tell me that she had never wanted to emigrate to the States with my father after the war. "I wanted to stay there with Zosia," she said with tears in her eyes. "And with Renzo. He was eight years old when I left." She shook her head. "It was Zosia who forced me to go."

"Why?"

My mother wiped her eyes. "Zosia knew Dad would never fit in in Italy. You know Dad. He would have been so unhappy there."

Remembering this now, I marvel at the guilelessness of my mother's stories. On the surface, her explanations are completely true. My father, with his mathematical certainty of right and wrong, would indeed have been driven crazy in Italy, where the laws of physics are so easily curved to accommodate the needs of personality and politics. But later I would come to realize that Zosia's reasons for sending her sister and brother-in-law overseas after the war were more complicated. After the war was over, the secrets took on a life of their own, and it would be decades before I could begin to piece together the whole story.

That fall, I applied to colleges, eager to launch. Now I looked beyond Wellesley—to Brown, Dartmouth, Bowdoin. My mother pretended that the choice was mine, but she dropped hints in case I made the wrong decision. "A women's college," she said. "You want to get an education, not a husband." In fairness to my mother, Kevin Flanagan wasn't the only boy she wanted gone; she seemed intent on removing the entire gender from my life.

My mother also helped me choose my career that year. Unlike Lara, a science geek, all I cared about was languages. I loved writing stories and dreamed of one day writing the story of my parents' lives. At the time, I didn't realize that my mother had created a fiction of her own life, but I was captivated by what little I knew of her past.

"I want to be a writer," I said. "A novelist."

"A foreign correspondent," my mother corrected. "You'll live in Paris, or perhaps Rome or

Heidelberg, and submit articles on art and culture to the *New Yorker* or the *Atlantic* or the *New York Times*."

Clearly, if you didn't write for the *New Yorker* or the *Atlantic* or the *New York Times*, there was no point in writing at all. I was going to be a huge disappointment to my mother, but neither of us knew exactly how huge at the time.

My mother drove me to my college interviews—in the end, I'd obediently applied only to two women's schools: Wellesley and Smith, where Lara was a sophomore now. She had finally settled into dorm life, and was actually sort of fun to be with, and I felt the familiar tug of sisterhood to join her. My mother kept dropping hints about how nice it would be if Lara and I were together. "Lara has a car," Mom pointed out, as she drove me to my interview at Smith. "You and she could come home together on weekends."

As it turned out, while I was being interviewed in the admissions office, my sister was two flights above me in the dean's office, being disciplined for breaking into the cafeteria with some classmates and raiding the ice cream bins. This caper had great appeal to me, and I pictured Lara and me bonding over similar adventures once I enrolled here. But another part of me remembered the volatility of our relationship. The urge to stay away from her was as strong as the urge to join her, and eventually I decided it would be safer for us not to go to the same school.

I was on crutches that fall, thanks to a field hockey injury that had torn my left quadriceps. Apparently, admissions committees could not resist a theatrical entrance; both colleges admitted me immediately, without waiting for me to finish my junior year of high school. And so, two weeks after my seventeenth birthday, in the fall of 1974, I became a high school dropout and college freshman.

Wellesley wasn't what I expected. I thought it would be like high school, only more beautiful, with better sports facilities. I'd gone to a semi-rural regional public school, so it was something of a jolt to find myself in a cerebral New England bastion of WASP privilege. Not that I knew what a WASP was; I only knew I was different. In my sweats and pixie haircut, I felt like an impostor, a kid from the boonies who did not belong with the sophisticated, sharp-dressed students on campus who called themselves "women" instead of girls. I wasn't used to this feeling of being a misfit, and it dawned on me that perhaps this was what Lara had felt like all her life. I felt a creepy shift in allegiance to her now.

Even more unnerving, the workload was killing. In high school, I'd never had to study more than an hour or two to outshine most of my classmates. But here, the syllabus for a single course listed more books than I'd read in the last two years of my life. One of the students in my literature class had read *Beowulf* in the original, and another discussed the political ramifications of nineteenth-century German philosophy over lunch. Cowed, I shackled myself to my desk and studied until the words on the page melted together.

My roommate was from the North Shore of Boston and had gone to a private boarding school. I liked her immediately—a tomboy in an oversize Brooks Brothers shirt, Levi's jeans, and Top-Siders without socks. She tied her limp hair in a ponytail and threw parties in our room for the whole floor, at which she served imported cheeses and bottles of gin. I'd never drunk anything more than a glass of wine in my life. Our room was small, so our classmates piled in, sitting on our beds and desks, on the floor, and even on the bookcases and dressers. Those who couldn't fit inside clogged the doorway and overflowed into the hall. At first, I liked being the social hub of our dorm. I could feel my coolness quotient rising. I passed the cheese and crackers, and quickly shed my unspoken identification with Lara. But after four or five parties in so many days, I started to worry about my studies. I couldn't figure out how to sneak off to the library without looking like a complete dork. So I played along and pretended to sip gin from my plastic cup of tap water, and tried to hide my growing anxiety over losing precious study time. But my affectation of a Fun Person was showing signs of wear.

Soon our parties attracted upperclassmen and students from other dorms. My roommate, flush with success, took periodic head counts of our guests. Later in the evening I would hear her talking excitedly on the phone with Mummy, proudly reporting the number of people who had attended our party.

That's when I understood that she and I were not so different after all. We were both desperate to impress our mothers; the only difference was how our mothers measured our success.

A few weeks later, my roommate and I were approached by some classmates who'd brokered a floor-wide freshman roommate swap to mix things up. I would move to a room at the end of the hall with another misfit, Janet Kairns, a public school kid like me in denim overalls, tube socks, and sneakers, who came from a hick town not far from my own. She and I bonded immediately over our common affliction of homesickness, something we hadn't dared admit to anyone before. And something else about Janet: in her geeky, good-natured way, she was a sweeter, simpler version of my sister. I felt comfortable and safe with Janet; she was like an overgrown eight-year-old boy mixed with a golden retriever. But strangely enough, I also found myself longing for the complicated edginess, the danger and sheer *Lara-ness* of Lara.

As if a switch had been flicked, I was now flooded with fond memories of skiing and hiking and swimming with Lara, of ganging up on Mom, who always seemed to delight in being the brunt of our silly jokes.

Here at college I was ashamed of this part of me, this childish, homesick Helen. It was time for me to become a successful adult in the world. So I spent my first semester holed up in the library and studied all weekend as if my life depended on it, which, of course, it did. Janet too disappeared into the stacks of the library, while the other women in our dorm smoked dope and drank vodka tonics from giant bowls, and fucked the boys from Harvard and MIT and Dartmouth and whoever else showed up on campus. I now missed my family in a way that took my breath away. I'd always been so self-assured, so hell-bent on getting out of there. But here in the world, I discovered I was more like them than like anyone else.

And now, for the first time in our lives, Lara and I started writing to each other—letters that were funny and self-mocking and oddly reassuring. To my surprise, we actually seemed to *like* each other. Perhaps now that we were both away from home, we began to see the possibility of friendship rather than rivalry. I took a bus to visit her over the Columbus Day weekend, and we had a surprisingly good time together, biking on country roads past tobacco fields and apple orchards, buying giant cookies at the country store. Lara was inexplicably good-natured and laid-back, no longer the dweeb I remembered from home. She nodded knowingly when I confessed to being intimidated by my classmates' erudition. Perhaps she was relieved to see that I was becoming less of an asshole—I could finally admit to cracks in my self-assured façade. In any event, it turned out we were very much alike, Lara and I—two college kids trying to impress our parents, for whom we felt a toxic mix of awe and love, and a sense of crushing obligation.

But over the next few weeks and months, it was precisely this similarity to my sister that began to gnaw at me. The pursuit of perfection was grinding me down. The fact that I'd managed to score straight As my first semester only plunged me deeper into despair. How was I going to keep this up? Now that I'd staked my claim at the top of the alphabet, anything else would feel like a failure.

This sense of implosion was new to me. It followed me everywhere—when I ran the tree-rooted trail around Lake Waban, when I tried to drown my anguish in ice cream sundaes in the dorm cafeteria, even when I shot hoops with Janet on weekends. *I'm sliding down the same chute as Lara,* I thought. Whatever "it" was that had tormented my sister since childhood, I had finally caught it. I was literally *turning into* Lara, or at least the version of Lara that was unglued. Somehow, Lara and I had quietly swapped places that winter. She had emerged the confident one, and I had turned into an insecure mess. I didn't know it then, but this was the beginning of a pattern my sister and I would fall into for decades to come.

It wasn't until the spring semester that I stumbled upon rowing. Or rather, first I stumbled upon Emma Dunlap, a tall, blond Californian with a goofy smile and calves the shape of mangoes. She seemed to breeze through campus as if she were on a surfboard—long athletic limbs, silky hair, aquamarine eyes. She and I were lab partners in Biology 100 that winter; we operated on the same frog and examined its tiny heart and kidneys. "He's beautiful," she murmured. This had not occurred to me. I had seen the frog as a speed bump on my way to a high-powered career of some sort; Emma made me see him as a lush country with rivers of life.

Emma was also a rower and had raced in the Head of the Charles in October. She showed me her photos of the regatta. I'd never seen a crew shell before. She'd developed and printed the pictures in one of the darkrooms in the art center. I caught my breath at the high-gloss images, stunned by her talent, her boundless energy, her off-kilter beauty. I imagined what it would feel like to fly across the water in one of those long, sleek racing shells with Emma and a team of women.

"You have to join the crew," she said. "We'll row together."

I pictured the mist rising at dawn as our boat unzipped the surface of the lake.

"Yes," I said.

Rowing was unlike any sport I'd ever done. The fastest crews are quiet and smooth, the perfection of power squeezed into as narrow and clean a line as possible, a speed seamstress streaking down the racecourse, stitching each stroke into the fabric of the river, and finishing before the water even knows it's been cut.

From the moment I tried it, I was in love. You take four strong women and blend them into a single motion. You slide together, catch together, breathe together. You lose sense of your boundaries. You become one with the boat, with the other rowers, with the water.

We would roll out of bed and stumble down to the boathouse before dawn, when the lake was just a dark smudge surrounded by the shapes of trees. We launched into darkness, our blades sailing over the water and punching holes in the lake. Now the first rays of sunlight seeped through heavy rags of mist. Behind us the shore was barely distinguishable from the soup of early morning. Soon the second boat joined us and we raced side by side.

The morning flew by as if on time-lapse photography. The sun rose like a gold coin in the sky, and the shore came into focus. The woods sprang up, dark limbs snaking through the sharp green of spring. The lake grew choppy, a slate color that turned blue-black, then gunmetal gray. Out on Route 16, cars began their slow descent into the city.

We spent an hour and a half racing each other from cove to cove, turning quickly at the end of each set and pausing—just long enough to pass the water bottle, wipe our foreheads on our shirtsleeves, and gasp for breath. We sat hunched over, shoulders soaked, legs quivering. Our fingers grew blisters and then calluses, hard and smooth.

By the time we docked, the world had awakened. Breakfast was cooking in the cafeteria. We threw on our sweats and ran up the hill to the dorm. Wet, flushed, stained with oarlock grease, we stormed the dining room, where a handful of our classmates sat slumped in bathrobes, sucking down coffee, stunned by the fact of morning. Flush with endorphins, we filled the room with roars of laughter, heaped our plates with food, and sat down to our meal like the victorious army we believed ourselves to be.

Passions crossed from one boat to another. Attraction was unavoidable. We were teenagers, we moved in sync, and it was all pretty much preconscious—most of us hadn't yet made the connection between love and Lesbos. It was 1975, but I don't think anyone on our crew had even heard of the Stonewall riots six years earlier. I certainly never imagined that the soaring feelings and giddy excitement I felt for some of my teammates could be more than the inevitable camaraderie of a close-knit team of athletes. My anxiety and self-doubt of the previous semester fell away. I grew closer to Emma. In the evenings she and I would sit on the floor of her room and talk about our families and our dreams for our future, as if our lives were a movie that could be previewed and condensed into tantalizing trailers. I barely mentioned my sister, and instead ratcheted up the romance and drama of our family story. After all, my parents had always been the real stars in my life; Lara and I were the tendrils you pushed out of the way to see them more clearly.

In her photos, Emma's parents and two brothers looked youthful and happy, bronzed by the California sun, while my family lurked in the shadow of its dark past. Her father had rowed for Berkeley in the fifties, while my father was still learning English and washing his gray hair in the residents' sinks at Mount Sinai Hospital. I wanted to be just like her. I wanted to grow a second skin like hers—smooth, strong, confident. She and her family hiked in the Sierra Nevada and rock-climbed in Yosemite, and her father was a helicopter pilot in his spare time, when he wasn't handling major financial deals for his bank. I fantasized about being adopted by the Dunlaps and tried not to think too much about my own family.

six

Lara came home from her junior year sunk in a soul-sucking depression. Her head hung to her chest, and she moved as if her feet were shackled together. She barely said hello to me as she shuffled through the door. I was shocked that the Lara of last fall had dissipated into this other Lara, someone I had buried deep in my memory of our unpleasant past.

She had gotten extensions on her final papers. Our family sprang into action, turned the dining room into our war room, and spread Lara's notebooks and research materials across the table. My mother prepared the plan of attack. My father did fact-checks, and I was assigned to editing. Lara perked up and got to work.

She completed her junior year with her fine grade point average intact. Then she fell apart. She disappeared into her room and could not be roused from bed for days at a time. It felt as if our house had closed around a festering wound, and my parents and I moved uneasily from kitchen to living room to bedroom, afraid of what might ooze out.

I'd returned home that May after my freshman

year with a broken heart. Emma was transferring to Berkeley to be closer to her family, and we wrote long, passionate, coast-to-coast letters over which I cried and cried. She sent me pressed wildflowers from the High Sierras and invited me to California. To my astonishment, I burst into tears at the mere mention of her name, and read and reread her letters obsessively. My mother thought this was perfectly normal. After all, it was the way she missed her sister, who was about to arrive from Rome to spend the summer with us, as she did every year now. During the winter months when she and Zosia were apart, my mother would run to the mailbox every afternoon for Zosia's letter as if it contained the oxygen she needed to get through the next twenty-four hours.

Now Mom made up the little couch in the television room as Zosia's bed for the summer. It was oddly sweet to see Mom dancing around Zosia like a puppy, bringing her tea, offering her fresh-baked linzer torte, and chattering away in Italian. Zosia was still groggy from the long flight, and it took her a few days to get over her jet lag, put on an apron, and start churning out choux pastry and apfelstrudel and panettone in the kitchen. My father, as usual, was at his office or at the hospital all day, stopping by for supper at four-thirty before rushing off for evening office hours a few minutes later. He seemed to accept that Zosia and his wife were a unit. He would join in their conversation in Italian at times—usually to correct them on some point of politics, history, or grammar, depending on the topic of discussion.

I can't remember exactly what happened to Kevin that summer. When I first came home in May, he'd proposed a summer fling, which I declined, having lost all interest in him. He seemed to be a dull shard from a distant past. I spent that summer of 1975 working the cash register at Herman's World of Sporting Goods. I was about to turn eighteen, still too young to work in a store that sold guns, but the manager was a Rotary Club friend of my father's, so he let it go. The rest of the employees, in their little mustard-colored vests with the World of Sporting Goods logo over the left breast, grumbled behind my back. I took my breaks with the High Adventure guys, who sold pitons and chalks and bright-colored climbing ropes. I listened to them brag about their winter assaults and Class 7 climbs. We sat on folding chairs around the dented table in the employee lounge and ate Clark Bars and Raisinets from the candy machine. Cigarette butts cascaded from a hubcap-size ashtray in the middle of the table. Bolted to the wall was the time clock, and next to it the metal rack with our time cards. If you punched in a minute late, you were docked fifteen minutes.

I spent most of my paycheck on climbing gear they recommended, and one of them, Joe Cantagna, asked me on a date. He had dark wavy hair and an uneven mustache, and he was always touching the calluses on his hands with his fingertips. Although I was in college, my mother still did not allow me to date, and boys did not understand my compliance with this rule. I had no interest in dating Joe Cantagna or any other guy. So I lied and told Joe I already had a boyfriend. It was easier all around. In my experience, going out with boys was not worth the acrobatics involved in lying to my mother. I needed my mother; I did not need boys. I didn't waste time wondering about this.

Lara wasn't able to do much with herself that summer. Mainly she stayed at home under the covers, playing games with the drugs her shrink prescribed—she'd take them, not take them, stockpile them, pretend to take them, fight with my father about them, etc. She would stagger from her room every day or two, dazed and barefoot. She dragged herself to the kitchen, collapsed in a chair at the counter, and picked at her fingers. She wore the same torn white T-shirt all summer, with a faded emblem of her Amateur Athletic Union swim team across the front.

We exchanged scowls. Would it have killed me to be nice to her? I was obviously in better shape than she was that summer, but it only made me more stingy with my tiny quota of kindness.

As soon as she sat down, my mother jumped to her feet. "Oh, Lara!" she said. "Coffee?"

Lara grunted, and my mother poured.

"Darling, would you like some panettone?" Lara picked at the coffee cake, then pushed it away, then picked at it some more. My mother leaned over her and whispered something in her ear. I refused to look at them, annoyed by the dance that bound them together. I did not want to be as miserable as Lara to deserve that kind of attention. But I wanted something too shameful to admit: I wanted my mother to myself. I wanted our long conversations about books and art and movies. I missed her laughter.

And I couldn't have said it at the time, but I also wanted my big sister back, the version of Lara who had reassuringly appeared out of the monster of childhood. I wanted the Lara who patiently listened to me and my problems, who took care of me and inspired me to go on adventures with her. I hated it when she was like this, so aggressively depressed, staring daggers and shoving me aside with a smoldering rage. Not only had this lout of a Lara taken my beloved sister away, but she had also taken my mother with her.

Zosia's presence added a new twist. Until this summer, my mother had managed to keep our family's misery a secret from Zosia. Lara had always been able to pull herself together around Zosia in the past. But by July, Lara had given up any effort at pretense, and she was having her meltdowns in plain view of all of us. Zosia seemed unfazed by this. "I'm tough," she would tell me. "I can take a lot."

"She's very fragile," my mother would say of Zosia. "She cannot take it."

And so we pursued our own ideas about ourselves and each other.

As the summer wore on, my father spent more time at his office. I wasted my days at the cash register, dreaming of someday busting loose. I had visions of running away to California to be with Emma, hiking the spine of the Sierras, climbing out of my life in the suburban Tri-City area. With my employee discount, I bought a backpack, tent, sleeping bag, headlamp, water bottles, everything I needed to get away from everyone and everything.

One day Zosia pulled me aside. "Your mother has her hands full," she said. "She doesn't have time for you. Tell me. I'm the auntie. Tell me what you did today." With her silvery hair and lined face, she seemed much older than last summer, when we had been together in Rome.

"I worked."

"What was it like?"

"I can't stand it," I said. "I can't stand watching

Mom pour herself into Lara, day and night. It makes me crazy just seeing them!"

"You have to be patient, darling." Zosia's voice dropped. "Lara is very sick, and your mother is doing the best she can. She loves you very much—"

"Oh, please," I said, turning away.

"No!" Zosia caught my wrist. Her eyes flashed. "You have to help your mother. You have to be as nice to her as you can. What she is dealing with is very, very hard."

Zosia's anger alarmed me. "If Lara's so sick," I said, "then how come she can be raving mad one minute, and then when the phone rings—if it's some friend of hers—she's instantly sweet and funny and fine, as if nothing's happened? Either she's sick or she's not! It's not like some spigot she can turn on and off at will."

"She's sick, darling. You have to understand."

My father agreed with me about Lara. But he took the discussion into dangerous territory that I did not wish to explore. "Mom is deranged," he said matter-of-factly. "She is damaged by the war." His face went solemn, and the creases around his mouth deepened. "She never recovered from the killing of her parents."

I kept silent. I refused to believe that my mother was deranged; I believed Lara was the problem. Remove Lara, I thought, and all would be fine.

I was just as deluded as everyone else.

• • •

One evening my father was driving Zosia and me down State Street to his office to fetch toilet paper for our house. He ordered it wholesale for his office, and we siphoned off the supplies for home use, keeping careful count for the IRS. We were riding in his new Plymouth Duster, and he recorded the mileage and gas expenditures in a little notebook, so he could monitor the engine's efficiency.

"She can't help it," Zosia was saying.

"Then she should be properly medicated."

I listened from the back seat. All we ever talked about was Lara. All day, every day, all my life. This summer was the first time Zosia was pulled in too.

"You can't just drug her into a stupor," Zosia said. "She has a problem. She needs help. "*P*sychotherapy," she added, coming down hard on the *p*. "She needs intensive *p*sychotherapy."

Wrong! I thought. Shrinks had been poking sticks at Lara for the past ten years, and they seemed to be part of the problem here. They could make anyone look crazy, especially someone as messed up as Lara. At least, that was Lara's position, and I was starting to agree with her. The more she saw psychiatrists, the worse she got.

"She needs patience," Zosia said.

"She also needs discipline," my father said. "She needs someone to lay down the law. Maria is too permissive. She gives in to Lara's every wish."

Although I was aligned with my father, his idea of discipline scared me; sometimes it looked a lot like sadism. He had Siberian standards of punishment. Once, when I was fourteen, he asked if I'd like to take a walk with him. It was August; we were on vacation in Maine. I chose to wear my new sandals—Dr. Scholl's knockoffs—of which my father disapproved. "Put on sensible shoes," he said. "But they're comfortable," I assured him. To teach me a lesson, he took off at a breakneck pace, walking as briskly as his long legs would carry him. I had to run to keep up, and by the time we got home an hour later, my feet were pulp, my sandals covered in blood. Neither of us said a word, but I had trouble walking for the rest of our vacation. I suppose I was more like my father than I liked to admit.

"Lara is a sick girl," my aunt said softly. "Kovik, remember, she's a child. She has a mental problem. I never realized it till this summer, you know. Maria didn't want to tell me. But now I see."

"She's twenty-one."

Zosia threw him a cutting glare. "A child."

"She needs to understand there are rules," he said. "And consequences." His hand came off the steering wheel and made a karate chop in the air. "If you separate Maria and Lara," he said, "then you will see."

"What will you see?"

"Without Maria, Lara will have no one with whom to engage. She will see that she gets nowhere with her tantrums and threats, and she will have to learn self-control."

I kept quiet, my default mode when my family talked about Lara. I knew that my voice in these matters was irrelevant, that I was better off listening and keeping my opinions to myself.

The sun dropped off the edge of State Street. In the midsummer dusk that gathered outside the windshield, the neon signs of fast-food joints and convenience stores popped to life. At home, I knew, my mother and sister would be speaking softly to each other. My sister would be in bed, and my mother would be sitting at the edge, stroking her hair, reassuring her of her love. This was their time alone, their moment together when they did not have to justify themselves to the rest of the family. They could love each other as they were meant to love: stubbornly, wholeheartedly, without shame or guilt.

August came. In another month, Zosia would be flying back to Rome, I would be returning to college, and if my parents could pull it off, Lara would return for her senior year. Lara had a knack for bouncing back from suicidal depression to successful scholar in no time flat. In retrospect, I can see the enormous pressure she was under, the rigidity of our parents' needs, and how impossible it must have felt to Lara to meet them. But at the time, I considered Lara's versatility in mood swings proof of her resourcefulness, evidence of the calculated power she held over us. Instead of feeling sorry for her, I was furious at her manipulation of us.

In mid-August, Dad and I came up with a brilliant plan.

"You need a vacation," he said when he picked me up from work one day. "You should get out of the house."

We were sitting in traffic on Drake Road. "What about you?" I said. "You haven't had a break all summer."

We were nearing home, the fun-less zone. It made us want to take care of each other.

"When does school start?" Dad asked.

"The day after Labor Day."

"How about the week before, then? We could take a trip."

A wild feeling of danger and hope surged through me. "I don't know about my job—I told them I'd work through Labor Day."

"I'll talk to Conklin," my father said. "I can get you out of it."

And so my father and I ran off together.

The great thing about running away with my father was that it was sanctioned by the family.

I could get out of the house without having to assume the label of Selfish Child. I could pretend I was doing it for my father, and he could pretend he was doing it for me.

The bad thing about running away with my father was that I would be stuck with him for ten days. Going on vacation with a sixty-year-old Holocaust survivor and former Gulag prisoner who tends to relive each moment of his six-year incarceration is not for everyone. But consider the alternative. If I had to spend one more minute at home, watching all of us move around Lara like deep-sea creatures, I was sure I would explode.

Dad and I packed a suitcase and two sleeping bags. He picked me up from work the next day and asked to speak with his friend Conklin, the manager. Mr. Conklin was a timid man with thinning hair and a sad little mustache that you had to look at twice to realize it was really there. He wore caved-in shoes and an over-all dreariness that made me feel sorry for him. You could see that he revered my father. When Dad appeared before him, Mr. Conklin's face lit up with wonder. He seemed not to mind my father's too-short clip-on tie that swung slightly to the right. Conklin's own fashion sense was not keen either. He wore the same thing he wore every day: a cheap maroon blazer with the Herman's World of Sporting Goods insignia emblazoned on the pocket. His shoulders swam in it.

"I'm sorry to ask this," my father said in a tone that suggested pain and dignity. "The situation at home is . . ." He paused and glanced down at his shoes. "It is extremely difficult. . . ."

I was curious to know what my father would tell my boss about "the situation at home." Conklin looked up at my father with genuine sympathy. You could see he would give my father anything he asked for. He would hand him the keys to the store, to the entire stockroom of goods. He would hand over his wallet, his watch, his wedding ring—*anything,* as long as my father didn't go into details.

"I know Helen agreed to work through the Labor Day weekend," my father said. He drew his lips into a thin line. "But the situation at home . . . I'm sorry that I must ask for Helen to step out of work a week early."

Conklin was already nodding his head before my father had finished his sentence. "Of course," he said. "Of course."

My father didn't stop there. "Someday," he said, looking wistfully over Conklin's head at the fluorescent lights gleaming in the Golf Department, "someday I will tell you about it." He sighed. "But I cannot now." He glanced briefly into Conklin's eyes. "It is too painful."

Conklin patted my father on the arm, a gesture that startled me by its intimacy and sweetness.

Conklin barely came up to my father's tie clip, and the sight of him extending his polyester arm toward my father broke my heart. "I'm sorry," he murmured. "I'm so sorry."

My father nodded. "I cannot talk about it," he said quietly.

I was suddenly annoyed that my father spent so much time saying what he could not talk about. Our forced silence about "the situation at home" drove me crazy. I wanted to scream it from the rooftops. Of course, it never occurred to me that maybe I could use some therapy myself. That would mean I was mentally ill, and I would sooner have died than see a shrink.

"If there's anything I can do," Conklin murmured, his small hand on my father's elbow, "please call me." His earnest face, those black horn-rimmed glasses, those broken-down shoes . . . I was embarrassed to see him give my father such support. And I was somehow ashamed of our performance, which was not a performance—our pain was genuine, yet it seemed so ridiculous played out in public. Did we really need to break my promise to my employer? I would never see Mr. Conklin again, but my father, no doubt, would see him at the Rotary Club luncheons, and would make some sad remark that would tell Conklin nothing and everything, and he would look at Conklin as a man who could not possibly imagine his suffering.

My mother and Zosia seemed relieved to get Dad and me out of the house. Now they could tend to Lara full-time without the nagging interference of my father and me. Lara was all-consuming, and now, at last, they could be fully consumed.

I let my father dictate our route. We drove north to the White Mountains and hiked in the Presidential Range, then drove south to Boston, where Dad spent a day in Harvard Square and played the Chess Master for a dollar per game. He kept winning his dollar back for hours, till it was too dark to see the board and they had to quit. Next we went to Cape Cod for lunch at a fish shack, and then to Falmouth, where we boarded the ferry for Martha's Vineyard. Armed with a map of the island, we drove from one cheap motel to another, and I would run into the office, ask the price of a room, and run back to my father. He shook his head if the price was too high. He made a soft whistling sound if the price was completely outrageous. After an hour or so, we found a campground. For ten dollars, they gave us a tent platform with an army surplus canvas tent that was mostly waterproof, albeit mildewed. We had brought our own sleeping bags and unfurled them across the wood-planked platform. Our sweaters and socks were our pillows.

It rained that night, and mosquitoes lined up and bit our necks, our ears, our eyelids. My father snored like a Cossack. I circled the tunnel of my sleeping bag and wondered whether I would ever find my way out of my family. I'd been in such a hurry to grow up and get out of high school, chart my course in the open world. But the world was full of mosquitoes and mildew and crap jobs behind a register. It was hard to choose the world when my family knew my name and the words to my heart. They could open and close it with the twist of a key. Would I ever get away?

Dawn finally broke and we went into town for coffee. A mimeographed sheet tacked to a bulletin board advertised a local chess tournament. The name of the contact person was familiar—I'd read a book about a disastrous climb up Everest by a guy named Woodrow Wilson Sayre. I called the number from a pay phone and said that my father would like to enter the tournament.

"Sorry, it's over," the man said. "I should take that flyer down."

"Um, are you, by any chance . . . Did you write *Four against Everest*?"

The man's voice warmed. "Why, yes," he said. "If you want to come over, I can sell you a copy." I was elated. "And tell your dad I'll play him a game, if he likes."

I hung up and ran back to my father in the car.

"The tournament's over," I said quickly, "but it's the same guy who climbed Everest and wrote a book about it! He said he'd sell me one if we go to his house!"

My father shook his head, unimpressed.

"And he said he'd play you a game, if you like."

At this, my father perked up. "Call him back and get directions," he said.

They played most of the afternoon and into the evening, while I reread Sayre's book. He happily sold it to me for fourteen dollars. Given his designer house with wall-to-wall windows, bronze sculptures, and family portraits by artists I'd studied in art history, I suspect he didn't really need my fourteen dollars, but it was well worth it for my father's six hours of uninterrupted chess.

In the evening we strolled the streets of Vineyard Haven staring at rich people who had puttered in from their yachts in the harbor. Art Buchwald waddled down the main street in a short-sleeved button-down shirt and shorts stretched over his round stomach. My father did not like rich people, whom he suspected of not having worked sufficiently hard or suffered enough (in his opinion) to earn their wealth. But he did like funny people like Art Buchwald, and he was willing to forgive certain funny people for being rich.

It was in Provincetown back on the Cape that he started talking about the Gulag. Stories and memories he'd never told me before. He talked about the cold in a way that made the Arctic take shape as an isolated world of blackened toes and endless ice and wind. He spoke of hunger, a constant drilling against the belly and the skull. Men went crazy from hunger. They daydreamed recipes and visualized beef stews. They salivated from memory and imagination. He told me more about himself than he ever had before, and I drank up his words with awe.

"In the Gulag, I learned to be an idiot," my father said. "The others tried to engage me in discussions, but I just shrugged and said, 'I know nothing. I have no opinion.'" My father looked so old to me then, more myth than man. I wanted to rescue him from his past, to absorb his pain and bring him back to life.

"I learned not to trust anyone," he said. "This was the most important lesson I learned. And that is the reason I was able to survive. That, and the fact that I was a doctor. Because as a doctor, I could work indoors. Everyone who worked outside died of starvation and exposure."

I spoke very little during these walks. I did not want my father to stop talking. I hoped he wouldn't notice me sucking up his life with a hunger I could not explain. It was important, I thought, for him to be able to unburden himself, and I wanted to be the one in whom he could confide. By the time I returned to school, I felt about a thousand years old. With zero sense of who I was.

seven

English had always been my favorite subject, but now I decided that the most impressive thing I could do for my father was to become a doctor. Never mind that Dad didn't *like* practicing medicine (he'd always wanted to be a violinist). He had no patience for people who complained; he hated practicing what he called "an imperfect science"; and he felt personally offended when a patient's condition got worse. Even so, he liked helping people, was proud of the status and income that his medical degree afforded him, and believed it was an excellent, if stressful, career choice. At eighteen, I didn't concern myself with the actual job description of being a doctor; I just wanted to pick the direct route to my parents' hearts. My sister was premed, and despite the fact that I'd never had the least interest in math or science, my scholastic achievement suggested I should be premed too. "Be a doctor," my mother had always advised us, "don't marry one."

"What should I take?" I asked Lara over the phone that September. Now that she and I were both back at school, she seemed to have reverted to her big sister role as fellow hunter-gatherer of good grades, and reliable provider of curricular information.

"Load up on chem," she said. "And get your physics out of the way. You'll need calculus too."

It was reassuring to have my sister back, to have her attention and advice. As a senior, she'd already taken this path, and could warn me of the pitfalls. I pictured us both hoisting our course loads like rucksacks and hiking along the precipitous path to an MD, just as we'd hiked across the Alps the summer I was fifteen, Lara in the lead. Only this time, instead of whining with exhaustion, I would embrace the suffering and conquer it.

The first inkling that I might have a problem was chemistry. I'd signed up for the survey course and took notes like a stenographer. I drew diagrams and graphs and charts with colored pencils, and labeled my beakers in the elegant penmanship for which I had won awards in grade school. My lab notebook could have been displayed in the Museum for the Anal-Retentive.

The problem was not my grades, nor my com-prehension of chemistry. The problem was new to me: it was a problem of *attitude*. Until now, it had been none of my business whether I liked a subject or not; my job was to study my brains out and get an A. Now, for the first time, I had *feelings* about it. I did not like chem lab. Lab started at one in the afternoon and lasted until nearly five. While I was indoors pouring liquids from one beaker into another, the lake was out there turning its smooth face to the sky, begging to be rowed on. The trails in the woods were just waiting for me to lace up my sneakers and run on them.

Chem lab was, quite simply, a crime against nature. Against *my* nature. I could feel my soul being sucked dry, one drop at a time. I faced a dilemma. I could strip myself of what I loved by turning myself in to the lab each afternoon, or I could skip lab sciences altogether and row my heart across the lake and back.

Within months, I made a decision that suited my soul: I decided not to be a doctor. The immediate pleasure I obtained by this decision: my afternoons would be free of lab for the rest of my life. I had, with the simple dismissal of a career choice, given myself the gift of light in the afternoons. Ironically, the career that had saved my father's life by keeping him indoors and safe from Siberian winters was precisely the career I rejected because it kept me inside a lab in eastern Massachusetts.

That semester I was also taking an English lit class taught by a battle-ax of a Chaucer scholar named Helen Corsa. In the middle of a lively discussion of *Moll Flanders* one day, she stood in front of the class with her fists on her hips and announced, "People always say, 'Don't major in English! What can you *do* with an English major?'" She rocked back on her heels and eyed us through thick glasses on her jowly face. "Well, who the hell cares whether it's *useful?* Major in it because it's *fun!*"

My heart leapt. I made an appointment to see her the following week, and asked her to be my advisor. Would she sign the paper declaring my English major? To my disappointment, she barely glanced at me as she scribbled her name on the document and handed it back to me. "There you go," she said, and returned to the papers on her desk. I felt foolish for having hoped she might take an interest in me, and I was too ashamed to ask for any more of her time. Despite my timidity, I reveled in Professor Corsa's belligerent take-no-prisoners attitude about choosing a field of study for *fun.* Here was someone as strong and opinionated as my parents, but with a completely opposite agenda. Of course, I didn't have the guts to stand up either to Professor Corsa or to my parents, but I was pretty sure that Helen Corsa could kick their butts, at least when it came to championing the importance of Chaucer in my life. The battle between my English professor and my parents took place in my mind, and I needed her in there.

Unfortunately, unlike Helen Corsa, who was a literary genius, I knew I was majoring in English because it was a breeze—only eight English classes and no lab component! How would I explain this to my parents? Taking the easy road was a felony in our family. Living up to my Potential, I understood, required hard work, pain, and suffering. My parents had talked about this magic Potential of mine from grade school on, as if it were some utopia that had been furnished and prepared for me with fresh linens and modern window treatments, and it was my responsibility to climb the stairs to get to this fabulous future of mine, a special deluxe suite at the top of the world. There was no time for dillydallying, as my father liked to say. If I didn't race up those stairs, if I didn't spend every ounce of my time, energy, and concentration on propelling myself upward, my Potential could simply evaporate, leaving me empty, alone, unloved, and worthless in a windowless studio with a Murphy bed.

October 1975

"Hold still," Harriet said, one callused hand on top of my head, the other holding a pair of scissors. I was sitting on a chair in the women's room of her dorm, with half of my hair scattered on the floor.

"You're scalping me!" I said. "Leave me *some*thing, will you? Like an inch?"

Harriet bent over, momentarily choked up with

laughter. "I left you way more than an inch," she said, pointing to a tuft of hair above my left ear. She stared at me in the mirror, trying to keep a straight face.

"Just wait till it's your turn," I said.

It was mid-October, six weeks into my sophomore year, and now that Emma had gone to Berkeley, I found myself (in that same cluelessly self-closeted way) crazy about Harriet Goodwin, a big-boned Minnesotan who rowed right behind me in our coxed four. She, in turn, had a crush on Jim, commander of the *Enterprise*—the character that William Shatner played in *Star Trek*. Harriet was a senior and captain of our team, a pure powerhouse of a rower who had been awarded a single racing shell by the U.S. Olympic Development Team. In practices, I could feel her drive with each stroke—she pried the lake open with her oar, propelling our boat forward.

It was her idea that we cut each other's hair. "We'll be more aerodynamic," she said. It was our private joke—we didn't include our teammates. Afterward, we both wore blue bandannas to classes, and laughed when we took them off. Neither of us cared, really, what we looked like. The idea was more of a bonding ritual, cutting our hair short in preparation for the Head of the Charles Regatta, in which we'd be racing in a few days.

I was slated to stroke our varsity boat, with

Harriet rowing in the seat behind me. My parents had offered to drive out to Boston to watch me race, and then to bring me home for the long weekend. At eighteen, I was overjoyed that they were coming, and eager to show them off to my coach and teammates. Although Lara and I had been playing on varsity teams all our lives, neither of my parents had ever watched us compete. Girls' sports were not considered important in those days, and Dad certainly never took time off from work to do anything as trivial as watch an athletic event. So I felt I'd scored the attention of the grand duke and duchess of my world. Later I would realize that they had arranged their visit for completely different reasons than I'd imagined. They had more important things on their minds.

I still hadn't broken the news about declaring an English major to my parents; I hadn't even told my sister about my decision to drop the whole premed thing. I was afraid Lara might feel let down. Weren't we supposed to be in this together? She and I hadn't spoken since the beginning of the semester, when she'd told me what science courses to take. In the meantime, I'd spent more time rowing and goofing off with Harriet than studying.

The morning of the regatta was a New England special: blue sky, trees in flame, river sparkling. Magazine Beach was covered with racing shells and men and women sporting muscle shirts and blast-off legs. When it was time for our race, we stripped off our socks and gingerly stepped on slimy rocks, carrying the boat into the water. We locked the oars, climbed in, toweled off our feet, laced them into the foot stretchers, and rowed down to the start.

We fought a brisk wind into the basin. When they called our start, we fairly exploded from the line, oars in sync, coxswain screaming. The crowds on the riverbanks were a blur, their cheers a dull roar. We were flying at an impossible stroke rate, and after a few minutes, I started to panic. *I can't do it,* I thought. *I'm going to let them all down.* I yanked wildly on my oar, my breath ragged. The boat lurched to port. "It's okay, just relax." Harriet's voice drifted over my shoulders. "Just settle down and drive with your legs." Her voice was calm and even, and it cut through my terror.

I found the rhythm again and we were back in the race. But my face burned with shame. What had happened? What was wrong with me? I poured my anger into each stroke. Soon we passed a boat near the Western Avenue Bridge, and another at Anderson. We did all right in the end, seventh in a field of some twenty crews. Seventh was perfectly respectable, but it was small solace for the realization that I could not rely on myself—that in a pinch, when push came to shove, when everyone was counting on me, I could not deliver.

"It's okay," Harriet said after we'd put the boat on slings and wiped it down. She patted my shoulder a bit awkwardly. We started derigging the boat. Despite my bravado, I knew I was weak at the center of my being. I was not reliable; I could not trust myself. It was at times like this that I felt a creeping sense of identity with Lara. She was the symbol of all that was scary and uncontrollable and irrational in our family. I felt myself slipping into that crater, and it was unnerving.

After our team loaded the boats back onto the truck, I found Mom and Dad waiting for me on the dock of the Weld Boathouse. Among the crowds of spectators in jeans and T-shirts, my father stood out in his dark business suit and my mother in a formal pantsuit.

"Do you have everything?" my mother asked, eyeing the small sports bag slung over my shoulder. I'd only packed two textbooks; I didn't feel like studying much over the weekend, and I was looking forward to spending time with my parents. Mercifully, my mother said nothing about my haircut, and I couldn't tell whether she'd even noticed it.

We walked to the car. I knew it was of no consequence to my parents how my team did. My father had been a decathlete on the Polish

Olympic team, but instead of competing in the 1936 Olympics, he had chosen to study for his medical exams. "Sports are an excellent outlet," he'd always said, "but a career is what matters."

It was fine if I wanted to row, as long as my studies didn't suffer.

One of my teammates' parents had invited the whole team to dinner at their home in Cambridge, one of those quiet multimillion-dollar houses three blocks from Harvard Square. It never occurred to me to be impressed by these folks. On the contrary, I wanted to show off *my* parents, who, I thought, were so foreign and exotic, so clearly extraordinary, everyone would admire me for my affiliation with them.

"We don't have time to stop," my father said.

"Oh, please," I begged. "Can't we just drop by for a couple minutes to say hi?"

We were the last ones to arrive. Mom and Dad stood stiffly in the foyer, politely declining offers to eat or drink. I felt inexplicably proud, simply because they were my parents. But their awkwardness was obvious, and we left quickly.

Night had fallen. Cambridge was strangely quiet, a planet of empty streets. My mother and I climbed into the Chrysler and my father started the engine. My eyelids closed of their own accord, and in the darkness I saw the racecourse again, the crowds cheering on the riverbank like colorful bits of confetti, crew shells skimming the water, fighting each other through the bridges. I was looking forward to the weekend at home. I would have a chance to rest and recover before returning to classes.

And I also wanted to talk to my mother about what had happened to me during the race. I didn't want to admit my weakness to my father, but I figured tomorrow, when Dad was at work, I could talk to Mom about it. She was better at that kind of stuff.

My father slipped the car into gear and we floated silently through the city and onto the Mass Pike. I began loosening the seat belt, longing to slide across the back seat and fall asleep.

"Helen," my mother said. "We have something to tell you."

I stiffened at the sound of her voice, and studied the outline of her head. Something was wrong. She didn't turn toward me, but stared straight ahead out the windshield. Stars had popped out in the sky, and we seemed to be driving into them, scattering them.

"It's about Lara," she said.

I held my breath.

"Lara has . . . well . . . you know she was having a very difficult time this summer." My mother's voice broke. "She's gone into an institution."

"What?"

"The Institute of Living," my mother said. "It's the best of its kind. Near Hartford, Connecticut."

"Of *Living?*" It made me think of death.

"It was last month. She just couldn't continue—" Mom paused to dab her eyes with a Kleenex. "She was terribly sick."

"But . . ." I gripped the seat as if it were a flotation device.

An institution?! I tried to organize this information into a logical beginning, middle, and end. While I'd been messing around in boats all fall, my sister had gone nuts. Why hadn't they told me sooner?

"She didn't want you to know," my mother said. "And there was nothing you could do anyway. She made me promise not to tell you. But in another month it will be Thanksgiving, and you would find out then anyway. . . ."

No no no no no. I'd spent a good chunk of my childhood hoping for Lara to get locked up someplace where she couldn't hurt me. But so much had changed since then—I *needed* Lara now. She and I were in this together, this terrible battle to grow up—and I couldn't lose her to the loony bin.

"She finally agreed to go," my mother said in a dead voice. "We took her to the Institute, and she finally agreed to sign herself in."

"There was no other choice," my father said bluntly.

My mother practically leapt out of her seat at him. "Oh, you've been wanting this for years!"

she hissed. "You've wanted to send her away since she was a child!"

My father stared straight ahead, the hairs on his head shining in the headlights of a passing car.

"How could you?" my mother shouted. "How could you do this to your own daughter?"

I'd never heard my mother speak like this—it was as if Lara's rage were spilling directly out of my mother's mouth.

I had the sudden impulse to flip open the door, jump to the side of the road, and run back down the highway to my dorm. My teammates would be sitting around in the lounge, laughing and talking about the races.

"You know that's not fair," my father said in a low voice.

I concentrated on sitting perfectly still and making no sound.

"It's true!" my mother cried. "You've wanted this all along!"

I stayed quiet and let my father take the rap, though I was the one who had always wanted Lara sent away when I was little. For a moment in the sixties, when Lara was fourteen and starving herself, my wish had almost come true. There was a hospital in White Plains, and the Hoffman Children and Family Center had made all the arrangements. They were just waiting for my mother to agree. It sounded good to me—I pictured a distant, desolate land stretched across a white expanse of New York State. She would be safely out of reach.

But it had never happened. Week after week, Lara always cleaned up her act at the last minute and ate something. I'd always imagined that with Lara gone, my parents and I could live in peace. It hadn't occurred to me that without Lara to distract us, my parents would turn on each other.

My mother was too angry to speak now. She stared ahead, and we plunged forward into the darkness.

We arrived at home late and my mother put the kettle on for tea. My father walked past us without speaking.

My room seemed so much smaller than I remembered. The blue shelves my father had built held the same childhood collection of figurines, some glued together after Lara's tantrums. They looked forlorn, remnants from a previous life.

Without thinking, I found myself walking into my sister's room next to mine. Her room was dark. I sat on her bed and lost all sense of time. She was gone, and I felt sick. I missed her. Her absence felt physical, a broken shell tumbling in my stomach. This couldn't be happening. I should have done something; I should have helped her.

From the kitchen I could hear my father murmuring and the staccato of my mother's response. The kettle screeched, and as I walked into the kitchen, my father brushed past me. "Good night," he said.

Mom and I sat at the kitchen counter, stirring our tea, staring at our reflections in the window. "It was very hard," my mother said. She unwrapped a hard candy and popped it in her mouth. "Want one?" She held the little bowl out to me. I shook my head.

"The doctor says she is doing better." She took a sip of tea, holding the candy between her teeth. "It was very bad the first few nights."

A light was on in my parents' bedroom, and I had the feeling my father was listening as he read the enormous black tome on psychiatry that he kept at his bedside.

"After Lara signed in, I hugged her good-bye, but when the aides came for her, she got very violent. She pushed them away and started screaming and fighting." My mother took a Kleenex from the cuff of her sweater and wiped her nose. "They had to wrestle her down and put her in restraints. There was nothing I could do. And Lara was yelling at me, 'You did this to me! It's your fault!'" Mom's voice cut off, and she brought the teacup to her mouth. "Eventually," she said, "they sedated her and took her to a room downstairs."

I put my hand on my mother's arm, but I didn't know what to say. I pictured Lara on one of her wild rampages. It must have taken half a dozen guards to bring her down.

"You know," my mother said, shaking her head, "I felt . . . I felt I'd betrayed her. Never again will I let that happen to her. *Never.*"

My mother took a sip of tea. She blinked away tears.

A chill crept down my spine. I had conveniently forgotten that Lara could get like that, and it was a jolt to be reminded. Why couldn't I ever hold those two parts of my sister together in my mind—Lara the beloved, and Lara the ballistic? When things were good between us, as they had been the year before, I simply washed her postal periods from my mind. Or rather, I tucked them into some hidden compartment called "the past," a chamber in which our family threw everything that was dangerous and scary. We pretended—no, we *believed*—that nothing from the past could ever return to haunt us. I rarely thought about our childhood fights, and when I did, I shrugged them off. Whatever had happened in the past, I told myself, couldn't have been as bad as I remembered. In any case, it was over and done with. We were fine.

But now part of me felt relieved that hospital staff—*people outside my family*—had seen Lara when she was like that. So it was real. There were witnesses. There was a record.

"The following day, they put her back on the

general ward," my mother said. "She called me afterward. She was very angry." My mother lowered her voice. "She demanded that I get her out of there, that it was all my fault."

I said nothing, but my heart broke for my mother, whom I held blameless. *Lara's crazy,* I thought. *How could she guilt-trip Mom like that?* But then again, maybe Mom wasn't so innocent after all. Why was she always catering to Lara's shit?

Sitting at the kitchen counter that night, I felt ashamed that I'd known nothing about Lara's hospitalization—I'd been encased in my own little bubble those past weeks while Lara and my parents had been flying through the woods of mental illness. My own meltdown during my race seemed so insignificant by comparison, it didn't even warrant mentioning. Instead I felt overwhelmed by the larger family drama—angry at my sister, sorry for my mother; angry at my mother, sorry for my sister. I couldn't sort it out.

"How long will she be there?"

Mom shrugged. "It all depends on how she does." Then she added, "You mustn't say a word of this to anyone."

Of course not, I thought. Secrets were the lifeblood of our family. No one must know that Lara was in a mental institution; her future was at stake, her brilliant career as a physician. Not even Zosia would ever be told.

It would be many years before I realized the connection between my mother's leaving Lara at the Institute that day, and an earlier separation that had occurred long before Lara was born. It was in October 1942, Mom told us, when she left her parents, cut her hair short, dressed up as an Italian soldier, and escaped to join Zosia in Rome. Her mother had talked her into leaving them and saving herself. Mom never saw her parents again. They were killed in a death camp months later. Mom had been twenty-three at the time—two years older than Lara was when Mom and Dad dropped her off at the Institute. Both separations, thirty-three years apart, were surrounded by secrecy, shame, and a sense of irrevocable loss. Leaving Lara at the Institute, I now realize, must have been excruciating for my mother, and she would never let it happen again, no matter how desperately ill Lara might become in the years ahead.

It cost a fortune, Dad told me years later. To prevent any record of my sister's hospitalization, my parents didn't file for insurance; my father footed the entire bill himself. My parents told Lara's college that my father had suffered a heart attack; they made this up as the reason for Lara's leave of absence.

Around the same time, my father installed a

single foldout couch in the basement of his office on State Street. Also a refrigerator and a little ice-cube-size shower stall. He drove me to the office to show it to me. "I did this for a reason," he said in a low voice.

I tried to read his face, the deep lines around his eyes, the sharp dagger of his jaw. He looked away from me. "Mom and I are going to get a divorce."

It took a moment for this to sink in. No one had mentioned divorce since I was little, at the Hoffman Children and Family Center. I stared at him now as he turned to face me. His eyes were red. Everyone I loved was falling apart.

It wasn't until Thanksgiving that I saw Lara. She'd gotten a pass from the Institute to come home for the holiday, and she sat hunched over the kitchen counter or in the living room—wherever we were—just picking, picking, picking at her nails. *Look what you've done to me,* she seemed to be saying. It didn't matter that she'd signed herself into the nuthouse; we were all accountable and we were all guilty.

At the end of the weekend, my mother drove Lara and me to Hartford to drop Lara off at the hospital, and then to Springfield, so I could catch the bus back to Boston. The three of us rode the Mass Pike in silence, Mom gripping the wheel at sixty miles an hour, my sister in the passenger seat, face hidden in a duck blind of dark-brown hair. And I sat in the back seat, staring out the window at the trees whizzing by.

What was going through my mother's mind, taking one daughter to a mental institution, and the other to an elite college, a school similar to one that my mother herself had dreamed of attending—if only she hadn't been Jewish, if only the war hadn't broken out? And what was my sister thinking, at the age of twenty-one, sitting in the nuthouse, while fifty miles away her college teammates were doing their workouts in the pool and snapping each other with towels in the locker room? It must have pissed her off that her little sister was sitting in the back seat, blithely returning to her undisturbed life with her friends and classes and freedom as a Wellesley sophomore.

And I, that lucky little sister, what was I thinking, in the heavy silence of that hour-and-a-half ride to the hospital on a cold gray November day in 1975? I remember only how lonely I felt, how bereft, how empty and angry, yes—*angry* at the oppressive ruins of my family, the violence and tragedy of its past, and the hopelessness of its present. My life, such as it was, belonged to them and not to me. I did not know who I was without them, and I hated myself for who I was with them.

It was around noon when we arrived at the

Institute and went up to Lara's floor, the solid *clunk-clunk* of doors locking behind us as we moved down the hall. The air was stifling. Wisps of mental patients in bathrobes drifted by with empty eyes. The shiny linoleum floors and the whispering sadness.

Lara showed us her room that she shared with another patient, who, thank God, was not there. My mother started putting away the clothes she'd washed for Lara. This made me inexpressibly sad, and I could not bear to watch. I turned toward the window, but it had black metal bars, and I could not bear to see that either. Lara didn't belong here any more than I did, I thought. It was such an obvious mistake—couldn't everyone see that? She was nothing like those husks of women sitting in front of the TV or standing around the common room like dandelion fluff.

Mom talked quietly while Lara and I stared at the floor. At last it was time to go. Mom left a tin of linzer torte on Lara's dresser and hugged her good-bye. Lara and I exchanged a quick nod, both of us ashamed to be there. Then Mom and I walked to the end of the hall where a nurse buzzed us through the doors, then down the stairs, and out into the exquisite blast of cold November air.

Mom and I said little as she drove me to the bus station. "She's doing so much better," she said when we hugged good-bye.

That night I lay awake in my dorm room, unable to scrub the images of the Institute from my mind. The barred windows. The dead eyes of the women in robes and slippers, sitting like stones on the dreary couch in front of the TV in the common room, staring at *Days of Our Lives*.

Another sleepless night, a mounting anxiety, and I felt a growing urge to tell someone. The more I wrestled it down, the more urgent it felt. What was I after?

Attention, I thought, horrified—the most shameful, weak, and egotistic form of self-indulgence in the world. What's more, I wanted attention for problems that weren't even mine! After all, *I* wasn't in the hospital. My parents were right—I was selfish.

At last I broke. In early December, I knocked on Carrie Hanson's door. She was our resident assistant, a slim-hipped psych major and natural-born caretaker of the needy and forlorn. I sat on her neatly made bed and told her my sister was in a mental hospital and my parents were getting a divorce, and I was breaking the rules by talking about it. She held me while I cried, and murmured reassurance. Still, I felt strangely detached from myself, afraid that I was making a big deal out of nothing. I felt vaguely false and guilty—like a well-fed dog scavenging for scraps from the neighbors, when I had it better than most.

"Helen, you know, maybe you should talk to someone at Campus Counseling. They're really good."

I reeled back. "No way!" I said. "That's exactly what got my sister into this mess! The shrinks *totally* screwed her up."

Carrie nodded, her eyes a beautiful blue that made me want to touch her face. "Okay," she said. "It's completely up to you. Anyway, you can always come talk to me."

I thanked her and stood, embarrassed and a bit confused. *What am I doing?* I felt the sharp bones of her shoulder blades as she hugged me again. Then I went out for a walk under the stars. The darkness felt good. But as the days went by, I still couldn't shake it—I felt haunted by my sister and trapped by my parents' insistence on silence. Finally I decided to tell Harriet, although I didn't know what I wanted or expected from her. Did I think she would love me more if I told her? Feel sorry for me? Hug me? At lunch one day I forced myself to say, "There's something I want to tell you."

Harriet cocked her head in the most adorable way—as a puppy might, waiting for what would come next.

"Um, my sister—she's in a mental hospital. I went to see her over Thanksgiving."

Harriet paused, knit her eyebrows together, and said, "I'm sorry." Then, a silence that was awkward for both of us, and I changed the subject. We never spoke of it again.

By mid-December, I had finished reading all 1,534 pages of Samuel Richardson's *Clarissa* for my eighteenth-century English lit class. Now I was chugging through *Pamela; or, Virtue Rewarded*, another overwritten brick about a teenager who gets abducted and locked up and endures repeated attempts at rape, until she falls in love with her captor. My English major exhilaration was wearing thin.

I moved joylessly from class to carrel and back to class. The snows came, rowing season was over, and I didn't go to Harriet's dorm anymore. She and I were both on the basketball team, but I withdrew into myself and she let me be. Mom called to tell me that Lara was improving, and the doctors were very pleased. "It looks like they'll release her in time for Christmas!" my mother said cheerfully.

The prospect of spending Christmas with my parents and Lara made me break out in a cold sweat. I wanted out from my family. I wanted to be free, light, unburdened. Long ago, Emma had invited me to California for winter break, and now Harriet invited me to spend Christmas with her family in Minneapolis.

I did the unthinkable. I wrote my parents a letter saying that I could not face going home, and that

I wanted to go to Harriet's for Christmas, and to Emma's for winter break.

My parents let me go. They did not forgive me.

eight

February 2002

A quarter of a century after refusing to go home to my family for Christmas as a college sophomore, I was driving to Schenectady on the Mass Pike as a disowned daughter. I'd gotten the name of the New York estate lawyer from a friend in Boston who had told me I should contest my father's will. I had never communicated with my family through a lawyer before—but then again, I'd never been legally pronounced dead by my family, so the situation called for adaptation all around.

I paid the toll at the exit ramp and thought about the nearby house in which I'd grown up, the house in which my mother was now sleeping. I no longer had rights to anything in that house—not to the artwork or the sculptures or the Oriental rugs or the Barcelona chairs or the piano that I'd dutifully practiced each day. Everything now belonged to my sister, the beneficiary, trustee, and heir to my parents' kingdom.

I considered following Natchaug Road north to the house. It was still early; the sun would be slanting through the pines outside Mom's window. I would creep in through the basement and steal up the stairs and remove the Emilio Greco drawings from their hooks on the walls and swipe the statues from the immaculate coffee table and leave in silence. My mother, who could have slept through the bombing of Dresden, would wake a few hours later and realize slowly that something had happened. But it would be so quiet, so dark, so free of any sign of overt violence, that it would all fit precisely into the contours of her own actions. She did not like to think of herself as an aggressor, but here it was: she'd effectively killed off one daughter. How fitting for the dead daughter now to strike before dawn, without a word, without a drop of blood, and take back what was hers—that is, the right to a piece of the past, the most beautiful piece, the part of my mother's life that had offered promise and hope and beauty.

Instead, I continued downtown to the lawyer's office. I arrived early and let the dog off leash for a romp in Central Park. He found a tree branch and carried it proudly in his mouth, prancing across the white expanse of snow. Less than an hour later, I left him in the car at a ticking meter on State Street, while I met with the lawyer on the top floor of an office building. His hourly rate was eight times more than I made as a public defender in Boston. He was terribly civilized, which, I came to realize, was worth paying for, under such circumstances.

1976

Lara managed to get herself sprung from the Institute after three months, which was sort of a world record at the time, when patients could linger for years. "That place was straight out of Kafka," she said. She sat slumped at the kitchen counter in her college T-shirt that was torn at the neck. Her arms were tanned and strong, and she sat with an athlete's disregard for space; her legs straddled the chair like separate beings, and although she was not particularly large, her limbs were everywhere. Her face looked thinner than usual, her mouth puckered so her cheeks puffed out. I felt a pang of regret for making fun of her chubby cheeks as a kid.

We were home at the end of my spring semester, sitting side by side at the counter, staring out the window. In the woods next to Mom's rock garden, my father had erected his latest squirrel-proof bird feeder—a giant spaceship-looking contraption suspended from a high tree branch, and draped with curving sheets of aluminum. Squirrels were leaping onto it from nearby trees, but they kept sliding off the aluminum and falling to the ground.

I shifted uneasily. Part of me wanted to pretend Lara's hospitalization had never happened. Another part of me wanted to hear all of it—every gruesome, painful detail—as if by absorbing Lara's experience, I could assuage my guilt for having skipped out on her. I still pictured those shiny corridors of the Institute, the barred windows, the provocative beauty of the landscaped lawns and gardens below. As sisters, we were supposed to get the same servings of meat and potatoes, success and failure, good and bad luck. Perhaps I feared retribution, since I believed—in my medieval sense of sibling justice—that now that she was out, she would make sure I suffered as much as she had.

"How come you signed yourself in?" I asked.

She didn't answer, and picked at a piece of skin on her thumb. "The whole place was a complete crock," she finally said. "I couldn't believe how crazy it was. I went to all their bullshit therapy and 'activities' classes, and just played along. I never told them anything I was really thinking or feeling." She snickered. "I learned to be a good little patient, and just said whatever they wanted to hear."

Lara's bitterness reminded me of my father's. I thought of the stories he'd told me about his years as a prisoner in Siberia, when he too had kept his own counsel. Lara's escape from the Institute sounded similar. She'd outwitted the

166

system, and I admired her for that. She hadn't let them swallow her whole.

"The real problem," she said, "is the shrinks. They have no clue what's going on, but they have all this power. It's like *Cuckoo's Nest*, you know?"

I'd seen the movie with Emma in Berkeley a few months earlier over winter break, and I'd felt as if the walls of the theater were closing in on me. The Jack Nicholson character, a puckish small-time criminal, gradually gets ground down by the rigid rules of the mental hospital. *My sister's in a place like that,* I thought. What right did I have to be at a movie theater in California?

A dull thump startled us; a squirrel had dive-bombed my father's bird feeder and now clung, spread-eagled, to the giant curved sheet of aluminum. The contraption swung wildly, and the squirrel hung on for a second or two before sliding off and hitting the ground. He shook his tail with irritation, then ran up the tree again, preparing for his next attempt.

Just like us, I thought. All four of us were throwing ourselves at one another over and over, desperate to get the goodies. Love, I suppose. Love was the birdseed we all wanted in my family, but we kept slamming into these crazy barriers between us.

"If not for swimming," Lara said, "I would have gone completely nuts."

"They had a pool?"

"No, they didn't have shit for exercise. But there was a Y a few blocks away, and as long as I behaved myself, they'd give me a pass, so I could walk to the Y and swim every day." She propped her elbows on the counter and held her forehead in her hands. "That's what saved me," she said. "If I hadn't found that pool, I don't know how I would have survived."

I nodded. I relied on rowing and running to protect myself from the chaos of my own mind. Lara and I were alike that way.

"I'll tell you one thing," she said. "I'm never talking to another shrink in my life." She looked me in the eye. "Just stay clear of them, Helen."

Psychiatry had certainly fucked her up; that was obvious. I took this advice to heart, since I was well aware of the deep cracks in my own foundation. Of course, back then, neither Lara nor I could have imagined that one day she would *be* a psychiatrist.

I never told Lara or anyone else what had happened while I was with Emma in Berkeley a few months earlier during my winter break of 1976. I didn't understand it myself, and I wouldn't admit it for years.

The day I arrived, a classmate of Emma's, Hugh Mattling, a tall, loose-limbed lunk of a boy, took us out to dinner in San Francisco. I sat in the back seat of his tiny Datsun as he circled the block, looking for a place to park. He wanted to show off a great little German restaurant he had found, and he made a big deal of ordering us Weissbier with raspberry syrup. We sipped and talked. I didn't like the way he looked at Emma, the way his blue eyes lit up, the way he blushed and smiled with those winsome dimples, the way his long dark hair fell over his face when he leaned in to her. He barely looked at me, as if I were a knapsack on the chair next to her.

A waitress came by in a dirndl, which I thought was overdoing it a bit. Fake grapevines hung from the ceiling to suggest a biergarten, and the menu was written in Gothic script. Hugh advised us what to order; he said the spaetzle were quite good.

I had flown across the country to spend my winter break with my best friend. I did not want to share her with anyone, and certainly not this guy, with his long, smooth arms and strong shoulders. You could see the muscles rippling under his shirt. Emma was mine, not his. But as I sat across the table from Hugh, I was surprised at the intensity of my feelings. Why did he grate on my nerves so? His head lolled, as if he had weak neck muscles. *He's lazy,* I thought. *Too lazy to lift his lovely head of hair.*

But now he was telling Emma about seat-racing on the Cal rowing team last semester, about getting up before dawn to lift weights and do sprints before practice. And he was going to double major in biology and environmental science and hike the Pacific Crest Trail.

Okay, so he wasn't lazy; I still hated him. What was my problem? He was a perfectly nice guy. Who cared if he was hitting on her? She too was long-limbed and athletic, and with her sparkling blue eyes and easy laugh, her silky blond hair that fell below her shoulders, she looked good sitting next to him. She was beautiful in an unself-conscious, almost accidental way. I was lucky, I told myself; I would always be her best friend, her *friend* friend. Hugh and I weren't rivals. Why did I always have to be so competitive?

After dinner, Hugh drove us home and invited himself in to see Emma's apartment near the university. It was a small studio with two twin beds. Her roommate was out of town, so I had spread my sleeping bag on her roommate's bed. While I was brushing my teeth, Emma came up to me. "Helen," she whispered. "Um . . . he wants to sleep over!" She laughed nervously. "I mean, I don't know how to get him out of here!"

What a jerk, I thought. I was relieved that Emma seemed to think so too. I felt for her; we were both young and inexperienced, and neither of us wanted to appear . . . well, young and inexperienced.

"Are you okay with that?" she asked.

I shrugged, affecting nonchalance. "Sure," I said. "I don't care." To say anything else would have been unthinkably uncool.

After washing up, I got into bed. Emma laid a sleeping bag on the floor for Hugh, brushed her teeth, and climbed into bed while Hugh took his turn in the bathroom. He came out and flicked off the lights. Next I heard them whispering. "Hugh! You can't just—" Then the rustling of sheets. "Ow! What are you . . ." My ears pricked up, every nerve in my body on high alert. I held my breath, listening: Snuffled giggles. Sheets swishing. My heart was pounding so hard it seemed it would fly out of my chest. Momentary quiet, then more giggles. What should I do? It was up to her to throw him out, not me. I remained tense, listening. It was nearly dawn before I fell asleep.

The next day, after Hugh left, Emma apologized. "I didn't think he was going to *get into bed* with me!" she said. "Not that we did anything— but that's not what I had in mind!"

I waved it off, relieved that she too had been shocked, but hadn't known what to do. It seemed obvious that now she would tell him she wasn't interested. But she didn't. Hugh came over the next day, and the day after that. He walked Emma to their first day of classes, and since I had another few weeks before my semester started back east, I tagged along. Soon it was apparent that Hugh was not going away, and despite Emma's assurances to me that she didn't like him "that way," his persistence seemed to be working. He and Emma became more or less inseparable. Not knowing what to do with myself, I spent hours wandering up and down Telegraph Avenue in Berkeley. I was utterly unconscious of my attraction to Emma; my feelings of physical longing were buried deep beneath the ocean floor of my awareness. Instead, what I felt was an insatiable hunger for sweets.

While Emma went to her classes, I started going from one bakery to another, eating pastries, cookies, muffins, chocolate—and washing everything down with ice cream sundaes. With horror, I saw myself as a giant steam shovel, rolling down the sidewalk, taking out entire city blocks of pastry shops.

I didn't gain much weight because in the evenings I went for long runs up the fire trails in the Berkeley hills, sometimes with Emma, and sometimes alone, trying to understand what was wrong with me. *Starting tomorrow,* I would tell myself reasonably, as if I were someone I could trust, *no more sweets.* The next morning, I would feel strong and good, and I'd eat breakfast with Emma and walk her to classes, and then I'd wander the bookshops and cafés of Berkeley. And then it would happen. Like a sudden tidal shift, some overpowering force rose up within me and drove me into a bakery. It was as if I'd lost control over where my feet took me. I felt like a serial killer—no, a serial eater—someone criminal, dangerous.

"Um, could I have a chocolate chip cookie, please?" I asked the girl behind the counter. My voice sounded like someone else's—higher, more tightly strained than my own. *It's okay. One cookie can't hurt.*

The girl slipped the cookie into a paper bag.

"Um, maybe two," I said, feeling my face burn. *I'll save one for later. I'll give it to Emma tonight.*

I waited till I was outside before opening the bag and peeking inside. I inched my hand in and broke off a small piece. It was still warm, and the taste was exquisite. But then I felt a prick of panic. *What am I doing? I'll get fat! Where is my fucking self-control?*

To shut myself up, I shoved half a cookie into my mouth and ate it so quickly I could not object. Without even thinking, I tore into the second cookie. In seconds, both were gone. I crumpled the paper bag and looked for a trash can to get rid of the evidence. Suddenly I was starving. I couldn't go back into the same bakery, the girl behind the counter would think I was a pig. I crossed the street to another shop, and bought a dozen cookies and brownies and chocolates. I walked down the street and ate everything, one after the other, until I had completely filled myself with shame and self-loathing.

Months later, Lara and I were sitting at the kitchen counter watching squirrels blitz Dad's bird feeder, and she told me about her experience in the Institute of Living. Of course it was the shrinks, I agreed. They had driven her crazy. Lara and I were in the same boat, facing the same pressures to succeed, to become superstars that our parents could be proud of. If Lara could go crazy, so could I.

"I quit premed," I told her, an offering of my own failure. "I decided to major in English." Maybe it wasn't as great a failure as losing a semester to the Institute, but it was an effort to bring us closer together.

"Good for you," she said.

"So I'm thinking maybe law school or something. You know, it's only three years. And there are no prerequisites."

She nodded. "Yeah, that sounds a lot better."

We fell silent, exhausted from our tiny admissions, and committed to our greater silences, allied in the daunting production of growing up.

part two

nine

Lara and I grew closer over the next few years, hiking and biking and skiing together on our vacations as if we'd never had a disagreement in our lives. By the summer of 1978 we were in nearly perfect alignment. We had both graduated from college. Lara had just been accepted into medical school, and I had gotten into law school, and we had almost a month to relish our good fortune—until September, when the grim reality of actually going to medical school and law school would drastically reduce our exuberance.

We decided to spend our last two weeks of August together hiking in the White Mountains. We crammed our tent, stove, and sleeping bags into two expedition backpacks, drove north to New Hampshire, and parked at a trailhead in Franconia. We hoisted our gear onto our backs and tore across the Presidential Range. Then we continued through the Mahoosucs into Maine. When we ran out of high peaks, we dropped into the valley, hitched a ride back to our car, and drove farther north in Maine to find another week's worth of hiking. We were in ridiculously good shape, and we galloped over the terrain, bagging peaks at breakneck speed. We wouldn't slow our pace until we reached the tree line, when we allowed ourselves a glance back at the view that had sprung up at our feet—rock ledges that cut the world in two: sky above, boulders below. At the summits we shrugged off our frame packs and guzzled water. Within minutes we saddled up again and scrambled down the trail until our legs burned and our knees felt rubbery.

There was a certain joy to this mad dash through the wilderness, a euphoric blend of mountains, wind, and endorphins run amok. There was no room for rumination. We had become bodies, pure and simple, and our bodies gave us pleasure. They took us through moss-green woods, lush as a fairy tale, and over mist-covered peaks. At the end of the day, we quickly pitched tent, ate a cold snack, and dropped into our sleeping bags like felled timber. Lara woke us at first light, and we broke camp by the time the sun nosed above the horizon.

As long as we kept moving, we were content. We ate little, spoke less, and disappeared into the mountains. Our bodies provided camouflage for our minds; it was our minds that were dangerous. We did not imagine that we were running from ourselves, from the history we held within us. We were only vaguely aware of a looming fear of failure that propelled us faster and faster along the trail. The result was bliss. The mountains gave us everything we needed: a place to run wild.

Toward the end of two weeks, a few signs of problems: Lara's knee gave out; my ankle puffed up. We pushed on until we couldn't walk, and then we limped back to the valley for our final day. When we got back to our car, we were shocked by what we saw in the mirror: dirt-smudged, sunbaked faces with crazy hair, bruised elbows, salt-bleached T-shirts and sweat-stained shorts. We drove the back roads of Maine, looking for the thrill of a general store, a cold soda, a pint of ice cream. We spent a few dollars on gas, a few more on food and two bottles of cheap wine.

Our last night in the mountains, we hiked to a lean-to on a remote mountain lake. The air was soft, and we slipped out of our packs and sat at the edge of the water. In another week we would be in separate cities, starting separate schools. We opened the first bottle and passed it back and forth. It was sweet and sharp, but after a while the taste didn't bother us. The sun slipped through the trees and dropped into the lake. The air turned cool and the water lapped the shore. Loons called to one another. My sister and I were grinning and talking, taking sloppy slugs of wine, and feeling woozy.

"I love you," I told her.

She seemed pleased, almost to the point of tears. "Yeah," she said. "Me too."

"It's like Zosia told me," I said.

"What?"

"Well, it was weird," I said. "The day before we left on this hiking trip, Zosia pulled me aside and said, 'You know, Helen, what the most important thing in the world is? The most important thing of all is the love between two sisters.'"

Lara nodded.

"She said the bond between her and Mom was stronger than anything else in their lives. And she said it made her so happy that you and I are finally devoted to each other, the same way they are."

Lara smiled. I felt very close to her then, brimming over with warmth and love and confidence in our future together. I felt at that moment as if we would always be like this; I dismissed all of the fights in our past in a heartbeat.

"We'll team up," I said. "You and me. Someday we'll go into business together."

"Yeah." She raised the bottle. "I'll take care of you. I'll be your doctor."

I giggled. "And I'll handle all your malpractice claims."

She shoved me playfully and I rolled to the side and bounced back, like those children's weighted punching bags.

"We'll be a 'loctor-dawyer' team," I said.

"Here's to us!" She raised the bottle again and took a swig. "The loctor-dawyer sisters."

We sat at the edge of the lean-to with our arms around each other and stared at the dark lake. Every so often we could see ripples where fish had jumped. The air smelled of summer and freedom, and I felt lucky and sure of myself. I wanted what my mother and aunt had: a sisterhood powerful beyond words. It was enough to topple nations and bring continents to their knees. My sister and I would rule the world. Nothing would separate us.

Lara and I got home in time to wash the mountains out of our hair and clothes, spend a night between clean sheets, and pack for our first year of professional school. Our parents beamed with pride that we were going to become a doctor and a lawyer, while Lara and I grew quiet under the descending blade of reality. We nodded to each other as Lara got in her car and drove north to med school in Vermont; I headed east to law school at Boston University.

I'd rented an apartment with two other women on the first floor of a triple-decker in Allston. Our landlady, a squat woman shaped like a jar of gefilte fish, lived upstairs with her two sons in their forties. A few blocks from our apartment, Harvard Avenue crossed Commonwealth Avenue, with its liquor stores and bars with boarded windows. Spanish grocery stores mysteriously opened and closed at will. Our street boasted the highest number of rapes in Boston that year—no small feat, since the competition was fierce. At night we'd run the few blocks from the trolley stop to our apartment with our keys clenched between the fingers of our fists. It took a minute or two to open the two dead bolts and the police lock, and then we were safe. We chained ourselves in till morning.

I wanted to like law school, but the Darwinian atmosphere got to me. In the hallways my classmates argued about the fine points of cases we'd been assigned to read, radiant with the sound of their own voices. It began to dawn on me that I'd made a serious mistake. I was studying law because my mother believed a law degree would come in handy; Uncle had a law degree, and he had used it to save my mother's life in 1942. My classmates, on the other hand, seemed to be in law school because they actually wanted to be *lawyers*. We had nothing in common, I thought.

Heavyweight, 1979

The eating problem I'd acquired in Berkeley three years earlier sprouted up with a vengeance my first year of law school. I would starve myself for days, run great loops around the city, drink liters of diet soda and nibble on iceberg lettuce—all the tricks I'd learned as a lightweight rower in college. A week later, or sometimes only a few days later, I would stuff myself with pints of Häagen-Dazs, unable to control the hand that held the spoon to my mouth.

I came home from my first year of law school in May weighing twenty pounds more than I had at winter break. My mother was alarmed. "Are you eating right?" she asked. "Yeah," I said with a shrug, "I guess so." I was too ashamed to admit my bingeing to anyone. But I could see that Lara, an Eating Disorder Lifer, was eyeing me with a knowing satisfaction; she knew exactly what was up with me. We silently sized each other up now, calculating who was keeping her weight down, and who was losing the battle.

My father sent me to see an endocrinologist, to rule out some kind of hormone or blood chemistry problem. I played along, and was not surprised when everything turned out to be fine. The doctor was about my parents' age—sixty-something—a tall, trim man in a starched white lab coat. He invited me into his office to tell me the results.

"Great," I said. "Thanks." I stood to leave, but he didn't, so I sat back down.

"Tell me," he said slowly, "are you happy?"

I nearly fell off my chair. This struck me as an inappropriate violation of my privacy. "Yes!" I said, shocked by the implication that I might not be. "I'm very happy." *Of course I'm happy!*

183

There's nothing psychologically wrong with me! "Except about my weight," I added.

"You're sure?"

"Of course!"

He shrugged and stood, shook my hand, and wished me luck.

My parents were relieved that nothing was wrong with me, and that was the end of it. I dropped the weight after a few weeks of virtuous dieting and running. But soon I found myself once again eating on the sly. I ate for solace and for company and for fun. I ate out of rage and fear and shame. I focused all these feelings into everything I ate and turned them into a larger, more undeniable problem: Helen the Overweight. In the month of August alone, I had gone from a trim 135 pounds to a shameful 150. Weight had become a measure of my self-worth.

As September approached, I finally confessed to my mother that I had a problem with eating. She consulted my sister, and they both decided that what I probably needed was a carefully circumscribed intervention.

"Behafe-your modifeecation," my mother said.

"Stay away from Freud," Lara said. "You don't want anyone messing around with your child-hood and all that crap. Just tell them you want behavior modification."

"Right," Mom said. "No digging up the past. Just to control the appetite."

"I'd like behavior modification," I told the Mass Mental Health Center when I called, as if ordering a lunch special.

They gave me names. Before fall classes started, I drove out to Newton to meet a shrink named Martin Flak in his psychiatric empire called Learning Therapies, Inc. It was a huge Victorian on Walnut Street, filled with therapists. I wore a large green tent of a dress and embarrassed myself by leaking tears when I told Dr. Flak about my problem with food.

"It's a question of who's in control," he said.

This struck me as the most brilliant thing anyone had said to me in my life. I thought he was a genius. I nodded and blew my nose. Then he suggested I might be a good candidate for psychotherapy.

"Oh no," I said, alarmed. "I just need to lose a few pounds."

He gave me an appointment for another session a week later. I left his office and went home, changed into running shoes and shorts, and went for a run. A thread of hope slipped through me, and as the traffic thinned and the sun rose higher, I ran with relief in my newfound mental health. I was cured. It was a miracle.

I returned home, showered, and made myself a salad. The next day I was fine. I ran. I studied. I ate sensibly. I was happy.

A week later I returned to the shrink, and

told him I was all set. He seemed surprised and pleased. He suggested I keep a daily log of my eating and exercise.

I met with him weekly all fall. I lost tons of weight. I increased my running to sixty-five miles a week. I chatted with Dr. Flak about my progress, and he chatted with me about his own running regimen, and together we spent a lot of Blue Cross Blue Shield's money, without ever having to look at what might be wrong.

Like my mother, I had always been able to arrange my denial in such a way as to enjoy the illusion that I was mostly just fine, at least compared to everyone else. Lara, on the other hand, was so painfully in touch with her feelings that she was incapable of self-deception. As long as I had Lara around to act like a maniac, it was easy for me to preserve my ignorance of the extent of my own problems. Perhaps the same was true for my mother. It would be years before I could see that our family drama served as a brilliant, albeit uncalculated, distraction from the past that Mom and her sister kept hidden from us. But all that would come later. Back in our twenties—the same age at which our parents had suffered through a *real* war—Lara and I found ourselves engaged in battles with ourselves that felt shameful, strange, and unjustifiable.

Another thing happened that fall. Right before classes started, Emma—more or less out of the blue—came to Boston. We hadn't seen each other in four years. She and her new boyfriend, Travis, an Alaskan bush pilot, had rented a Cessna, flown from Berkeley to Boston, and landed at my doorstep. Emma was starting grad school at BU while Travis finished up college in California. "You and I can room together!" she said.

Seeing her again was like being blindsided by a Mack truck of joy. I felt as if I'd spent the past few years living in a tunnel underground. She'd flown east, and the sun came up.

We waved good-bye to Travis and set up house together. I was ecstatic. Every morning we bicycled to classes, and at the end of the day, after my run, we fixed dinner and talked. We spent our weekends together when we weren't studying. Gone were my eating problems, gone was my excess weight, life was good. At twenty-two, I still wasn't aware of wanting to hold her hand, or drape an arm over her shoulders, or touch her face, her neck, her arms. I was happy just being with her. The fact that she had a boyfriend in California was fine with me. Even law school was tolerable now, and I started thinking maybe I'd actually be a lawyer after all. I was doing an internship with Greater Boston Legal

Services that year, so after classes I biked to the GBLS office, put on a suit, and picked up cases assigned by my supervisor. I liked my clients; they mattered to me in a way that my equity and evidence classes did not. When I won a case, I felt I'd actually helped someone; I felt important and grown-up, with just the hint of an underlying feeling that I didn't know what I was doing.

But a few weeks before Christmas, Emma came running into my room to tell me her good news. "Travis and I are getting married!" she said. "Next summer! Oh, H, I'm so excited!" She did a little dance of joy.

Oh, wow, I thought. My life was over. *Over.*

"It's a secret, okay? We're not going to tell my parents or anyone till Christmas. Promise me you won't say a word."

I nodded. I still didn't know why Emma's news was so devastating to me.

"Travis is flying out here to take me home." Her eyes lit up, and her blocky nose was strangely endearing. "We're going to drive back to California together. And I'm going to take next semester off and prepare for the wedding!"

I forced a smile, and in a fit of friendship, I stood and embraced the love of my life. I was stunned with grief.

"That's wonderful," I said. "I'm so happy for you."

I *was* happy for her. It was me I felt sorry for.

"Let's have some champagne." I searched the refrigerator, although I knew we had nothing but a heel of white table wine.

"H, you have to come out next summer, okay? It'll be our last time together, just you and me, before the wedding in August."

"But I have to get a job," I said. "With a law firm or something."

"My dad knows tons of lawyers in Sacramento," she said.

This was encouraging. I could spend the summer with her, and maybe then I'd just move out to the West Coast myself. Maybe I'd get a job there after law school, and I could be near her all the time. My heart opened to the possibilities.

But the fact was, Emma was going to leave me. In three weeks she would be gone, and I'd be alone with my equity and evidence notes and Greater Boston Legal Services. I didn't really understand what I was losing, but I knew that the loss was almost too much to bear.

When Travis arrived a few weeks later, Emma seemed to burst into flower. She wore a goofy grin on her face all the time. She was unbearably happy. So was Travis. They were in love, they did not even see me, and that was probably a good thing. I helped them pack up the car with her backpack, clothes, books, hiking boots, running shoes, and tennis racket. I waved to them as they backed down the driveway.

Then I laced up my sneakers and went for a two-hour run. I studied for finals. I went to the legal aid office and helped poor people fight their landlords and the government and their lousy lot in life. I went to therapy and talked about moving to California.

Two weeks later I went home for the holidays. On Christmas Eve, my father and I were sitting around the fireplace reading. Lara flopped into the green sling-back chair next to me, one leg hooked over the chair arm. My father hated it when we didn't sit properly in a chair. He believed it was bad for the furniture. But Lara was twenty-five years old; he glanced at her swinging foot and said nothing. She'd come home the day before, absorbed in a corona of her own rage after squeaking through her fall semester of medical school on the slimmest margin of mental health.

"Helen!" She kicked the leg of my chair.

"What?"

"Helllenn. . . . Helllenn. . . . Helllenn. . . ." She punctuated each word with a kick.

"What do you want?"

"I want to go out and do something with you." Her voice was angry; it sounded like an offer to throw me off a cliff.

"I don't feel like going out," I said. "It's freezing outside."

Mom brought out a tray of cheese and crackers,

set it on the coffee table, and sat down to join us. Lara leaned forward as if to take a cracker, but instead picked up a paper napkin. Very slowly, she tore it into small strips, and let the pieces float to the floor. When she reached for another napkin, my mother placed her hand on Lara's. "Darling," she said. "Talk to me. I know you're upset. Please tell me what's bothering you."

Lara yanked her hand away. "Leave me alone! Go cook your precious Christmas dinner!"

My mother's eyes welled. She stood and retreated to the kitchen. Soon we could hear her chopping vegetables and preparing the turkey. My father, sitting across from me, said nothing, but his hands tensed on the business section of the *Times*. I picked up my book and reread the same paragraph.

Lara started kicking my chair again, and I asked her to stop.

"Make me," she snickered.

I ignored her. The words on the page ran together and I couldn't concentrate on the sentences. I let my eyes ride the coattails of the words, hoping to pick up their meaning as I went along. Lara kicked my chair harder. I could feel the heat rise in my ears. I closed my book. Night had fallen, and our living room was reflected like a Rembrandt in the floor-to-ceiling windows behind the fireplace. I got up and went to my room, locked the door behind me, and flopped onto my bed. I opened my book and began again.

Within minutes, I heard a thump on my door. I sat up, and it came again. *Thunk.* It sounded like Lara was pounding the door with something— her fist? Her foot? I tried to keep reading. The noise grew louder, more rapid. *Thunk. Thunk. Thunk.* I closed my eyes and waited. How many years? My sister was a second-year med student, learning to save lives. Her classmates at school liked her; she was thoughtful and considerate, an ideal roommate in the house she shared with half a dozen other budding doctors. How did she pull it off? *Thunk.* Maybe the supreme effort of holding herself together in the world was so exhausting, she simply fell apart when she got home.

Thunk. I fought the urge to scream now, to blast from my room and bash her head against the brick wall. Instead I remained on my bed, book open, eyes closed. The pounding seemed to make a small explosion at the base of my skull every two seconds. I had nine more days of vacation before I was due back at school for the second semester. I wasn't sure how long I could hold out.

I finally opened the door and found Lara sitting on the floor in front of it, legs splayed, a tennis ball in her hand. So that's what she'd been doing—throwing a stupid tennis ball at my door, over and over. I stepped over her legs and returned to the living room, where my mother was picking up the shredded napkin from the rug. I sat in the chair across from my father. Lara followed me and collapsed into the chair next to mine, and started kicking my chair again.

"Lara," I said in a tired voice, "cut it out." It took all my concentration to keep my voice calm.

She took a balled-up Kleenex from her pocket and tossed bits of it at me, laughing.

"Come on, Lara, just leave me alone. I want to read."

"So read," she said.

I glanced at my father, who sat stone-still, holding his book in his lap, pretending to read. His newspaper had already gone up in flames in the fireplace. I returned to my book, resolute. Bits of Kleenex landed in my hair and on my shirt and in my lap. Finally I got up and went into the kitchen. "Can I borrow the car keys?" I asked my mother.

"Why?" she asked, alarmed.

"I want to go for a ride," I said. "I want to see if I can find something."

"What?"

"It's a surprise." In fact, I wanted to find a coffee shop where I could sit in peace and read my book. But I knew this would upset my mother.

"It's Christmas Eve," she said. "Stay here with us. Let's be together as a family."

"She's driving me crazy," I said.

A sad look came over my mother's face, and my heart ached for her. "Oh, Helen. She can't help it. She's not well."

A wave of guilt washed over me. If my parents had to deal with her, then so should I. After all my parents had been through—the war, the camps, the killings—I owed them my loyalty. The least I could do was be with them now.

"We all have to try," my mother said. "We have to do our best."

I took the car keys. I drove through the empty streets of town in a snow squall, and headed east toward the shopping mall. I pulled into the Tri-City Diner, open twenty-four hours a day. A glass tower of pies and cakes rotated at the entrance. I slid into a booth near the window and opened my book. And I began to cry.

Years later, during an interval when Lara and I were the best of friends, I sometimes broached the subject of those times when she had acted like this, when she'd soaked our house in her silent rage. The few times I tried to talk with her about it, her body sank as if I'd struck her: her head dropped, face drawn in pain, and she squirmed with such discomfort, I could not bring myself to pursue it further. It was too painful to talk about the damage we had all done to each other in the past. Like our parents, Lara and I left those storms alone, survived them as best we could, and tried to enjoy the moments of reprieve when we got along well.

Christmas morning the sun crashed through the woods outside our house. I could hear the coffeemaker gurgling in the kitchen. The news was on the radio: the Soviet Union had invaded Afghanistan. From the living room, I heard a violin sobbing on the hi-fi. I found my mother in the kitchen in her home-sewn bathrobe, her hair standing up in stiff peaks like whipped egg whites. "Oh," she said, "put on slippers!" Then she tilted her chin up, kissed me on the cheek, and said, "Good morning, how did you sleep?" Before I could answer, she pointed to my feet. "Slippers!"

The heat came through the floor and felt good on my bare feet. I went back to my room for slippers.

My father joined us in the kitchen. He'd been up since six, as usual. He'd shoveled the path around the house, filled the bird feeder, brought in another load of wood, and built a fire. Now he pulled out a stool and sat at the kitchen counter as my mother poured us coffee. We stared out the window at the squirrels stealing seeds from the bird feeder. This drove my father crazy. He jumped to his feet and reached for the kitchen door.

"It's Christmas," my mother said. "Let them eat."

· · ·

At noon Mom went to check on my sister. I followed quietly. Lara's bedroom was dark, drapes drawn.

"Lara?" My mother's voice sounded tentative. She leaned over my sister. "Lara, darling? It's noon. Come to the living room. Come join us. It's Christmas."

"Mrrrrmph." Lara rolled over under the covers.

Mom waited another minute, then turned and stepped out of the room.

We didn't speak until we reached the kitchen. "Let's have a cup of tea," she said. Mom and I divided time into cups of tea. She placed the kettle on the stove and we began to fill the kitchen with chatter. We loved to talk, my mother and I. She could be so animated, so funny, so opinionated and lively. We would talk about books and movies and opera singers and people we knew and people we didn't. She and I were, as they say, *verbal*. We hid things with words.

The kettle sang. My mother took a used Lipton tea bag from the saucer by the sink. Its waist was cinched by its string, which had dried and turned rust-brown. We could afford a fresh tea bag, but it was a point of pride for my mother to extend the life of a tea bag from hours to days, so as not to waste even a single leaf. I loved this about her, and I followed the ritual in my own kitchen, much to the horror of my roommates over the

196

years. My mother ceremoniously unfurled the string and let the tea bag drop first into one cup, then into the second. She coaxed a bit of color from the bag, then scooped it up, strangled it with its string, and set it on the saucer.

"Do you have a bird feeder?" she asked.

I nodded. Emma had bought us one, and filled it regularly. She cared about living things in a way that I didn't. Something was missing in me.

Behind us we heard the soft scuffing of my sister's bare feet. She rubbed her forehead with the heel of her hand and seemed to be emerging from the bottom of the ocean.

My mother jumped up. "Darling," she said. "Sit! Would you like some tea? Stollen?" She bustled to get the coffee cake from the serving tray. "Let me heat it up for you."

Lara staggered to the counter and collapsed on a stool. It was too soon to tell what would happen. Would she perk up and decide to open presents? Or would she tear her napkin to shreds? I pretended not to care. Everything depended on not caring in our house. You had to suspend all hope. You watched the signals carefully, and tried to assess her mood from moment to moment.

Lara let my mother cut her a slice of stollen. That was good. She let her serve her a cup of tea. That was good. She sipped her tea and blew her nose. All good.

Twenty minutes passed. My father tiptoed into

the kitchen. "So are we opening presents?" he asked.

My mother shook her head and motioned him to leave.

Lara finished her tea, rose, and walked into the living room where the Christmas tree was drowning in a sea of gifts. She pushed the hair from her face and straightened her back. A light came into her eyes, and her face was suddenly transformed. She leaned over and picked up a gift. "Here, Helen," she said brightly. "Open this."

For the next few hours we opened presents. We burned the wrapping paper in the fire and put on another log and our faces glowed in the warmth. The floor was covered with our spoils: cross-country ski gloves and glacier goggles and lip gloss. My aunt had sent checks; my mother had bought sheets. My father flipped through the pages of the books we got him, and finally settled on the book about quarks and hadrons. The dog, exhausted, lay at his feet, jowls sunk over the arch of his shoe. A miracle had occurred and we had all pulled it off: we had gone from danger to delight. While it lasted, it seemed that our family had always been this way, that we could never be anything else.

Trouble didn't start until the next day. You could feel it when she walked into the kitchen. It was in her posture, the angle of her head, the scowl on her face. Lara dropped onto a kitchen stool, propped her elbows on the counter and scuttled her fingers through her hair. When I left the room, she followed me into the living room, and demanded that I do something with her. I declined and went to my bedroom, closed the door, and locked it.

I was a crucial member of this family, and I was expected to do my part. If I took her out hiking or skiing, at least it would give my parents a few hours' reprieve. But I couldn't rise to the occasion. I didn't *want* to rise to the occasion. I had been through my own semester with my own problems.

Thunk.

I sat up with a jolt.

Thunk.

The tennis ball again. "Helen," she called. *Thunk.*

I opened the door, stepped over her, and went to the telephone. I looked up Greyhound in the Yellow Pages and called for the schedule of buses. Then I told my parents I planned to take the bus to Boston the following morning.

My father looked up, alarmed.

"What?" my mother said.

"I want to go back to Boston."

"But you just got here!"

"I know," I said. "I'm sorry, but I can't take it anymore."

"You and Lara should do something together," my mother said. "Take her skiing."

I bit my lip. The realization that I could actually take a bus and leave home was both heady and disturbing. I couldn't bear to disappoint my parents, and I felt ashamed to leave them alone with Lara. I was shirking my duty as one-third of the family reserve to cope with her.

The next morning, my father drove me to the bus station. We said little. "Do you need money?" he asked. I shook my head. "She is not well," he said.

We hugged outside the bus. He slipped twenty dollars in my pocket.

Boston was bleak after Christmas. The students had disappeared overnight and the streets were empty. My apartment was dark; it accused me of family desertion. Emma was gone. I was alone.

A day later, the phone rang. It was my mother. "Helen," she said, "I wish you would come home. Please, darling. Take Lara skiing. Or hiking. It would do her so much good."

I listened to my mother with a growing sense of shame. It did seem like very little to ask of me. Why couldn't I just go home and help my parents out? Last March I'd sped across Massachusetts at midnight, rushing to my sister's side when she'd called in tears. I'd felt proud of my virtue— the heroic daughter, rushing to the rescue—and had taken a perverse satisfaction in my own sacrifice. The glow from mild martyrdom was not so different from the pride I took in not eating, in pushing myself to run farther and faster than ever before. It was mastery of the *self,* and it was precisely this self of mine that had always caused me so much difficulty in my family.

But now I found myself unwilling to sign up for another tour of duty at home. It was hard enough to sort out my own life. I didn't even begin to understand the depth charge of Emma's engagement and move to California. At twenty-two, I had about as much self-knowledge as a seedpod.

"Mom, I can't," I said, trying the words out to see if they would stick. "I'm really sorry."

"Why? What are you doing there?"

The fact was, I was trying to preserve my sanity. "I have some cases I'm working on," I lied.

"Please, Helen. Just take the bus. Let us know when you're coming, and Dad will pick you up. All right, darling? It would be so good for Lara if you could—"

"Mom, I just can't," I said. "I really need to be here right now."

There was a silence on the other end of the phone, and when my mother spoke again, her voice was cold. "All right," she said. "I'll tell you what happened!" I was stunned by her sudden anger. "I didn't want to tell you, but you've left me no choice! After you left, I walked into Lara's room, and do you know what I found? I walked in, and she was lying in the bed, and her arms were covered in blood! Yes! She had cut herself up, and she was bleeding!"

A chill came over me, and I squeezed my eyes tight. Without even thinking, I could feel my arms outstretched to catch my mother's perfectly thrown pass of guilt.

"Do you know what it's like," my mother said, "for a mother to walk in and see her daughter like that? Do you have any idea?"

I was crying now, and rocking myself on the floor. Lara had cut herself up. Because I'd left home. These two thoughts were connected. *Proximate cause. Damages.*

"Now, get on the bus," she commanded, "and you come home."

I pictured my sister in the darkness of her room at the far end of the house. Her arms on the sheets, blood oozing from her wrists, streaming over the covers. Had she passed out? Was she conscious? I couldn't ask.

"I'm sorry," I said weakly, squeezing each word out like dots of glue from a tube. "But I can't come home."

"What?"

"Mom, you can't ask that of me." I didn't dare

open my eyes. I was already drowning in guilt, and my mother's pressure felt cruel.

"You have always been selfish," my mother said coldly. "You've always only thought about yourself."

It was true. I did not want to go home. I did not want to save Lara's life. Although I couldn't be sure at the moment, I didn't actually believe that I had caused Lara to cut herself up. Had I? It wasn't my fault, I thought. But part of me believed that it was. Part of me felt that I must now undo what I had done. I did not know whether I could resist the pull to go home and redeem myself. I didn't know if I would be able to live with myself if I didn't.

Looking back on those years, I'm struck by how Lara was the focus around which our family revolved. She was our Id du Jour, the gasket we blew when the pressure got too great. Yet Mom and Zosia had always been at the center of the production, pouring all their energy into sealing off the past. Together, we were all sucked into a performance of aggression and loss and fear and betrayal, but the stage on which it was set—suburban America in the late twentieth century—made no sense at all. In the context of our lives in 1980, Lara looked crazy.

It wasn't until a dozen years later, in 1992, that Lara and I would begin to research our family history and discover the secret that our parents and aunt had hidden from us all our lives—that we were Jewish, not Catholic, and we'd lost our entire family in the Holocaust. This revelation in our midthirties would radically change the way we understood our family. Maybe we weren't so crazy after all; maybe it was just our history that was crazy.

ten

Boston, January 1980

It was already late at night when I put on my sweats and sneakers and ran down the empty streets to the river. The skin of the Charles was blistered with ice, and the path was rutted with frozen ski tracks and footprints from what seemed like prehistoric runners.

I was running from the image of my sister, blood pouring down her arms and over the sheets. From the image of my mother walking into Lara's room, the shock of that first impression. I ran past the frozen playing fields and boat slips and tennis courts, deserted and windblown at this time of night. I turned at the Museum of Science and ran back, listening to the river groaning under ice. An occasional car sprayed salt from Storrow Drive.

I spent the next two days running. I found that I could not bear to be still; I couldn't be alone with myself in my apartment. I could not read. As long as I was on the move, sweating, heart pounding, I could hold the feelings at bay. The minute I stopped, I was flooded with guilt and a terrible anxiety.

Emma seemed a world away, on the sunny West Coast of happiness, preparing for her wedding, joyfully in love. I'd lost her not once, but twice. I was in a permanent posture of losing her. Even now, five years after I'd lost her to Hugh in Berkeley, it still did not occur to me that I might be queer or that I was in love with her. I knew only that I was achingly lonely and that I was an impostor—a law student who did not want to be a lawyer, a woman who did not want to date men, a daughter who would not go home. The gap between Emma and me now seemed impossible to bridge. I didn't call her.

And I didn't even consider calling Flak, who was on a ski vacation somewhere. What could he do anyway? This was my problem, and in the grand scheme of things, it really wasn't such a big deal. After all, I wasn't living in a bombed-out building or freezing in a forced labor camp above the Arctic Circle. I needed to grow up and get a grip. It was time to prove to myself and to Flak that I had outgrown my weakness, my dependence on others. Last year I'd lost control and gained weight, but now I was fine. I had to be fine.

Except I was scared of the telephone. Nobody had answering machines in 1980; if the phone rang, you picked it up. I was afraid Mom would call again, and that I'd be sucked back into the vortex. So I took myself to matinees, sometimes one after another. I spent my days in coffee shops, reading novels that failed to distract me. I wrote in my journal. I went to the Greater Boston Legal Services office and pretended to work on my cases. There was nothing, really, that needed my attention.

I kept running: midnight, one, two in the morning. I had no reason to follow the sun. I slept long and hard and dreaded waking. Days flipped over on themselves. I began to nurse my anxiety with coffee cakes and ice cream. I was starting to lose my sense of self-control. I ran and ate and slept and fretted.

And I could not hide from the phone altogether. One evening it rang and rang and rang; I held my breath until it stopped. Then it rang and rang again. I finally unplugged it, but could not remain in its company. I drove aimlessly through the streets of Newton, Brighton, Allston. I wanted desperately to prove that I could survive without my family, that I could flourish, but it was an impossible test. I was sunk from the minute I'd left Schenectady. I was going to have to sabotage everything I did from now on. I did not deserve peace.

Reflections on Suicide

Despite her years of violent moods and crazy behavior, I still had trouble believing Lara had a bona fide mental illness. In public, among friends or acquaintances or even strangers, she was always charming. "She's sick," my mother would tell me in a low voice. "She can't help it."

I believed she was only selectively sick. If I were sick, I thought, I would not do it in such a pantywaist way. I would not limit it to my family or my home or my loved ones. And if I were suicidal, I vowed, I'd do it right. I wouldn't spend all that time threatening to do it, or making half-assed attempts that made everyone wring their hands and talk about "cries for help." Mental illness, I believed, came with moral imperatives. If you were going to kill yourself, you should stop dicking around and just do it.

A week after school started, I received a letter from my father. His sharp handwriting on the envelope seemed to cut my hands. I opened the letter, took a deep breath, and read.

Lara's condition had gotten worse, Dad wrote, and she would not be returning to medical school that semester. They used the old excuse that my father had had a heart attack, and Lara had to stay home to tend to him. The irony was almost too rich, but I recognized it as my family's quintessential solution to the truth.

Lara's psychiatrist had advised my parents to handle Lara with "kid gloves." *She is homicidal,* my father reported, *and suicidal.* Mom was calling Lara's doctor two, three, five times a day: Lara won't get out of bed. Lara won't eat. Lara has found where I hid the knives.

We are closely monitoring her medications, to make sure she doesn't hide them. Mom has taken over the role of full-time nurse, to prevent her from having to go into a hospital. Her condition is volatile. She could snap at any minute.

It had been three years since Lara was institutionalized during college, and it had nearly torn my parents apart. Lara had never forgiven them. My mother would never let it happen again—and despite my father's overbearing presence, it was Mom who held the power in our family.

As I reread Dad's letter, my heart went out to him. What I loved most about it was that he did not suggest that I was the cause of Lara's breakdown, or that I should come home. He simply wanted me to know that their home life was hell. He asked how I was, how my studies were going. *Lara is very angry at you,* my father wrote. *She is fixated on you. Write me at the office.*

I folded the letter and replaced it in its envelope, grateful that my father had extended a hand from behind enemy lines. The suggestion of using his office address was a relief. My letters would be safe there; Lara wouldn't even know about them. I wrote my father back, telling him that I was fine, that I was busy with classes and studies. I tried to make my life sound interesting and upbeat.

But soon my eating disorder was back in full swing, and I didn't want to admit it to Flak. It was too humiliating to tell him how many gallons of ice cream I was eating, or that I'd missed days and then weeks of running. I gained weight—a pound or two at first, and then a surge: ten, fifteen pounds. I missed Emma. I was listless and losing control, and although I would never say this to him, I was ashamed of letting Flak down. I was afraid that if I didn't perform well, Flak would give up on me.

"Does your father know?" Flak asked.

"Know what?"

"How you are."

I shrugged. "We write. My parents are having a horrible time with Lara."

"Maybe we could have a session with him," Flak said. "Do you think he would be willing to come out and have a session with us?"

The idea appealed to me. I knew my father would never go to a shrink for his own sake, but I was pretty sure he would do so for me. Now that my mother had turned against me, I needed Dad more than ever.

· · ·

My father and I sat next to each other in identical chairs facing Flak. Dad had driven to Boston that morning in his brand-new Ford Escort, a car that did not do him justice, but one that appealed to his sense of economy.

"Thank you for coming," Flak said. "How are you?"

"The situation at home is very bad," my father said, wasting no time on pleasantries. "We are keeping Lara under twenty-four-hour supervision." His voice was quiet, deep, and matter-of-fact. "My life is anguish."

"Oh, I'm sorry."

"The home is essentially a mental institution."

Flak nodded. He already knew this from the letters I'd been getting from my father. "How do you feel about that?" he said.

My father gazed at the ceiling for a moment. "What I wish for, quite simply, is to put an end to it all."

This sounded pretty normal to me. I too had often wished that we could simply remove Lara from our midst and put an end to our agony. I was only surprised that Dad would say this to a stranger, to Dr. Flak.

"Yes," Flak said, as if he'd been hoping for precisely this sort of confession. "When do you think of this?" He leaned forward and gazed at my father.

Dad's broad forehead was creased now.

"Do you think of this often?" Flak said.

My father shrugged. "Most of the time."

Flak was sitting so far forward in his chair, he was in danger of falling onto the carpet at my father's feet. "And have you thought about how you would go about it?"

Flak's question alarmed me in a way that my father's words had not. Flak, I suddenly realized, was talking about *suicide* here. It had never occurred to me that my coolheaded father was in danger of killing himself. My mother was the one who always wished she'd died with her parents. And it was Lara who was now recuperating from her recent adventure with razor blades. But Dad?

I stared in shock at the two men. Everything else in the room seemed to fall away, and all that was left was the line between their eyes. Neither of them looked in my direction. I had ceased to exist. I was the Soviet bug in the chandelier, the unseen, unacknowledged eavesdropper.

"I'm a physician," my father said. "I have all the means at my disposal."

I felt as if a vacuum cleaner had sucked out my insides. I couldn't listen to this.

Flak nodded. "How close have you come to doing anything?"

His eyes were riveted on my father. Dad was staring out the window now, and I followed his gaze. Suddenly I wanted to bolt from the room, get out of Newton, get out of my own skin.

"You've come pretty close, haven't you?" Flak said.

I looked from my father to Flak. I could barely breathe. Although it didn't occur to me at the time, my claim to pain had been preempted. Dad didn't appear any more depressed than usual, but his declaration of the wish to kill himself was new, and it scared me. He was in worse shape than I was.

My father tilted his head. White hair rose in a column from the top of his head and was combed straight back. "I'm a physician," he repeated. "I have all the means at my disposal."

I pictured Dad in the little lab of his office, concocting a potion that would remove him from his misery. He would calculate the dosage, titrate the chemicals, prepare the syringe, the pills, the *means*.

Flak nodded. Here we were, in the shrink's office, mano a mano with death. The deeper my father and Flak explored his suicide, the more I needed to remove myself from it. I transported myself in my mind to a palatial movie theater with stadium seating; I looked down with a critic's detachment, and considered the performances. The struggle was an ancient one: a father's wisdom and patience succumbing, in the end, to psychological torture. The able young psychiatrist using all of his Harvard training to contain the threat, to ascertain its dimensions, and then, very carefully, to disarm the overwrought hero.

"Have you thought about what it would be like?" Flak asked. It was so lovely, so intoxicating, the degree of attention Flak packed into those words. His entire body—his shoulders, his waist, the muscles in his legs—was poised.

"Yes. Yes. It would be an enormous relief," my father said. He did not sound terribly upset. You could see him going over the steps in his mind. Opening his office door, striding to his lab, flipping on the light switch . . .

"Do you ever think how it might affect Helen?" Flak asked.

My father glanced at me, then back at Flak. "Yes," he said. "That is why I haven't done it yet."

Holy shit, I thought. *I'm the only reason he's still alive.*

My sense of self-importance bloomed, but the pressure made my knees buckle.

After the session, my father and I drove in silence back to my apartment. The plan was that he'd return to Schenectady that afternoon. I wondered whether he might put himself out of his misery that night or that week or that month, but I was afraid to ask. I sat up straight, as if to demonstrate reliability and strength. I knew that my own problems—whatever they were—were nothing compared to my family's drama. Now I needed to focus all my attention on helping my father not kill himself.

My father turned left off Comm Ave and wheeled onto Algonquin Road with élan, which is hard to do in a Ford Escort. Then he pulled into the driveway outside my apartment, but declined to come in. "I don't want to get caught in traffic," he said.

"You should call him, Dad. Call Flak."

My father shook his head. "What for?"

"Just to talk about stuff. He really wants you to. I think he wants to help."

"Well, are you feeling better?" he said.

Was he kidding? Was I supposed to feel *better* now? "Yeah," I said. It was the required answer. And relatively speaking, I was in no position to complain. I was the only one in my family, it seemed, who did not have the immediate urge to kill herself.

"That's what matters, then." He put the car in reverse. "Okay, well. Good-bye."

I went into the apartment and stared at my tax and commercial paper casebooks. I felt nothing, just numb. I considered changing clothes and going for a run. You didn't have to solve anything on a run. Just breathe in and out, put one foot in front of the other. It took up all the concentration in the world; it kept you safe from feeling.

Instead, I opened the freezer and found a quart of Brigham's ice cream. A package of Chips Ahoy! in the cupboard. A bag of Doritos. I was suddenly starving. I could always run later, I reasoned—after dark, when there was nothing left to eat.

eleven

Labor Day 1980

The following fall, before starting my last year of law school, I spent the Labor Day weekend with a friend on Martha's Vineyard. We walked for miles along the shore, swam in the ocean, and talked late into the evenings. Obeying my family's rule of secrecy, I didn't mention a word to her about my summer—I had been exiled from home by my parents, who were still caring for Lara around the clock. The last time I'd called home, Lara had grabbed the phone from my mother and screamed that she would kill me, and Mom too, if I ever called again.

The Labor Day traffic back to Boston was heavy. When I finally pulled up in front of my apartment, I froze. There in my parking space was my mother's Plymouth. *Lara's killed herself,* I thought. *She's finally done it.* I jumped out of the car and ran up the steps. *Breathe.* I fumbled with the keys, then burst into the apartment. My mother was lying on my bed reading the *New Yorker*, and rose to greet me.

"Hi, darling," she said pleasantly. "Your land-lady let me in. She's very nice."

"What happened?"

"What do you mean?" My mother gave me a hug and took my knapsack from my shoulder, as if it were the most natural thing for her to be in my apartment on a Monday afternoon.

"What are you doing here?"

My mother shrugged. "I just thought I'd come for the weekend."

Mom had never shown up unannounced before. She sidestepped past me into the little kitchen. "I'll make tea," she said. "Are you hungry?" She flipped on the electric hot plate and filled the kettle with water.

"Why didn't you tell me you were coming?" I asked.

My mother shrugged. "I didn't even know till Saturday morning, and when I called, there was no answer."

"I'd just left for the Vineyard—"

"It's all right," Mom said. "I was fine here. I had a very nice time. I read and relaxed."

"Mom, what's going on? Is Lara okay?"

She narrowed her eyes and picked her words carefully. "Well . . . last week was very difficult. But everything is all right now. I think I'll be able to go home tomorrow."

I didn't know what to make of this. My mother didn't just drive three hours across Massachusetts and show up out of the blue for no reason. The last time I'd seen her was three months ago, when I'd driven home for the summer. Before I could even get out of the car, she and Dad had intercepted me in the driveway. "You can't stay here," Mom had said. "Lara is too unstable. She's very angry at you." Stunned, I'd driven back across the river, got a room at the Y, and started my summer clerkship in Troy the next day.

"Where's Dad?" I asked my mother now.

"He's fine. He's at home."

"And Lara?"

"She left for Burlington this afternoon. She's going back to medical school."

My mother set two cups on the table and poured the tea. "You see, darling," she said, "last week with Lara, it was very touch-and-go. You know how hard it's been for us."

I nodded and leaned toward her, a flower to the sun.

Mom cut two micro-slices of lemon and dropped them in our teacups. Lara had intended to return to medical school for the fall semester, Mom said, but last week she suddenly took a turn for the worse. So my parents and Lara's shrink came up with a plan: they decided that my mother would have to leave the house. "As long as I was there, we knew Lara wouldn't leave for school," Mom explained. "So we told her that I was going away."

"What do you mean? You told her you were coming to visit me?"

"Oh no!" Mom said. "She would have been furious! No, she must never know that I'm here!"

I rolled my eyes.

"You must promise never to tell her!"

"Okay, okay," I said.

It seemed so bizarre, so crazy, the lengths to which my parents went to keep Lara out of the hospital, and now en route to medical school.

"And the plan worked," my mother said proudly. "Dad called me this afternoon and said that she had just left. She's gone back to school."

"So Dad knew you were coming here?"

"Of course! But he couldn't tell Lara. Otherwise she wouldn't have gone back to school. She must never know."

This is nuts, I thought. My mother always insisted on secrecy, as if we would all die from the truth. "So where did she think you were going?"

"We wouldn't tell her. Just *away.*"

My mother left the next morning, once she'd gotten the all-clear signal from my father. Lara had started her third year of medical school.

Dr. Flak asked me to join a new group he was starting that fall. On Tuesday and Thursday evenings, we sat in a circle on hard plastic chairs. The good thing about group therapy was that it was cheap. The bad thing was that it didn't work. Each of us went up in flames that fall. Terrence had a psychotic break and landed in a mental institution, Edgar wound up in the ICU after a near-fatal car crash on the Mass Pike, and Gwen wrestled with her husband and manic depression. I was fine, I decided, and I spent weeks listening to everyone's woes, believing that I would win Flak's love and respect by helping them with their problems.

But in the quiet of my apartment, I started having completely random bouts of shaking and hyperventilating that brought me to my knees. I didn't know what to make of them. In the beginning, they always struck when I was alone—usually at home, or sometimes outdoors at night. After the initial few minutes of slam-dunk terror, they felt strangely reassuring to me—at least they signaled to the tyrannical Helen sitting at the switchboard of my mind to back off; I was suffering enough already. In the aftermath of the attack, I didn't hate myself quite so much; I treated myself gently, with care. I was ready to be a little nicer to myself.

I kept meaning to bring this up in group, but I could never find the right moment. We spent our evenings talking about Gwen's husband who had grabbed her (we agreed it was good that she'd told him, "You're hurting me!"); we questioned Terrence about his plans to marry his girlfriend, and the pros and cons of paying for sex with men. We tried to help Edgar, whom we considered boring but not utterly undatable, and we offered strategies for meeting women.

None of these seemed like a natural segue to a confession like, "I collapsed on the floor and hyperventilated this afternoon." So I stayed quiet.

One night as I was driving home after group, the attack hit like a karate chop from God. I was suddenly doubled over at the wheel, shaking uncontrollably. I managed to pull over to the side of the road. When I finally calmed down, I turned the car around and gingerly drove back to Flak's office. His little VW Bug was still in its spot in the parking lot. Through the bay windows, I could see that he was running another group, and I decided to wait for him. It would probably go till eight-thirty or so.

I walked around the block and tried to figure out what was wrong with me. I could not make any sense of my distress. I decided to ask Flak for an individual appointment. I rehearsed what I would say: "Doctor Flak"—I was very respectful—"I'm sorry to disturb you so late, but I just wanted to ask if I could make an appointment with you sometime this week. A private session." I ran these lines over in my mind, and waited.

It was almost eight-thirty; I watched the door to Flak's office open. His patients spilled out like supplicants after communion with heads lowered. One by one, they filed out, climbed into their cars, and drove off. But the parking lot was still pretty full. To my amazement, Flak's office door remained open, and another seven or eight patients from the waiting room piled into the room for the next group session. I looked at my watch. Flak wouldn't get out till ten. The guy was practically working around the clock, a real-life Energizer Bunny for mental illness.

I stood on the sidewalk, trying to make myself go home, but my agitation was too great. I was afraid that if I waited till tomorrow morning to call, I would lose my nerve. So I walked out to the empty soccer field, and practiced my lines. The more I walked, the more anxious I got. "Doctor Flak," I repeated over and over. "Doctor Flak . . ." My hopelessness finally knocked me down, and I found myself on my knees, heart racing, unable to catch my breath. The earth was soft, and I felt momentarily comforted by the fact that I was a complete wreck.

I finally walked back to Flak's office at ten and stood outside the building. I was too ashamed to go inside and wait in the waiting room. I did not want to be seen by the other patients. I checked my watch. Five after ten. Nothing happened. Ten-ten. Nothing. Was he going to keep them there overnight? What if he literally never stopped working?

Suddenly the door opened and people came out. They were a livelier group; they chatted with each other as they tramped down the three stairs to the parking lot. I waited for them to sing their good-byes before approaching the door.

My hands were sweating, and I had trouble turning the knob. Once in the foyer, I heard Flak straightening chairs and turning out lights. Before I reached the hallway, he was right in front of me, and we both jumped back, startled.

"I'm sorry to disturb you," I blurted, staring at my feet. "Um, I know it's late, I was just wondering if I could make an appointment for a private session with you."

Having recited my lines, I looked up. Flak was slowly shaking his head. "What's this about?" he said coolly.

His reproach threw me off; I didn't want to get into it now. I didn't even know what *it* was.

"I don't know," I said. "It's just that . . ."

"Well you need to bring this up in group. Talk about it on Thursday."

"But I can't," I said. "I can't talk in group. I mean, it's like everyone has worse problems than I do. Compared to them, you know, I don't feel like I have the right—"

"Whoa," he said, holding up his hands. "You're making this larger than life."

"I know! I know I am! It's just—" The words caught in my throat. I felt tears on my face, and I quickly wiped them away with my sleeve. It had never occurred to me that he could just say no like that. After all, I wasn't asking for free advice. I was asking for an *appointment.* During normal business hours. He couldn't even give me that?

And then, to my horror, I started shaking. The shame and frustration were a brushfire in my chest, rising, heating my face. My lips started quivering, and soon my legs and shoulders were shaking, and I couldn't stop. "Sorry!" I mumbled, and started to run out the door, but Flak grabbed my wrist.

"Wait a second," he said. His tone was completely changed. He sounded warm, caring. His hand on my wrist sent a shock wave through my arm. I looked up at him now with uncertainty. Tears were pouring down my face, and I wanted to wipe them away, but Flak was trying to hold my hand. Despite my humiliation, I was stunned by his sudden change, as if a light had switched on behind his eyes. He was smiling and looking at me with genuine concern. I stood shaking before him for some time, unable to speak, trying to catch my breath.

"You're feeling scared," he said quietly. "You're very frightened."

And I thought, *No, I'm not frightened, I'm frustrated.*

"You're having what's called a classic panic attack," he said.

The term was new to me. I was pretty sure I felt no panic, but now was not the time to quibble.

225

His eyes gazed into mine, a calm, heroic beam. "It's all right." He adjusted his grip on my hand. He cared. He actually cared! I felt slightly dishonest, knowing I didn't feel the slightest bit of panic or fear—just shame at being so out of control.

But I let him talk on in his soothing voice, and he was so gentle and kind, and the touch of his hand was so warm, I was reassured, even if his words didn't exactly make sense.

"And I'm sorry," he said. "I didn't realize it was so bad. How long have you been having these?"

I rolled my eyes. "All along," I squeaked. It was true—not only did I have them at home, but I'd started having them at moments when I was about to get on the T, or sometimes in the hallway outside court. I was working as a student defender that semester, and I liked my clients who were charged with breaking into houses, beating up their girlfriends, or slashing tires on police cruisers. But I had problems with my heartbeat. Sometimes I would step into the hallway on the thirteenth floor of the Cambridge District Courthouse and stare out the window, at the wild expanse of the city spread like a series of dioramas below me—the Necco factory and the triple-deckers of East Cambridge, the river beyond, and the skyscrapers of Boston. And I thought about soaring over all of those chipped rooftops and rusted handrails, the poured concrete and the nailed porches, how pure the air would be and how soft the landing.

Then my case would get called and I would return to my life as a baby lawyer, a buttoned-down, briefcase-toting kid playing grown-up.

"And you're right," he continued. "We should set up an individual session. Let's meet tomorrow, okay?"

I nodded, unable to take my eyes off my sneakers.

"Tomorrow, two o'clock?"

I nodded, but still couldn't look at him.

"You going to be okay?"

I nodded again.

"Okay, then. I'll see you tomorrow at two."

I flew out the door. When I got around the corner, I fell to my knees by the side of the street, unable to breathe. My heart was pounding as if it would gallop out of my chest and down the street. I curled into a ball, clutched my head to my knees, and waited out the storm.

Suddenly I heard footsteps behind me. "Helen?" It was Dr. Flak.

I leaped up and tore down the road as fast as I could. When I reached my car, I fell again, shaking and sobbing, and waited a long time till I felt calm enough to stand. Then I opened the door and slowly drove home.

What had just happened? What a pathetic ruse

to get attention! How wonderful Flak was! What a worthless fuckup I was! My neediness was an oozing wound, and because of my failure to control myself, I had snared the god's attention. What a manipulative bitch. What dreamy eyes he had! What was wrong with me? Jesus! But how lovely to feel his gaze on me, to feel him hold my hand.

I fell into bed, but couldn't sleep. I kept replaying those few moments over and over in my mind. It seemed important, a *breakthrough,* as they said in the movies. Everything would be all right, I thought. I would place myself in Flak's hands. He would take care of me. Everything would be fine.

Flak and I met the next day, and he persuaded me to tell everyone in group about my attacks. I even gave them a demonstration, since it took almost nothing to set me off. I think I scared the shit out of one of Flak's new recruits, a pretty young Harvard boy whom Flak seemed crazy about. But the whole thing felt fraudulent somehow—a little performance that Flak and I had staged for the others. I was so removed from my own experience I had trouble feeling anything but disgust at the entire charade of my suffering. Group, it seemed, was just another dysfunctional family in which I didn't know who I was or how I really felt.

twelve

The Confusion of Sex

Years earlier, when I was still in college and things had been good between Lara and me, we never talked about boys or romance or sex, perhaps because the topic was just plain taboo in our family. Besides, I didn't really know what to make of romance. When I was a junior in college, almost all the women on my rowing team were paired off with one another. Even our pixieish coach lived with another woman. Through the powerful magic of denial, I never realized that these relationships could be sexual in any way. It was as if gay sex were an insoluble solid suspended in the solution of my mind—it was right there in front of me, but I couldn't absorb it. Sure, my friends cuddled and hugged and wrestled with each other, but I never saw anyone kiss or act in an *explicitly* sexual way. So it never dawned on me that my friends might be lesbians.

I only knew that I felt terribly lonely my junior year. Harriet had graduated the summer before and moved back to Minnesota, and Emma was at Berkeley. All my other friends seemed to be involved in passionate friendships that made me feel left out. I had no words for this, just a vague sense of loss.

I decided to go on exchange to Dartmouth College in the spring of my junior year, and over the summer I met Philip, a tightly muscled, curly-haired guy in the Outward Bound program. We spent ten weeks learning to rock climb, to portage canoes across miles of muddy bogs, and to survive alone in the wilderness for days without food or shelter. Although I was much more drawn to my roommate, Claire, it was Philip who kissed me at the end of the summer.

A few months later, with grim determination, I decided it was time to lose my virginity. Philip and I succeeded at this task in workmanlike fashion, and we more or less stayed together for two years, portaging our relationship like the bulky canoe of good intentions that it was. I found sex a colossal disappointment. The entire human race—centuries of literature and art— had led me to believe that sex was this thrilling experience of galactic proportions. Instead, the best thing I could say about sex was that it was mercifully quick work. I managed to fake my way through it, which was how I got through much of my life in those days. I didn't talk about this with any of my friends. I simply decided that romantic love and sex were ridiculously overrated and unimportant to me. I liked Philip well enough; he was a Russian studies major, and he was fascinated by my father, with whom he conversed in Russian when I brought him home for Thanksgiving. I, in turn, was fascinated by Philip's tales of working on an offshore oil rig in the Gulf of Mexico, and his love of Texas, a place as remote as Siberia to me. Philip and I protected each other from loneliness. But over time we got on each other's nerves, and I refused to move in with him after college. He went to Germany for the summer and had a fling with a girl, which gave me a legitimate excuse to stop seeing him. I still didn't know I was queer; I just knew that I didn't care for Philip nearly as much as I did for my girlfriends.

I never brought any of this up in group, because the great landmass of my family seemed to block out whatever other problems I might have.

Fall Semester 1980

In the evenings that fall, after I'd prepared my cases as a student defender for the next day, I found myself getting into my Plymouth Duster and driving aimlessly through the dark residential streets of Newton and Chestnut Hill. Usually I would stop at a convenience store and pick up a package of chocolate chip cookies, which I would then eat methodically through the western suburbs, while trying to figure out what was wrong with me. I was too depressed to talk to my law school friends; I had to figure this out for myself. Eventually I would turn over in my mind the magic card that Flak had given me. It had his telephone number, and he had encouraged me to call him anytime I needed to.

Problem was, that word *need*. The daughter of Holocaust survivors, I was a strict constructionist of the word. As my father had always told us, all one really "needed" was:

a. food and water
b. shelter
c. clothing, a means to stay warm

I had yards of everything I could possibly need. I fairly reeked of privilege. So why, in the midst of my riches, did I still hold out my beggar's bowl for some unidentified "more"? After all, I thought, sizing up my circumstances, I already had a heated apartment, a closet of clothes, a refrigerator of food, a registered car, a right of free speech, a right to bear arms . . .

Don't think it didn't occur to me.

Inevitably, thoughts of what I needed led me to consider what I would do with a gun. Every morning in court, I watched the slow shuffle of prisoners in and out like cattle before the auctioneer in the black robe. Evidence: all the pretty guns, assault rifles, sawed-off shotguns,

.45s. All the ways to bear arms and bear them poorly. If I had a gun, I would be efficient. I would not fall into that unseemly, bogus bucket of would-be suicides. I would distinguish myself from Lara. No half-assed cutting up my arms or swallowing a bottle of pills. *This is how you commit suicide, you dipshit,* I would say with my elegantly dead body, a single breathtaking bullet to the skull.

But I knew I would never get a gun.

All the guns in court were sealed in clear plastic evidence bags and fondled by cops; I was certainly not going to get my hands on a gun in court. And I would never ask a client for a gun. I had a hard enough time convincing them I was their lawyer. Besides, like most law students, I had an exaggerated sense of professional ethics.

Buying a gun legally was also out of the question—I had no patience for applying for a license and registration, the sheer bureaucracy of preparing for violence. I could not picture myself walking into a gun store, asking for advice from the sales clerk at the counter, discussing different models, making sure I would get the best quality for the lowest price. All of this was too mundane, too public, too time-consuming. But I also knew I'd be inept at getting a gun on the street—I would get one that malfunctioned; I would get arrested before I could use it; I would not know how to load it properly, or how to release the safety.

The whole point of suicide, I thought, was to succeed at it. My sister's completion rate was pathetic. She would never get into the Suicide Hall of Fame with her record of attempts and failures.

And so I finally decided that the way to kill myself would be in my Plymouth Duster. A midnight high-speed single-car crash into a rock wall. This had a number of advantages: it involved heart-thumping action, collision, blood, and a pretty quick resolution. It also seemed a likely success, and in any event, it would be colorful, and it would put Lara's paltry efforts to shame.

I cruised around the Chestnut Hill Reservoir in search of optimal conditions to carry out my plans. Too many intersections, not enough walls. I would have to go out of town, perhaps even out of state—to New Hampshire, where one was encouraged to live free or die. But thinking about New Hampshire always put me in a good mood. I'd take my snowshoes, go camping for the weekend, and feel better. I'd forget to kill myself till I got back to Boston Monday morning, and there, in court, would be all the pretty guns.

At last I called him. Not because I needed to. Not because I had really scared myself into thinking I would kill myself, but because I finally grew tired of myself. It was a Friday evening when I left a message for Flak to call me. This was an extraordinarily bold move, and my heart was racing at the sheer audacity of calling a doctor—an important man! A man with patients, employees, a wife, children, countless pressures I could only guess at. And here was I, Little Helen of the Perpetual Worries, adding one more complaint to his burden. And what was it, exactly, that I wanted from him?

I couldn't admit it, but what I wanted, quite simply, was a bit of his warmth and attention. Or maybe more than just a bit. I wanted him to say, "Helen, I love you. You are the most amazing person in the world." Or maybe he could just say something reassuring, and we would talk like coach to athlete: he would tell me I was brave and strong, and I would be fine. "Now, just go back out there and stay loose," he would say. "You'll do fine, I have every confidence in—"

The phone rang. I practically jumped out of my skin.

"Hello, Helen? This is Dr. Flak." He sounded brusque, all business.

I sat with the receiver pressed to my ear, paralyzed for a moment, before a stream of words rushed from my mouth. "Thanks for calling back," I said. "I'm sorry to bother you—I mean, it's really not a big deal, but, um . . ."

He was silent. A cold emptiness on the other

end of the line. He was probably listening, I thought with rising alarm, in that shrinky way—with narrowed eyes and pursed lips, evaluating my sanity.

"I'm okay," I said quickly. "I mean, I guess . . . maybe it's getting worse."

"What's worse?"

"I don't know! I'm not sure what I expect you to—"

"Where are you?" he asked.

"At home." I was sitting on the mustard-colored shag carpeting, propped between my desk and my bed. "I don't know what I want," I said. "It's not like I—"

"Well, I expected this," he said flatly.

This was disappointing. He didn't sound the least bit loving.

"I think you need medication. I thought you needed this before, but I figured we'd see how it goes, and—"

My face went cold. Everything in my body lurched forward. "No!" I said.

"Listen to me," he said. "This is what I want you to do. I'm going to call in a prescription for imipramine to the CVS on Charles Street, near Mass General. It's open till midnight. Do you know where that is?"

I did. I often went to the movie theater a few blocks down the street. But I was horrified to think that I was being sent downtown to get psycho medication on a Friday night, like it was some kind of emergency.

"I don't want any drugs," I said in a thin voice.

"Well, I think you need them." He'd turned into Dr. Authority. No more Mr. Nice & Listen. I was mortified at what I had unleashed. If only I'd kept my big mouth shut! What had compelled me to call him? I was never satisfied, I thought. Always wanted more.

"Please," I sniveled. "Please, no drugs."

"Can I trust you to pick these up?" he said.

I held my breath. What could I say to start this conversation over again?

"Helen?"

"Yes," I said meekly.

"Can I trust—"

"Yes." I was the obedient, good girl after all. I would have no tantrums, no hysterics like Lara. I would gather whatever dignity was left me and drive downtown to the drugstore, where I would wait until they bagged my prescription and cashed me out.

Once home, with a sense of resignation, I read the label, swallowed a pill, and chased it with a glass of water as instructed. Then I allowed myself the unsatisfying indulgence of hopelessness. I would sink now, I thought. There was nothing left of me, a hollow shell. Flak was no different from my father, from anyone else. They were autocrats and they would treat me in the order in which I placed my call. Like anyone else who asked for help, I would be given the dosage recommended by the *Physician's Desk Reference*, and left to live somehow on my own.

Sleep hit at some point in the middle of the night, and knocked me to the side of the bed, where I stayed until late morning. Groggy, I stumbled to the bathroom, turned on the shower, and then felt the world tip on its side. I grabbed the edges of the spinning shower stall and gradually dropped to the floor. *Side effect: dizziness.* I was a mental patient. Just like Lara, I was now taking a mind-altering drug that would make me crazy.

A few weeks later Lara called and asked me to go hiking with her in Vermont. I hadn't spoken to her in half a year, and the sound of her voice— so friendly and gentle—made me cry. It was like hearing the voice of a long-lost love.

I didn't want her to hear me sniffle—it seemed weak and shameful. Neither of us said much. She asked me how I was. "Okay," I said. "And you?"

"Okay."

We were both lying, pretending that nothing had happened over the past six months: her suicide attempts and threats to kill me, my panic attacks and exile from home, my parents' insistence on secrecy—it was safer to say nothing. Instead we agreed to meet at the Appalachian Trail south of

Bromley Mountain for a weekend in the woods.

I got up before dawn, threw my gear in the trunk, and drove to Vermont. A nor'easter was thrashing New England, and the wind hurled sheets of rain onto the roads. Three hours later I was sitting in my rusting Plymouth at the trailhead off Route 8 in the pounding rain. In another five months I was supposed to graduate and become a lawyer—a ludicrous idea to me at the time. I was much too young and immature to be a lawyer. I couldn't even figure out how to be me.

Headlights turned into the parking lot. Through the driving rain, I could barely make out the shape of my sister's drab-green Chevy Malibu with its dented fenders and broken defroster. She rolled up beside me and lowered her window an inch. I did the same. We eyed each other across the no-man's-land of angry rain. She did not look any different than she usually did, except her hair was combed, and although it billowed out behind her ears, it looked quiet. And she looked lonely and a little scared; her shoulders were hunched as if she were protecting herself from a blow. Under her mountaineering parka, I could see her stretched-out cotton turtleneck. She was a third-year medical student, but she didn't look any more like a doctor than I looked like a lawyer.

"Hi," she said.

"Hi."

"This sucks."

I nodded.

"Want to get a cup of coffee and see if it lets up?"

My face brightened. We wouldn't have to trudge out in this mess, slip on rocks, and crawl into soaked sleeping bags at the end of the day. We didn't have to hurt ourselves too badly. The competition was postponed due to good sense.

I followed Lara's taillights down the mountain, through the lashing rain. We parked at a coffee shop in Manchester, bought coffee and blueberry muffins at the counter, and slid into an empty booth. We were the only ones there. A long-haired boy drifted behind the counter, scruffy and sleepy-eyed. Somewhere in the back, the Stones were on, Jagger singing *I sit and watch the children play. . . .*

Lara looked thinner than when I'd last seen her in the spring, when she was so angry at me. She seemed gentle now, with a shy, sweet smile, and warm green eyes and a perky nose. I suddenly realized how terribly I'd missed her. I had felt part of myself sliced off, an arm, or perhaps both arms, and as I'd wandered through my days at law school and through the streets of Boston, I had felt stunned by my loss, unable to grasp anything, clumsy and mute with pain. And now she was here. She was whole—her round face and strong shoulders, the terribly ravaged fingers; my sister was here before me, sipping coffee from a tall paper cup.

"I don't know where to begin," I said. And then we began, patching together the intervening time.

"I wasn't allowed home last summer," I said. "As long as you were there, Mom and Dad said I couldn't set foot in the house. I guess they were afraid of what you'd do."

Lara looked bewildered.

"You were in really, really bad shape," I said. I stared at my coffee, unable to meet her eyes. I was burning to talk about the past summer, about meeting my father on the sly at the hospital coffee shop to get updates on Lara's condition. About Mom showing up in my apartment over Labor Day. But it seemed cruel now to remind Lara of how she'd acted, of how frightened we'd all been. I separated the wax paper from the muffin and broke off a piece. Lara tore into hers, spreading crumbs across the table. "Mom and Dad said you were . . . well, they said it was very, very dangerous," I said carefully. "They were afraid you'd kill yourself. You were furious at me." I took a sip of coffee and sneaked a glance at Lara to see how she was taking this.

Lara shook her head slowly. "That's nuts," she said. "That's completely wack. They told me you wouldn't have anything to do with us. That you refused to see us."

241

What? Did she really believe that? "I used to meet Dad," I said.

Lara's eyebrows went up.

"We'd have coffee at the hospital."

I used to get up before six on Sundays and drive through the sleepy streets of Troy and west to Schenectady, and I would park on the opposite side of the hospital parking lot, so as not to be seen. And I would go into the familiar halls of my father's hospital. He would be standing there in his gray suit, waiting inside the doctors' entrance next to his nameplate, on a wall panel of all the doctors' names. He would flick the little switch, lighting up his name to show that he was there, he was on the premises, and if anyone needed him, all they had to do was page him over the loudspeaker.

I always felt a surge of pride at seeing this, the simple flick of my father's index finger lighting up his presence in the world. It spoke to his importance, that he was actually ingrained in the walls of this hospital, that he was part of the edifice of healing. I followed him down the hall to the coffee shop, and people stopped and greeted him; everyone knew him, everyone admired him and joked with him and smiled at me and shook my hand when he introduced me as his daughter. And my head swelled to think that I was attached to this great man, and through no credit of my own, I had managed to gain this exalted position as my father's daughter. It wasn't just doctors who stopped to talk with him, but nurses and orderlies and cafeteria workers and janitors and patients and volunteers who worked the gift shop and the flower stand.

"We got together once a week," I told Lara.

She stared at me. I couldn't tell whether she was puzzled, or angry, or what. My father had told me he'd had to sneak out of the house unnoticed, to prevent Lara from finding out he was meeting with me.

"In the beginning, I called Mom," I said. "I wanted to see her. But she said you were too sick, and she couldn't leave you alone."

"Sick?"

I nodded. "And she said I couldn't come home because you were ready to kill me or something. And you'd flip out if you found out she was even *talking* to me. So she hung up."

"What?" My sister fidgeted. Her fingers found each other on the table and she began tugging at the skin over her cuticle.

How could Lara have forgotten how crazy she'd been? I glanced at her shaggy brown hair falling over her face. She looked like one of those lovable mutts in Hollywood movies that chew up the carpets and then win you over with their sheer scruffiness. *Oh, who cares?* I thought. *Let it go.* I was exhausted from years of trying to make sense of Lara and my family. All that mattered now was that my sister was here, sitting across the table from me, and that we were friends.

Lara got up to get more coffee, and when she sat down again, I realized that she and I were no longer in competition; we had both failed to make our parents happy. As I had done so many times before, I now rearranged what I knew about my sister to accommodate my loneliness, my need to be aligned with her. Perhaps, I now thought, it was our parents who were nuts, and it was Lara who was my real friend and ally.

"They had me drugged to the gills," Lara said, staring at her coffee. Her fingers picked at each other as if they were separate entities beyond her control. "I didn't even know what was going on."

There was something so plaintive in her voice, I felt the solidarity of a fellow sufferer. I could no longer pretend that I was the healthy one, the normal one, and she the crazy one. I had finally joined her ranks in the battle for mental health: I was a walking, talking psych patient, with a panic disorder and imipramine running through my veins. I had lowered my head and offered it to the profession, and I was now in their clutches, just as she was.

"That must have been awful," I found myself saying.

She shrugged. Her hair had begun its outward stretch, growing like a hydra as it absorbed the humidity in the air. "I missed you," she said.

I nodded, and smiled. "Well, you were also really pissed at me."

Her head snapped back as if struck, and her brow furrowed.

Alarms went off in my head. *Just like always,* I thought. *She's conveniently forgotten everything she did.* "At the end of May," I reminded her. "When I called home from the mountains— remember?"

Lara was shaking her head and slouching lower in her chair. She seemed to grow smaller before me, a snail curling into its shell. I couldn't bear to see it. I changed the subject. I told her about my panic attacks. It was an offering—to show her that I too was crazy.

"They come out of nowhere," I said. "I'll be standing on the subway platform, and all of a sudden, I'll get a tingly feeling. And then I can feel my lips trembling, and I know it's coming. It's like holding your breath underwater, right before it hits."

I could see that she wasn't listening to me, she was still lost in the words I'd left in the air before. I could see her working over the details of that phone call in May, when she'd screamed that she would kill me, and Mom too, if I ever tried calling again. So complete was her grip on me then, I'd been certain she would kill us. But now, sitting across the table from her, with her hunched shoulders and bleeding fingers, it seemed impossible that she could have ever struck such fear in me.

"Lara, you listening?"

She rolled her shoulders wearily and brought her eyes even with mine. "Yeah."

I didn't know where she'd gone, but I tried to get her back. "Listen, never mind about last summer. It's over. It doesn't matter. I'm glad you called me. I'm glad you took that chance."

And at this moment, sitting in a coffee shop in Manchester, Vermont, I was so grateful to have my sister with me, to have the warmth of her presence, the light in her soft green-brown eyes, her shy smile. I needed her, pure and simple. I did not understand my own unhappiness, but I knew this much: I loved my sister and had missed her terribly, and something of that wound was healing here at this table. I felt myself being repaired by her presence and by her friendship. I might not be able to solve the problem of my life, but I could bask in the glow of our friendship. We were together again.

thirteen

Rubin Vase

I first saw the image in my psych textbook in 1974 as a college freshman—a stark white goblet on a black background. The caption under the picture asked whether you could see the two faces in profile, facing each other.

All I saw was a white goblet. I read further, and it said to focus only on the black "background" of the picture and bring that image forward. It took me a few minutes before I could find the two identical faces in silhouette, their noses almost touching each other. Seeing these two faces was like an electric shock. How could I have studied the picture so closely, yet missed something so obvious? Once I found the two faces, the goblet simply disappeared.

The text went on to talk about human perception; about how the brain receives stimuli and matches patterns to make mental interpretations of what we see. When you look at the picture, you cannot simultaneously see both images at once. It was called a Rubin vase after the Danish psychologist who had developed the image and similar optical illusions.

The goblet with the two faces became an image for my relationship with my sister. When I was younger, I saw Lara as the goblet filled with some toxic fluid that would burn on contact. But then, for no apparent reason, my image of her would flip, and all of a sudden I would see my sister and me as two identical faces, joined together, aligned. The goblet was gone. It was just the two of us—Lara and me looking directly into each other's eyes with love and devotion. She and I were exactly the same.

These two images of our relationship kept flipping back and forth on me throughout our lives. There was never any transition—no warning, no sense of in-between. It was always black or white. One moment we were best friends, two sisters seeing eye to eye. The next, mortal enemies, the vase of poison.

1980

Lara and I spent hours on the phone that fall, finding companionship in suicidal thoughts. At twenty-three and twenty-six, the obligation to make up for our parents' unspoken losses was too great. We owed them our happiness and our lives, and suicide seemed like the fastest way to get out of debt.

Also, there was the terrible burden of make-believe—the pressure of pretense—that we could no longer sustain. Our family had always looked fine from the outside. Our surfaces sparkled. Our lawn was green, our grades were good, our expenses paid. A double suicide by the children would certainly give lie to all that. We were frauds—desperate to appear successful and well-adjusted on the outside, while harboring the rage and grief of a destroyed people. Suicide would be more honest. My sister and I felt a certain sense of entitlement to apocalypse.

My father had always dismissed our unhappiness as the ennui of privileged youth. We were bored and restless and unhappy, he explained, because we had too much of everything. And he seemed to be right: our lives had become too easy to bear, and therefore unbearable in light of all that had come before. Hardship would do wonders for us, Lara and I believed. But neither of us wanted to give up too much comfort for the sake of happiness. We would rather be miserable.

"I think a car crash," I said. I was sitting on the shag carpet of my one-room apartment across from Boston College. I cradled the phone receiver against my ear while doodling on my tax notebook. "What about you?" I asked.

Lara sighed. The world turned on its axis with that sigh, wind fluttered through the trees, stars died. "I think knives."

Lara, the doctor, scalpel in hand. She had taken

anatomy twice—her first year in med school, and then the summer afterward, for good measure.

"Or drugs," she added.

"What drugs?"

"There's zillions of meds. I can get anything I want."

Medical school had its advantages, I could see that. I tried to imagine swallowing a bottle of pills and lying on the narrow bed against the wall of my room. It seemed too depressing. "I want more of an impact," I told Lara. "I want something noisier, faster, explosive. Drugs are so . . . passive. So quiet. It's like, why bother?"

She didn't answer.

"A car crash would be fast, it would be active. It wouldn't be like lying around, waiting to die." Listening to myself, I wondered how serious I was. Would I really kill myself? I didn't think so, but I thought Lara might.

"It doesn't matter how," she said. "It's all the same. Nothing matters."

"Okay, but I'm just saying—"

"It doesn't matter how you do it."

When my mother was my age, she'd been smuggling food to her parents in the ghetto by night; by day she worked for the occupying army in Lvov; and by October 1942, she'd escaped Poland altogether, posing as a young Italian infantryman. She had lost her fiancé to the Russians, her parents to the Germans, and her sister to the Italians, until finally she had lost herself as a person whom she could recognize at all.

And now, as a third-year law student, I did not know who I was or what I was doing. No one was trying to kill me, no one was shooting my friends or gassing my loved ones. What right did I have to be unhappy? My inner and outer worlds did not match. I was starting to break down, and I turned to my big sister as my model of decompensation.

"Let's just do it," Lara said. Her voice was so low I could barely hear her.

"Yeah?"

"Yeah," she said.

"Okay." The idea of killing ourselves together had growing appeal. It would be more like a mission, a bond we would share. Something that would draw us together. "When?"

"This weekend," Lara said.

I had nothing planned this weekend. It would be a perfect time to kill myself. "You serious?" I asked. My sister was the most unreliable person I knew. It would be so like her to set something up, and then back out at the last minute with some lame excuse.

"Yeah."

"Me too," I said. I wondered what my obligation was. If we agreed to do it, and I finked out, would I be responsible for her death? If I went through with it, she'd better kill herself too. Otherwise, what was the point?

What, exactly, was the point?

"All right," I said. "So what day? Saturday?"

"I don't know. Maybe. Or maybe Sunday."

Here we go, I thought. *She can't even commit to the day. She's never been able to make a decision in her life.* I felt my irritation rising. "Well, pick one," I said.

"I'm not sure yet."

"But you're sure you want to do it, right?"

"Oh yeah."

"Well, I don't want to talk you—"

"I said I want to do it."

The sun was out. In two hours the Patriots would host the New York Jets at Foxborough. It all sounded so crazy. Lara and I were being dramatic. She had tried to kill herself before, but my depression was sharp and fresh. I wanted to be serious enough to go through with the plan, but I was pretty sure I didn't have the guts. It all seemed so unreal. "Then we'll do it," I said.

"Together," she said.

"Well, you do it your way, I'll do it mine." I didn't think we should have to synchronize our acts. But I needed her support, and she needed mine, and together we might be able to pull it off.

"All right," she said. "This weekend."

We were quiet for a moment. "So what are you going to do now?" I asked.

"I don't know."

"Are your roommates around?"

"No. They're never here."

She lived with a group of med students who barely skimmed the surface of the planet. They studied all day and night; they partied and slept with each other between classes. My sister was isolated by a scrim of gloom that her roommates could not guess lay behind her convincing smile. I had spent my life distancing myself from her, and now I was closing the gap. We were not so different after all. We were both lost.

"You all right?" I began to worry that she might kill herself ahead of schedule.

"I'll be all right once we do it," she said.

We hung up, and I felt better. Maybe it was not the healthiest of relationships, but Lara and I bonded well over suicidal depression. It felt good, knowing that she was also depressed. I didn't feel so alone. And there was something we could do about it: we could kill ourselves. I felt an obligation to her. I would have to find a road on which I could really slam into a wall without killing anyone else. I had to do it responsibly. I would not be a menace to other drivers. When I did it, I would do it right.

The weekend came. My conversation with Lara seemed ages ago. I wasn't in the mood for suicide, and I was pretty sure she wasn't either, and anyway, neither of us called. I didn't even think about it until Sunday night, when I vaguely wondered whether maybe she'd gone ahead and done it. But I knew she hadn't.

It wasn't until a week or two later that Lara called. We talked for a while, both of us miserable, but neither of us mentioned our suicide pact. Apparently it had expired for lack of interest.

Looking back now, I think we needed our pact to get us through whatever blackness had descended. For that half hour or forty minutes, we'd gotten some relief, some acknowledgment that we weren't alone, that we were, in fact, "normal" sisters, since both of us were suicidally depressed. If we weren't both feeling exactly the same way at the same time (whether up or down), the vase of poison would come between us.

A dozen years later, in 1992, after we discovered that Mom and Dad were Jewish Holocaust survivors, Lara and I never discussed those times in our twenties when we had been so troubled. Just as our parents had avoided talking about their war, Lara and I avoided talking about ours. Instead, we searched for clues from our parents' past, and tried to find people who had known them before and after the war. We even tracked down Dr. Grokle, the shrink at the Hoffman Children and Family Center, who was now seventy-five, to see if she could shed light on our family.

"I remember your family quite well," she said,

sitting in a wingback chair in her living room in Schenectady. Lara had contacted her twenty-five years after we'd seen her as children. "I have seen so many patients and families over the years, you know, and I'm more or less retired now. . . ." She looked down at her hands. They were thin, spotted with age, free of jewelry except for a gold band. "I've forgotten a great deal, but you and your parents stuck in my mind."

She looked at Lara and smiled. "I'm afraid we didn't really do much for your family," she said.

No shit, I thought.

"You see, family therapy was in its infancy in those days," she said. "In the sixties, we really didn't know that much about family dynamics or treatment techniques." She paused, perhaps remembering the low-lit room of the Hoffman Center, where my family took our appointed seats each week and waited to be cured. "I must confess that I was a bit intimidated by your parents," Dr. Grokle said. "I mean, given what they'd gone through in the war. I never tried to ask them about their past. Frankly, I was relieved that they didn't talk about it. In those days . . . well, none of us wanted to talk about the war. We were all too happy to sweep it under the rug."

fourteen

I was home for winter break during my last year of law school. The phone rang and I picked it up. The voice of my high school boyfriend, Kevin, surprised me; we hadn't spoken in years. I still had the leather belt and wallet he'd made for me. Our romance had been doomed for a number of reasons—first, my mother forbade me to date boys, and second, I'd lost interest in guys altogether when I went off to college. But over the past few years, Kevin sometimes came over when Lara was home and they'd run a five-mile loop together.

"Helen? I didn't know you were home."

His voice was sweet, and it made me think, suddenly, of Lake Tear of the Clouds in the Adirondacks. In January six years earlier, he and I had climbed to its frozen shore, just below the final pitch up Mount Marcy.

"How are you?"

"Good," I said automatically. Actually, considering I'd contemplated suicide with my sister a few weeks ago, I *was* pretty good. "How've you been?"

"Okay," he said. "I'm taking some classes at SUNY, you know, doing some work for Greg Crump, just hanging out." I remembered coming home for Thanksgiving three years earlier with my then-boyfriend Philip, and the awkwardness when Kevin joined Lara, me, and Philip for a run. Philip had felt the need to sprint past us all at the end. I was ashamed to think of it.

"Well, look," Kevin said. "I was going to invite Lara for dinner—I've been working on a couple quiche recipes I got out of the *Times*, and they're pretty good. You know, Craig Claiborne's column. You want to come too?"

"You're cooking quiche?"

"Yeah, I know, I'm a total Renaissance man."

My mother was a huge Craig Claiborne fan. She clipped his recipes and folded them into her little metal recipe box. It would blow her mind if she heard Kevin was making Craig Claiborne's quiche lorraine. She had always considered Kevin some sort of blue-collar rapist.

We made a date.

Lara seemed relieved that I was coming along for dinner at Kevin's. She and Kevin had been uneasy classmates in high school, and although she didn't mind him coming over for a run now and then, she still suspected him of being a jerk.

She and I put on clean jeans and sweaters and drove out to Kevin's. He lived in a little apartment above Crump's Garage, an old truck repair shop near Verdoy, with dead engines and parts out back and a retired 1960s gas station in front. In the winter of 1980, Kevin was the tow-truck driver in residence. He received free use of the premises and a regular paycheck in exchange for responding to calls for disabled tractor-trailers. In bad weather, he often spent entire nights in subzero temperatures, hauling out rigs that had skidded on ice and snow off the Northway a few miles away.

Kevin served us a knockout meal of quiche, salad, and hot rolls with a bottle of chianti. We ate by candlelight, killed the bottle, then opened another. Lara, as usual in the presence of others, was perfectly polite, drank half a glass, and watched Kevin and me get blotto.

To my delight, Kevin was exactly my size of silly. We entertained ourselves with a free-wheeling sense of humor that swung dangerously between the sublime and the ridiculous, often crashing into delicate subjects, doing damage to friends, loved ones, and entire segments of the population.

"Worth it!" he said.

"Who needs friends?" I agreed.

By nine o'clock, Lara had had enough. She signaled toward the door with her eyes, and poked me with her elbow to get me to leave. But I didn't feel like going.

"I'll drive Helen home," Kevin offered. "Don't worry—I'll wait till I sober up."

Lara frowned. Her self-appointed responsibilities as big sister included preventing me from having too much fun, or, alternatively, from getting splattered across Route 7 in a drunken car crash.

"Go ahead," I said. "I'll catch a ride with Kevin later."

Lara clomped down the stairs and out the door. We heard the Chevy's engine struggle in the cold, then the wheels crunching on the snow as she turned onto Route 7. Kevin put the Stones on the turntable and opened another bottle of wine.

"This is just temporary," he said, meaning his life. "Crump pays me pretty good money, but I just don't know what I want to do yet—you know, like a *career*."

We put our feet up on the coffee table and talked about the future, which scared us with its sheer size.

"I can't really see being a lawyer," I said. "I don't know if I can survive wearing pantyhose for the rest of my life."

"At least you're close to finishing school." Kevin was taking the scenic route through college, a few courses here, a few there.

"Well, I've had some real problems this year." I told him about my odyssey through the land of psychiatry: the panic attacks, group therapy, medication. I told him Flak had now proposed I might be *uni*polar, which was like bipolar, but without the benefits of mania. I just had depression, with intermittent breathers of okay-ness.

You could say I put Kevin on notice.

But he did not seem shocked or uneasy with my revelation of crazy. On the contrary—he was interested and sympathetic. "That sounds really rough," he said. "I'm glad you're feeling better."

He was no stranger to unhappiness. I liked that about him.

We talked for hours. He told me about his former girlfriends, what he had hoped for, and why they hadn't worked out. We looked up, and it was already past midnight. By then we were kissing, and then we found ourselves on the bed, and one thing led to another, and by the time he drove me home at two-thirty in the morning, I couldn't wait to see him the next day.

And so, absurdly, over winter break, I fell in love.

When I got up the next morning and came into the kitchen, my mother's face turned to ice. She watched me pour my coffee in silence, then left the room. Zosia was staying with us over the holidays, and I could hear the staccato of their voices as my mother intercepted her in the hallway. I knew, without her saying a word, that she was furious at me for having stayed out late with Kevin. I had violated the solemn law of family loyalty.

"You left coffee for Zosia, didn't you?" Mom asked, staring daggers.

"There's a whole pot, Mom."

She brushed past me, too angry to speak.

"What's the matter?"

She said nothing.

"Mom?"

She took the coffeepot and a mug out to the dining table for Zosia. I left them alone.

Kevin called, and I drove downtown to meet him at the library. We both had classwork to do, so we studied for a few hours and grabbed lunch at the Lark Street Grill. I told him my mother and Zosia weren't talking to me.

"I do have that effect on your mother, don't I?" he said. "But what did I ever do to your aunt?"

"Package deal." I finally didn't care what my mother thought of me and Kevin, or at least that's what I told myself. Being with him these two days had felt like opening the curtains after a long hard winter. I think I was happy. I think that's what was going on here.

The problem with falling in love was that I was starting to separate from the family, and that was not okay with them. And it put a crimp in my sisterhood with Lara; our bond in the fall had been based on mutual depression and anguish, neither of which I was feeling at the moment. Now when she called in a blue mood, I listened and sympathized, but it was disconcerting for both of us that we didn't match. I think it fueled her resentment.

Despite her wild rampages, Lara's loyalty to our family had never been in doubt. She might try to blow us up, but she would never run away. I, on the other hand, was always trying to duck my family to be with my friends. "Escape artist," my mother always called me. "You're always trying to get away!"

Many years later it would occur to me that what my mother most resented about me was precisely what she saw in herself. Throughout her life, she was racked with guilt for having abandoned her own parents in order to survive the war. She had built the façade of a new life on top of the secret of her old one, and from the outside, it looked smooth. But within our family, her invisible past filled our rooms. She had nothing left but her children, and she watched in shock as we dismantled first the walls she had built, and then ourselves.

fifteen

L aw school graduation was less than a month away. Between me and graduation lay three weeks of classes and four final exams—a mere hop, skip, and a jump before launching my career as a word-wielding lawyer.

But the closer graduation loomed, the more I dreaded the prospect of being a lawyer: the suits, the seriousness, the world of corporate finance and commercial real estate. I was not interested in money; I was interested in mountains. Perhaps it was just starting to dawn on me that law, for the most part, was practiced indoors, and this seemed to have been a terrible miscalculation on my part.

Although the conflict between me and my career path seems pretty obvious now, at the time I didn't know what my problem was. I was holding my entire life in the fist of my mind. Any effort to loosen my grip felt dangerous—as if the contents of my life would simply blow away, and there would be nothing left of me.

During this time, I was seeing Kevin on weekends, taking my meds, and attending individual and group therapy, the purpose of which eluded me. I was on autopilot, fulfilling my mandate to live up to my Potential. I needed to get my law degree and satisfy, if not exactly impress, my parents. I had a desperate, prenatal need for their approval.

But despite my love for Kevin, the panic attacks came back in March with a vengeance, and I found myself in a free-fall funk. There are no precise words for this feeling, and even less reason, but feelings often find rooms that reason cannot enter. I reported this to Flak, who, in those pre-Prozac days of psychiatry, prescribed another drug, Thorazine. I was a walking pharmaceutical experiment, a panic-attacked, unfocused twenty-three-year-old.

"Tell me about your schoolwork," Flak said one day in late March.

I examined his sharply creased gabardine trousers and pressed shirt. He had the most beautiful liquid-brown eyes. I wondered where I had gone wrong in my life. Lara was right. I *was* a fuckup.

"Are you keeping up with your classes?" he asked.

We'd never talked about my classes before, and I wondered why he wanted to know now. Flak was not a detail-oriented guy.

"I'm not sure," I said.

"When are exams?"

I looked at my watch as if exams might happen any minute. "A few . . . um, three weeks."

"Well, are you able to study?"

I shook my head.

"Have you thought about taking a leave of absence?"

I jerked to attention. "No, I would never do that."

"Why not? It might make sense. You know, rather than failing to complete the semester."

The thought of interrupting my education was shocking. How would I ever explain it to my parents? Suicide was one thing, but in order to really get attention in our family, you had to drop out of school.

"Do you feel like you can complete your exams?"

I dropped my head and fought back tears.

"Helen?" Flak's voice seemed to come from very far away. He sounded kind. I started to cry.

"Look," he said, leaning forward. "Here's what I think you should do. Go see the dean, and explain that you've got some medical issues that prevent you from completing the semester. Just ask to take a leave of absence."

Outside the window, buds dotted the oak trees across the road. There was a baby-green newness to the world; it looked foreign, even psychedelic.

"I'll write a letter for you," Flak said. "I'll recommend a medical leave from your studies."

• • •

It all happened very quickly. I walked into the dean's office the next morning as if in a dream. I had put on a new pair of corduroys and a freshly washed shirt. I had even combed my hair. The dean was an energetic man in striped suspenders, with a warm smile and youthful exuberance that I envied. He seemed genuinely happy to see me, and he offered me a seat in a shellacked black chair with the university's seal embossed in gold.

"What can I do for you?"

I felt strangely old, like a soldier returning from a distant war. "I need to ask for a leave of absence," I heard myself say.

He smiled. "It's that time of year, isn't it?" he said cheerfully. "This is when the pressure gets to people, with exams looming." He crossed one leg over the other and clasped his knee with his hands. "I think you'll find that if you just take a deep breath and get through the next week or two, you'll do fine. It's always this time of year when people panic."

I looked at him, realizing he couldn't possibly comprehend what I had been going through. I had traveled a long distance from the bloody battlefield of my heart to ask for a furlough. He, on the other hand, was used to students who were simply afraid of exams.

"I don't think so," I said, looking down.

266

My lower lip started to tremble, and I felt the beginnings of an attack rising. When I glanced up, I knew that he saw it too—a look of terror spread across his face.

"It's okay," he said quickly, unclasping his hands. "Please, it's okay."

I tried to speak, but my head was beginning to shake, and I had trouble getting the words out. "My psychiatrist advised me to do this," I said. My hands and shoulders were quivering. Soon, I knew, I would have trouble remaining in the chair.

"It's okay!" the dean said again. "Really, please, don't worry."

"He'll write you a letter."

"Okay, that's fine," he said, jumping to his feet. "I'm so sorry. You just take all the time you need, and feel better, okay? I'll see to this, and you just take care of yourself and feel better."

I hadn't meant to scare him, but I was relieved that I didn't have to explain further. Panic attacks had become my most eloquent form of speech.

I nodded gratefully and walked out of his office. It had taken nothing to drop out of law school. It seemed so strange and unreal and liberating. *Too easy.*

The hard part was getting up the nerve to tell my parents. They would be devastated. And I cringed at the thought of Lara finding out, her smug satisfaction that I had finally gone up in flames, after all those years I'd acted so superior to her. She and I were connected to each other as if we were on a seesaw. I was falling fast; Lara would get a nosebleed from her sudden ascension in my parents' eyes.

"This is because of Kevin!" my mother said when I called her. "He got you to do this, didn't he?"

"No, Mom, that's completely—"

"Kevin is a dropout," she said. "You're stooping to his level." She hung up.

The next day, my father called. "We need to meet with Flak," he said. "Schedule an appointment. Mom and I will drive out Saturday."

I was used to being told what to do by my parents. At this point, I even welcomed my father's directions—thinking had become difficult for me these days. It was easier just to follow orders. He also told me to get a consult with another psychiatrist. Flak and I had botched things on our end, and he and Mom were going to have to come straighten me out.

They arrived at my apartment Saturday morning, and we drove to Flak's office.

"You have failed in your treatment of my daughter," my father said as soon as we were seated. He enumerated the conditions of employment, the expectations of services, and the glaring disappointment in results. "She was better off at this time last year than after a year of treatment with you."

No one could disagree, so my father continued: "She has taken up with this Kevin, who has distinguished himself by reaching the age of twenty-seven without securing a college degree."

"He drives tow trucks," my mother added.

I knew better than to say anything. By quitting law school, I'd forfeited my right to speak on my behalf. Besides, I felt oddly proud of my parents' ruthlessness—they were certainly a force to contend with, and I didn't think Flak stood a chance. As usual in family therapy, I was once again a spectator, watching the adults duke it out.

Afterward, in the car, it was my turn to get the law laid down. "No more Kevin," my father said. "From now on, you will not see him or speak to him."

"You can't do that!" I was shocked by my father's ultimatum. "Kevin had nothing to do with this. Besides, it's my choice who I see!"

"Not anymore," he said.

My mother said nothing and stared straight ahead.

"First thing Monday morning," my father said, "you'll make sure the law school credits your tuition for the semester toward next fall, when you will repeat the semester and graduate. Then call and get a consult with another psychiatrist before the end of the week."

My parents dropped me off at my apartment and drove back to Schenectady, leaving me with a to-do list and instructions to report back to them.

Dr. Russell's office had a giant aquarium of neon-colored fish and a long wall of books behind it. I had gotten his name from a friend, and I liked him immediately. Paul Russell was the opposite of Flak: a little shy and very sweet. Although he was easily as tall as my father, with the same stork-like legs, he lacked my father's fierce athleticism. Smiling, he offered me a chair and sat across from me. I noticed he wore a pair of high-top suede Clarks Wallabees, the exact color as mine in high school.

"Tell me why you're here," he said.

And so I did. I told him about dropping out of law school weeks before graduation; I told him about the panic attacks, about all the medication Flak had prescribed for me, and how I didn't think it was working. I told him about my older sister's hospitalization and suicide attempts. I told him I entertained myself with thoughts of crashing my car. I told him about group therapy, which I believed was pointless; I told him about Kevin, whom my parents hated. I told him I'd skipped my senior year of high school to go straight to college, and that I'd gone immediately from college to law school. I told him my parents' story, how they'd been engaged to marry before the war. That they'd been separated by the war in which everyone was killed. I told him how my father miraculously found my mother in Rome and married her ten years to the day after they'd first met. I told him about the Hoffman Children and Family Center where we'd gone to family therapy when I was a kid, and how—

"I think we need to schedule another appointment," Paul said, opening the calendar on his desk. I'd been talking nonstop for nearly seventy minutes.

The following day, to my amazement and delight, Paul told me he didn't think I needed medication; he thought "there's enough other stuff going on." And if I didn't want group therapy, he said, I should just quit. He encouraged me to trust my instincts and figure out what I wanted.

This was a radical idea. I was fairly blown away by professional advice *to do what I wanted*.

When I got home, I tossed my meds in the garbage and called Flak to tell him I was quitting group. It was a heady feeling, just doing whatever I goddamned pleased. I called the dean, and he assured me he would credit my tuition for next fall. Then I packed my hiking boots, sleeping bag, and backpack into the trunk of my Plymouth and drove north to New Hampshire. All I wanted to do was get out of Boston and head for the hills.

My parents insisted that I find a new shrink to see over the summer, but I figured I'd deal with that after I found a job. I arrived at Dartmouth after dark, sneaked into a dorm, and crashed in the lounge. The next morning, I showered and walked into town to look for a job. I tried the bookstore on Main Street, the hardware store, the sporting goods store, a couple of restaurants, and a pizza joint. No one needed help. Finally I sat in a coffee shop with the local paper and checked the Help Wanted ads. There were ads for auto mechanics, secretaries, and nurse's aides. And this:

Farmhand: dairy farm, Woodstock, Vt.
$50/wk + rm/bd. (802) 555-6745

I knew exactly nothing about farming, had zero experience with livestock, agriculture, or manual labor, but the ad instantly appealed to me. Without thinking, I walked to the pay phone on the street corner, plugged in a dime, and dialed the number. A woman with a scratchy voice answered the phone.

"I'm calling about the ad in the paper," I said. "I'd like to apply for the farmhand job."

"Ya ever worked on a farm?"

"No, but I'm a hard worker," I said. "I'll work one week for free, and you can decide if you want to hire me after that."

She gave me directions. "Come tomorrow morning, around seven," she said. "We'll talk."

The farm lay four miles north of Woodstock, on a frozen dirt road rutted by tractor wheels. It was early April, twenty-eight degrees Fahrenheit, sugaring season. The old farmhouse lay in a crook in the snowy hillside, and I pulled into its gravel drive.

At my knock, a bulldozer-shaped woman who looked to be about 104 years old yanked open the front door. Her long gray hair was braided and pinned to her head, and she stood stoutly, eyeing me up and down. "Come in," she said gruffly, brandishing a wooden cane. Her arms, hefty as a butcher's, emerged from the short sleeves of her cotton housedress. A faint pattern of indeterminate color was barely visible on the threadbare fabric. I followed her across the room to a wooden table crowded with doilies.

"Where ya from?" she asked.

"Schenectady," I said. "But I just drove up from Boston—I went to school there."

"Ya ain't in college, are ya?" Her voice rose, and behind her thick plastic-framed glasses her eyes were fierce.

"No," I said. "I was in law school."

She seemed relieved. "That's good," she harrumphed. "We got no use for them college kids. All that fancy schoolin'. Think they know

273

everything." She narrowed her gaze. "So you're a flatlander!" she said with a mischievous grin.

"What?"

"FLATLANDER," she bellowed, laughing now. "That's what we call folks ain't from around here."

I smiled. "Well, I lived in New Hampshire for a little while," I said, careful not to reveal that I'd gone to Dartmouth College as an exchange student.

"Well, you're a flatlander all the same. Ya ever worked on a farm?"

"No, but I'm pretty strong."

"Well, I can see that," she said, sizing me up with a critical eye, then grumbled, "Probably eat a lot too." After a moment, she added, "My name's Edwina. Randall's my son. You'll have to talk to him about it. I don't have no say in it, but I like ya okay."

With that, she stood up painfully, and I followed her into the kitchen. "That's my sister Darline," she shouted, waving her cane at a small woman scrubbing clothes on a washboard and wringing them through a hand-crank into a large metal bucket.

"Go out there to the barn," Edwina said, waving her cane in the direction I should walk. "Talk to Randall. You'll have to see what he says."

She threw open the kitchen door and sent me off across the yard.

Inside the barn, the thick odor of cow milk and manure swallowed me whole. It was warm and musty, an altered universe of low ceilings and worn floorboards. Once my eyes adjusted to the dark, I spotted a man at the far end of the barn. I walked past the long row of cows' hindquarters. He was leaning over a cow, and straightened to his full height when I approached. Randall was a lanky man in his fifties, with a chiseled and clean-shaved face, very short-cropped gray hair, and the same plastic-rimmed glasses his mother had. He was wearing a worn-out zippered jacket covered with the short hairs of his cows.

I introduced myself, and he looked me over carefully. "Ya know anything about cows?" He pronounced the word with two syllables; it sounded like "cayoos."

"No," I said. "But I like hard work."

He nodded slowly. "Ya Catholic?" he asked.

"Um, yes," I said, surprised, but I figured it couldn't hurt my chances.

"I don't trust Catholics," he said.

"Well, I'm not much of a Catholic," I said quickly. "I mean, I haven't been to church since I was, like, six. It really doesn't mean anything to me."

"Catholics are always tryin' to convert ya," he said, studying me closely.

I shook my head and laughed. "I don't even

know enough about Catholicism to tell the difference."

He nodded. "Well, I believe ya," he said.

And so in March 1981, within ten days of dropping out of law school, I became my mother's worst nightmare: I became what she would have referred to as a *peasant*.

"I've got a job," I told my parents when I called to check in. I gave them Randall's phone number. "I'm helping out on a farm—it's really beautiful up here."

I heard my mother suck in her breath.

"You will finish law school," my father said from the other phone.

"Of course. My tuition for the fall semester is all set."

"Have you found a psychiatrist?" he asked.

I had forgotten about that. "Um . . . not yet. But, you know, I really don't think I'll have time. I mean . . . well, maybe I'll just take the summer off from shrinks."

I waited for a response, but there was none. I think my parents were worn out. Perhaps they were simply relieved that I would be returning to law school in the fall. And that they had effectively gotten rid of Kevin, whom none of us even mentioned.

We also said nothing about Lara, though I was pretty sure she would rise as Star Achiever, now that I had crashed and burned. I hadn't heard from her since spring break, when she'd blasted me for choosing to spend the week with Kevin instead of her. Lara and I wouldn't speak again until the following fall, and by then we'd both pretend that nothing at all had come between us.

I slept in the spare bedroom of Randall's ranch house perched on the steep hillside above his mother's farmhouse and the cow barn, with a view across the valley to the blue waves of mountains beyond.

At three-fifteen each morning, Randall and I slipped through his house in stocking feet so as not to wake his wife, who worked as a bank teller in town. We pulled on our boots in the basement, refilled the woodstove that heated the house, and trudged down to the barn by moonlight. The nights were well below freezing, and my fingers and toes were always numb. When we stepped into the barn, the damp heat of the cows hit us like a soft wall of warmth. Randall went for the milk cans, while I hooked up the crapper barrel, hefted the shovel, and started lifting a few metric tons of shit.

Mucking out and milking the cows—our three hours of "chores"—were the bookends of our days. In between was the work. In April Randall and I spent the daylight hours climbing up and down miles of his wooded hills, flushing out maple sugaring lines, bundling them, tagging them, and carrying them back to the sugarhouse for storage until the following spring. The snow was still knee-deep on the northern slopes, and by the time we returned to the barn for evening chores, I could barely walk. Three hours later, at seven, after the last can of milk was poured into the enormous holding tank, we staggered back up the hill under the stars to Randall's house, where his wife was preparing dinner.

My body felt as if every muscle had been beaten with a rolling pin. It's hard to say which I loved more—dinner or sleep—and although I showered in seconds and we ate quickly, I often had trouble keeping my eyes open through dessert. Falling into bed was like diving directly into a dream. Minutes later, it seemed, my alarm clock jarred me awake at 3:15 a.m.

I was so fully occupied, and so completely exhausted, I couldn't even think about Kevin or law school or my parents or anyone. After that meeting with my parents and Flak, I had called Kevin to tell him my parents had ended our affair. "I don't know what's going to happen next," I said. He seemed to take the news as if he'd seen it coming. We hadn't spoken since then. My life before the farm slid out of my mind into some slag heap that I had no energy to visit right now.

My schedule was simple: I worked sixteen

hours a day, from three in the morning till seven at night. Every two weeks I got a Sunday off. Never before had I relished the Lord's wisdom in commanding rest on the seventh day—or in my case, on the fourteenth. I used those Sundays to sleep and do laundry. The rest of the time, I worked alongside Randall, a brilliant self-taught engineer, mechanic, and farmer.

And I fell in love with the cows: thirty-five big-boned hulks standing in their stanchions, butts out, tails swishing. I loved their clammy breath from giant nostrils, and the steam rising from their slops. I would lean my head and shoulders against their warm, massive flanks, and they leaned gently against me out of friendliness, while I washed their udders with a soapy cloth. Then I'd slip the suction cups onto their teats, and set up the next cow. My favorite was a giant Holstein with a head like a boulder and a whiskered pink muzzle. Hey You was her name. And Gert, the big beautiful Guernsey, with her strawberry-blond eyelashes.

We poured the cans of milk into the giant stainless steel tank, then took apart the milkers, washed everything with soap and a chlorine rinse, and hung them up to dry in time for the next milking, which started nine hours later.

By May, the snow was gone, the days were longer, and we let the cows out each day to graze on the hills. During the hours that I was working the distant fields, I had time to reflect on the wisdom of my chosen profession—law—compared with the joy of my current employment—shoveling cow shit, posting fences, and harrowing hillsides. I began to think that maybe I wasn't crazy after all; maybe I just didn't want to be a lawyer. Over the past month I had grown attached to Randall, who cracked me up with his taciturn one-liners. And I loved the hard work and fresh air, the rhythm of the days, and the warmth of the animals.

One day in May, when evening chores were over, I stopped at the farmhouse for a glass of water. "Ya boyfriend's here," Edwina said with a grin. "Seems like a pretty nice fella." I rushed up the hill and saw Kevin coming out of the basement door of Randall's house. He smiled and wrapped me in his arms. I was relieved he wasn't angry at me for having disappeared.

"How did you find me?" I asked.

"Well, it wasn't easy!"

He'd called Flak, who told him I was working on a farm near Woodstock. So he drove up and started going from farmhouse to farmhouse. "I had no idea there were so many farms out here!" he said.

Randall let him camp out in the field below the house for a few days, and Kevin helped with the farmwork before returning to Crump's Garage outside Schenectady. This became my destination every two weeks for my twenty-four hours off. As soon as the last cow was milked every other Saturday night, I'd run up to Randall's house to shower and change, jump into my Plymouth, and speed down the dirt road toward Schenectady.

Kevin would be sitting up waiting for me, nursing a Rolling Rock and listening to the Who, reading the *Times*, or studying *Foxfire* for ways to build an eco-friendly underground dwelling. We would collapse into bed together, thrilled to have outwitted the forces of nature (my parents) by managing to be together after all.

Best of all was sleeping in the next morning. For the first time in two weeks, I was not awakened by my alarm clock at 3:15 a.m. We slept till the sun spread itself across the room, till hunger finally forced us out into the world in search of breakfast. We'd go to a small diner in Cohoes and read the *Times* over pancakes and eggs. Eventually we'd go back to Kevin's place, usually to bed, until about four in the afternoon, when I had to get back on the road and return to the farm.

I don't remember how the topic came up, but as the summer wore on, Kevin suggested we get married. The idea began to grow on me; it made the prospect of becoming a lawyer more tolerable—I figured I could balance doing something dull and dreary (law) with something fun and comforting (Kevin).

"Are you going to tell your parents?" he asked one Sunday afternoon as we lay in bed, dreading the moment I would have to drive back to Vermont.

Just thinking about my parents made me break out in a sweat. "Sooner or later, I'll have to."

"How do you want to do it? Do you want me to be there?"

"No way," I said.

Kevin looked relieved.

Two weeks later, on my next day off, Kevin and I went to his parents' house to announce our engagement. His father jumped up and gave me a big bear hug. Mrs. Flanagan pecked me on the cheek, and I blushed, wondering if I could really pull off something as surreal as marriage. I liked the Flanagans, and they liked me, and in any event, they did not consider it any of their business whom Kevin married.

I drove straight from the Flanagans' to our house to tell my mother. I knew my father would be at work, and it was always easier to talk with Mom than Dad. She could break the news to him later.

But when I came up the stairs from the driveway, her face was stony with anger before I'd even opened my mouth. She didn't even offer me tea—instead, we sat in the living room at a chilly distance from each other.

"Mom," I said. "Kevin and I have decided to get married."

She stared at me.

"I know you don't approve, but I wanted you to know."

I could see her face shut down, as if a steel grate had just been lowered.

"Why are you doing this to us?" she said in an ominous voice.

"What am I doing to you?"

"Oh, you know perfectly well!" Her eyes narrowed. "Look at yourself."

I glanced down at my T-shirt and jeans. This was how I always looked. "What do you mean?"

My mother scowled. "As if you didn't know."

"Because I want to marry Kevin? That's why you're so angry at me?"

"Well, isn't that what you wanted?" My mother's lips came together in a tight pinch. "Ach," she said. A Prussian spitting champion. "Do whatever you want, I don't care. Go ahead. Throw your life away." She stood and walked out of the room.

Shaken, I drove back to Kevin's above Crump's Garage. He was happily inebriated after spending the afternoon at his cousins', celebrating his betrothal. He welcomed me with a goofy grin. I burst into tears.

"What?" he said.

I shook my head. We were miles apart, I thought. What had made me think this could work? I sank into the couch, put my head in my hands, and sobbed.

Kevin stumbled into the kitchen and cracked open a beer. "Wanna brewski?" he said.

What an idiot, I thought.

Kevin's good mood could not be undone. He told me how happy the rest of his family was when he announced our decision to get married. His cousins had gotten a keg of beer, and all the aunts and uncles and kids had come over and sat around the yard in lawn chairs, talking and drinking the afternoon away.

"I'm really sorry," he said when I told him how it had gone with my mother. "At least you got it over with."

He was right. But long after he went to bed, I stayed up, milking my loneliness, realizing that what I'd *actually* gotten over was the desire to get married in the first place.

It would be months before I could admit this to Kevin. I've always tried to avoid acknowledging my mistakes. By the time I brought it up, Kevin was neck-deep in a ROTC program, slogging through the swamps of Ranger School, and seemingly unsurprised by my latest reversal. I couldn't explain my sudden change of heart, and I was ashamed of it. It would take me several more years to grapple with the fact that I was gay. But being queer was only part of the problem; at the age of twenty-four, I still didn't know much of *anything* about myself. That summer I'd latched on to the idea that maybe I could stow myself away in marriage, but almost immediately I realized it wouldn't work. I still didn't really know what I wanted, much less who I was.

part three

sixteen

1982

Lesbian coming-out stories tend to be similar in at least one regard: most women figure out they're lesbians when they fall in love with a woman. Usually the body knows what the mind denies, and the body manages to wake up the mind to its needs and desires. In my case, however, there was a complete disconnect between my body and my mind, a sort of Iron Curtain between the Wild West of my heart and the Stalinist regime of my brain. That dividing line was my mother. Or rather, it was my mother in me.

Like my mother, I had the uncanny ability— well, disability, really—to believe what I wanted to believe about myself, and then to act the part, to direct myself in such a convincing performance that I lost track of who I really was. I was able to fool myself, resulting in the charade that was my life.

During the winter of 1982 I was studying for the New Hampshire bar exam in Concord. I still hadn't found a new shrink, so out of laziness, I returned to Dr. Flak for a few months. Once a week I would drive the hour and a half from New Hampshire to Boston to his office, and it was there, suspended in the middle of nowhere in my personal life, that I came upon the realization of my sexual orientation, as one might come upon a large outcrop of rock in the middle of the woods that had been sitting there all along, but had gone unnoticed because it was covered with leaves. I don't remember how that session started, but I found myself talking about my college days, about the intensity of my feelings for Emma Dunlap, and then, and then . . . As I talked, my mind unspooled, and a light flickered on, and then another, and another—a little string of lights snapping to attention as I listened to what I was saying. Like a surprise party in my head.

I didn't want to admit it to Flak, but as I talked about the women I'd been crazy about, I realized that I'd always been a boy at heart; I'd always played war and football and hated the onslaught of breasts and hips, and I realized I had never liked sex—not with Philip, not with . . . well—but I did love Kevin. Okay, I really did love Kevin, and sex was even nice sometimes, but setting Kevin aside for the moment, I realized it was tomboys I'd always loved, just like Lara—she and I had been rough-and-tumble kids who loved sports and tests of strength, and it wasn't just our attraction to starvation and grueling workouts and punishing hikes in subzero temperatures; it was our love of *guy* things and our disgust for *girl* things; we didn't care about makeup or dresses or fingernails or jewelry or any of the stuff girls were supposed to like.

And setting Lara aside, I kept coming back to the overpowering passion I felt for Emma my freshman year. And then for Harriet as a sophomore. And then, junior year, for Claire! And long before college—in a line going all the way back to first grade—I'd always had a best friend, a girlfriend with whom I'd wrestled and played catch and stayed up late at night talking and laughing and planning daring escapades.

So my coming out was a process of elimination—I sorted through all my experiences with boys, and realized they didn't amount to much.

But. Yet. There was Kevin. My lone straw in the other juice box. He was proof that I was not quite 100 percent lesbian. He was my holdout for bisexuality.

I drove back to New Hampshire from that session with Dr. Flak giddy with excitement. Of course! All the evidence came rushing in, flooding the "queer" side of the scales. *I'm queer! I love women! What a relief! I'm a dyke!* My elation was through the roof. It explained so much! After so many years of not understanding what was wrong with me, I finally made sense to myself.

Not that I knew what it meant to be queer. I

just knew that I was, sort of. I tried to attach a feeling of attraction retroactively to Emma. It was a process of reconstruction in my mind. As I said, it was a head game; my body was barely implicated.

But now I started looking around me, and there they were, everywhere! The girl at the register at the grocery store—we exchanged a knowing smile. The woman at the post office. The woman who sat three seats away in the bar review class. Everywhere I looked I saw lesbians.

I told my sister about my revelation that winter, and she nodded and smiled with what I took to be recognition and something like relief. A few years earlier, she had told me about a brief flirtation she'd had with another woman in med school, but Lara was crushed when the woman decided to remain faithful to her girlfriend back home. Being gay—or bisexual, or whatever I was—was something Lara and I had in common, something that brought us closer together, something we shared as sisters. Neither of us had ever dated a woman, but we both knew this about ourselves, and that knowledge was huge.

Of course, we didn't breathe a word about any of this to our parents, or at least not until many years later. It was hard enough figuring out who we were and what we wanted while our parents were still calling the shots in our lives.

. . .

As soon as I decided I didn't have to be a lawyer, my panic attacks simply melted away. In retrospect, I think I had to go a little crazy my third year of law school in order to give myself permission to disappoint my parents on a grander scale. Maybe that's what Lara had been doing all her life—acting psycho to earn the right to catch a break and figure out her own path. Not that any of this was conscious, but looking back, I think our family relied on mental illness as a sort of free pass from our responsibilities as members of our Family Cult of Success.

Years later, after we learned that our parents were Holocaust survivors, Lara and I immersed ourselves in the psychiatric literature about children of survivors. *Often in families of survivors,* we read, *"separation" becomes associated with death. A child who does manage to separate may be seen as betraying or abandoning the family.* It was oddly reassuring to realize that Lara and I fit a pattern carved by a history of genocide. But that still didn't explain the secrets that Mom and her sister continued to hide from us throughout their lives.

seventeen

Fall 1982

After passing the bar, I applied for the Peace Corps. I told my interviewer I wanted to go to Nepal or anywhere in the mountains, and he laughed and assured me that no one was actually sent to a country he or she requested. In September, I received my assignment: I would teach science and English in Lesotho.

I had never heard of it, and looked it up: a small black mountainous kingdom in the Drakensberg Range, completely surrounded by the Republic of South Africa. This was back in the days of apartheid, when Nelson Mandela was still in prison. A few days after I arrived in the country, special forces of the white South African regime invaded Lesotho and assassinated several members of the African National Congress. Later I would live in the midst of the bloody infighting between the African National Congress and the more radical Pan Africanist Congress.

My parents considered my decision to serve as a Peace Corps volunteer in Africa a giant fuck-you to them. Of course I'd known they would disapprove; but what I didn't expect was that they would cut me off altogether. Not once while I was in Africa did I hear from either my parents or my sister.

To complicate matters, I had injured my knee playing basketball shortly before leaving for Africa and was on crutches for two weeks. The orthopedist in Schenectady, a friend of my dad's, grudgingly cleared me for the Peace Corps. I'd had sports injuries all my life, and I wasn't about to let this hold me back.

My last day at home was Thanksgiving. As usual, my mother roasted a huge Butterball for the four of us, complete with enough side dishes and desserts to feed . . . well, a small African nation. After we ate, I stuffed my backpack with everything I thought I'd need for the next two years. A nervous energy ran through me, as if I had just launched myself from a very high diving board, and now hovered in midair—that delicious but nerve-racking moment of suspense before falling headlong into the water below. Something about my decision felt desperate—I was more afraid to stay on firm ground in America, where I would have to figure out what to do with my life, than I was to catapult myself into the unknown, halfway around the world. The Peace Corps, I thought, would give me a chance to grow up, something I couldn't seem to do here in America. My attraction to deprivation was at once punishing and hopeful—I assumed it would toughen me, I later realized, as Siberia had toughened my father.

Lara had arrived home the day before. She was working as a general practitioner in a rural county upstate, not far from Evans Mills, where my father had first put out his shingle in 1953. She described her practice as primarily tending to fishing accidents—sewing up every imaginable part of the body where a fishhook could get stuck. But she was growing tired of the drudgery, and she had finally decided to accept a residency in psychiatry to begin the following summer.

It was in the evening—the night before I was scheduled to leave—that my parents and sister summoned me into the living room. "Sit down," my mother said. All three of them stared at me as if I were being arraigned on criminal charges.

"What?"

"Don't go to the Peace Corps," Mom said. "We are asking you to reconsider."

"What do you mean? My flight leaves *tomorrow.*"

"You're only doing this to hurt us," my mother said. "You have no right!"

I shook my head, amazed that after months of explaining myself, she acted as if I'd just sprung this on her a minute ago. "Mom," I said. "We've been talking about this since August! This is what I really want to do. I have so much to learn and—"

"What, a law degree and a Wellesley education, that's not enough? You're throwing it away to go to the jungle?"

"I'm not throwing anything away, Mom. And it's not a—"

"You will get sick," my father said. "You will get sick in the middle of nowhere. What will you do then?"

"Peace Corps will take care of it. They have a nurse—"

"And your knee is not healed. You should not go in this condition," he added.

I was worried about my knee, but I didn't want to admit it.

"I don't understand why you're doing this," Lara said. She shook her head. "I just don't get it."

I was surprised by Lara's response. She had never said anything one way or another about the Peace Corps, and I had assumed she'd be on board. Unlike my parents, surely Lara would get the lure of adventure, the tantalizing hardship and challenge of it.

Then again, I thought, looking at her in her tidy white turtleneck, Lara was anything but an adventurer. She played things safe; she stayed close to home. Yes, she was an outdoors woman and more or less indestructible when it came to feats of physical strength and endurance, but at the end of the day she liked to come home to a shower, family, and friends.

"After all the sacrifices we've made," my mother said. "After all we've gone through . . . this is how you repay us?"

We argued for hours. I was foolish, I was selfish, I was trying to destroy them. Nothing I could say would change that, and eventually I gave up trying. By the end of the evening, I couldn't wait to leave.

The next morning, we drove in silence to the airport. Like robots, we hugged good-bye at the curb, and I promised to write regularly. Then, with my crutches as carry-on baggage and a sinking feeling in my heart, I flew halfway across the world to southern Africa.

Twenty years later, when I was disowned by my family, I realized that they had done something similar to me, back when I had gone into the Peace Corps. My crime in both instances was the same: I had chosen to do something so perfidious, so beyond the pale, that in their eyes, it was I who had effectively severed our relationship. Later, with the codicil to my father's will, my parents and sister would simply make the break final.

After six weeks of in-country training, the other trainees and I were asked our preferences for permanent assignments. I wanted *adventure*, so I asked to be placed in the most remote part of the country, far from any other volunteers. A week later I found myself sitting in the passenger seat of a jeep on an eighteen-hour, teeth-jarring journey across mountain passes and deep gorges to a tiny village in Mokhotlong. Two men with machine guns hung off the back of our vehicle as protection, in case of ambush by rebels. In the higher elevations, the wheels of the jeep barely clung to the edges of precipices, and when you looked straight down, you could see the twisted metal carcasses of other jeeps that had not negotiated the track as well. At last we arrived at my site: a hut perched high on the escarpment, overlooking endless miles of mountains. Massive and rocky, their sides plunged like green velvet drapes to a narrow sliver of a creekbed, invisible from my hut. I felt I'd arrived in heaven. The weather was sunny and cool; every afternoon, a brief hail- or rainstorm blew through, leaving brilliant, glistening rainbows behind.

In the morning I woke to the acrid smell of breakfast fires of burning dung, shrouding the village in a bluish fog. I was one of the only white people within half a day's travel, and people wondered at my skin, my hair, and touched me gingerly, as if I might disintegrate or explode upon contact. During the day I taught science and English at the local mountain school and grew inexpressibly fond of my students, especially the older ones, who had outgrown the wide-eyed shyness of their youth, and who laughed uproariously at my fledgling Sesotho, a language so tricked out with grammatical twists and noun declensions that it made my head spin. And my pronunciation of words containing the impossible letter *x*—a sort of clucking sound made by snapping your tongue on the roof of the mouth, while somehow uttering the word with the rest of your mouth—made them literally roll on the floor laughing.

But as time went by, I grew lonely. Occasionally I made the half-day hike across the mountains to the regional camp where four other volunteers lived. They invited me to stay the night, and the following morning, I bought supplies—a candle and matches, a head of cabbage, tins of sardines—and hiked back to my village. I was troubled to discover how much I missed the company of Westerners. As much as I loved my students and the villagers and other teachers, I felt more alone than ever before in my life.

I wrote upbeat letters to my parents several times a week, hoping to appease them, to reassure them of my safety and well-being. I also wrote to Lara, describing my isolation and the beauty of the mountains, the double rainbows that sprang up in the midst of afternoon showers. I wanted to be blameless, even though I knew that they blamed me for deserting them. The silence of their rage felt natural and familiar to me. This was simply how my parents were, and it didn't occur to me that their reaction was particularly unusual. Although I sometimes hoped they would send me something—even a postcard, some token symbol of connection—I was not really surprised that they didn't. What did strike me as odd was that every other volunteer in my training group received regular letters and packages from their families.

And I was surprised and hurt that Lara didn't write. Perhaps it pissed her off that I could so neatly remove myself from her for two years. I don't know; we never talked about it. Perhaps Lara simply needed to align herself with my parents out of loyalty. If my parents refused to recognize my existence, then Lara needed to follow suit.

I had trouble imagining what Lara's life was like in those days, working as a small-town doctor. I tried to picture her in a white lab coat, seeing one patient after another, writing notes in their charts. But what I saw, instead, was an image of my sister and my parents turning their backs, closing ranks against me. After all, what right did I have to complain about their silence? Wasn't I the one who had left them?

The emptiness of the mountains, beautiful as they were, crept into me and left me hungry, ravenous. I longed for the voice of a friend. I wrote hundreds of pages in my journal and exchanged long letters with Kevin and other friends in the States, and with fellow volunteers scattered across the country. Mail was sporadic, depending on the weather, the availability of petrol, and the chance that a Land Rover could manage the arduous day's journey from Maseru. It was in one of those letters that I learned of the death of my college roommate, Janet. She and I had bonded as freshmen over our shared homesickness and fear of inadequacy at Wellesley. The cancer had announced itself and killed her in less time than it had taken the letter to arrive, and by the time I received the news, she had already been dead for months. Like me, she was twenty-five. I sat on the floor of my hut, lit by a single candle, and cried in shock and disbelief. I moved through the next few days in a haze, standing in front of my students in science class and teaching them about gravity, velocity, the forces that act upon us without our even noticing.

eighteen

Over the next few months in Africa, instead of healing, my knee got worse. Without warning, it would suddenly buckle and I'd find myself on the ground—sometimes on the trail outside the village, sometimes in the classroom. I hobbled around like that for another half year, and (as I would later learn) succeeded in tearing three of the four ligaments in my knee, completely severing the anterior cruciate. In a letter to the Peace Corps nurse, I finally admitted that I was having trouble with my knee, but I certainly didn't want to make a big deal about it. In my experience—perhaps having learned from my parents' dismissal of Lara's attacks on me as a child—complaining was shameful, and certainly didn't help your case. In any event, my self-image did not allow for weakness; my body was expendable in the interest of my self-esteem.

Despite my effort to downplay my condition, the wheels of the U.S. government had been set in motion. One evening I was writing in my journal by candlelight when the school director appeared at my door. "Hurry," she said. "You must get to Mokhotlong by morning. A plane is coming for you." The Peace Corps had lined up surgery for me in Washington, DC, so I could recover in time to return to Lesotho for the start of the next school year six weeks later. The news reached me by pure chance; someone in a nearby village had overheard it on a shortwave radio and ran to tell my director.

I barely had time to throw some clothes into my backpack before starting down the path from my village in the dark. The trail was studded with loose rocks that skidded off into darkness with each step. Although I had a headlamp, I turned it off because it was easier to see by moonlight. This was the sort of harebrained adventure that Lara would have dragged me into during one of our hiking trips, but now it was pure Peace Corps. To meet the bush pilot at dawn, I'd have to hike four hours in the dark on a busted knee.

At last I arrived at the airfield and was weighed on a giant scale together with my backpack and a couple boxes of cargo. The bush pilot flew me and a few other government types to Maseru, the capital of Lesotho. From there, it was another flight to Johannesburg, then twenty hours to Liberia, and finally another twenty-hour flight to Washington. When my plane touched down in DC, I was sent to the Peace Corps office, where they had already typed up termination papers for me to sign.

I burst into tears. "No," I said. "My director

told me Peace Corps was arranging surgery here and would send me back in a few weeks."

The Peace Corps administrator, an impossibly white woman with gold earrings and a bright-green dress, scanned the papers. "I'm sorry," she said flatly. "I have instructions to terminate you."

"But—"

"Sign here, please."

"What about surgery?"

"You'll have to look into that yourself. Contact OWCP to have your medical bills covered by FECA."

I was in shock. The fluorescent lights of the office were too bright. The street traffic outside was freakishly loud. I had come from silent long-distance landscapes to this cacophony of ear-splitting noise, blinding lights, too many white people, and everyone moving and talking at an incomprehensible speed.

"Where do you want to go?" the woman asked me, signing the papers below my signature. Her words came out as quick and sharp as the clicking of a typewriter. It took me a moment to understand her.

"Can I . . . I really want to go back to my site. I'm supposed to be there in time for the school year."

Without looking up, she shook her head. "You're terminated."

I couldn't make sense of this. I didn't move.

She finally glanced up at me. "You can stay at our residence hall for tonight only," she said. "Tomorrow we will fly you home, or wherever you want to be sent in the United States. Where do you want to go?"

I stared at her.

"I need to issue you a plane ticket. I don't have all day. You're flying out tomorrow. If you don't give me a destination, you will need to make your own arrangements."

Tears poured down my face. "I don't know," I said. The last place I wanted to go was home; I couldn't bear the thought of facing my parents. Boston had good surgeons, I thought, but I hadn't lined up anywhere to stay. I didn't even have enough clothes in my backpack to live for more than a few days. "Schenectady," I whispered.

"New York?"

I nodded.

"Your parents have been notified of your return to the States," she said, stapling copies of forms and filing them in a drawer. "If you want, you can call them on the WATS line in the other room." She pointed to an adjacent room with a desk and telephone.

I picked up the black receiver, such a foreign object in my hands. This was all so surreal. I dialed my parents' number, and my mother answered the phone.

"Hi, Mom. It's Helen."

"Oh, Helen. Where are you?" She sounded relieved, and I nearly burst into tears. I did not want to be here, I did not want to be calling my mother, I did not want to be sent home, but I tried to keep my voice steady.

"In Washington."

"When are you arriving?"

"Tomorrow morning at ten-fifteen."

We hung up.

I stumbled out of the Peace Corps office into the stifling heat of Washington, DC. The streets were a blur of noise and light—cars and buses flashing in the sun, engines roaring, brakes squealing—I had to lean against the building to get my bearings. It was as if the world had cracked open, people rushing up and down the side-walks, running for their lives. Yet no one looked frightened; they all looked purposeful—going to work, to shop, to meet, to eat. They rushed past me as I walked to the residence hall where Peace Corps had directed me to go. My leg felt fine, and I could almost believe there was nothing wrong with it. I climbed the stairs to my room. It was mercifully dark and quiet—so quiet, in fact, that I didn't realize at first that I had a roommate—a very pale-skinned blonde around my age who was lying on the other bed, staring at the ceiling.

I introduced myself and told her I'd been a teacher in Lesotho.

She looked at me blankly.

"Are you okay?" I asked.

She told me that she'd been psycho-vac'ed from her village in East Africa because her school had been overrun by marauders. The men had raped and killed many of the local students and teachers, and Peace Corps was letting her hang out for a day or two before sending her home to the Midwest. I wondered whether she too had been raped, but I didn't ask any questions. She seemed grateful for the silence.

The next morning, I took the Metro to the airport and flew home, where my mother was waiting for me at the arrivals gate. She was wearing her no-nonsense brown slacks and a button-down shirt. "Do you have luggage?" she asked. I shook my head.

"Lara is starting her residency in a few weeks," she said.

I resented the pleasure in her voice, the pride she took in Lara's success.

"She got into a very good program!"

I didn't want to talk about Lara, and apparently Mom didn't want to talk about me. We drove home in silence, but the air around us crackled with tension. I'd refused to heed my parents' warnings, yet here I was, crawling back to them, dragging my ruined leg behind me.

"Are you hungry?" my mother asked when we got home.

I nodded. We sat side by side at the counter, eating babka and sipping tea, but could not find a way to talk to each other. She and I had always had a talent for chatter, for covering over everything with words, but now it was as if weights were tied to each word we uttered. They dropped at our feet like dumbbells, and we could not pick up the strand of a conversation.

My father returned home from work that evening and eyed me carefully before speaking. "How is the knee?" he asked.

I shrugged. "I'll look for an orthopedist in Boston," I said. I couldn't bear to be at home another moment.

The next morning, I drove to Boston and started shopping for surgeons. I crashed on the couch of friends in Cambridge; they were working and studying and we barely saw each other.

After a few consults, I realized my prospects were grim. All the surgeons said I'd be lucky if I could walk again without a limp, but none of them could get me into an OR for months. I was devastated. And I was overwhelmed by the sheer noise, speed, and shiny surfaces of America, which after Lesotho felt as foreign to me as the inside of a combustion engine. Michael Jackson's "Thriller" was blasting from the speakers in every store; people spoke so quickly I had trouble understanding them.

After a few days, I returned home to

Schenectady in defeat. I was angry at the Peace Corps for dropping me like a piece of sheep dung; angry at myself for getting into this mess; angry at my knee for betraying me. And I was angry at my parents, who rose before me, a formidable force of reason and experience that I could not get around. Whenever I mentioned anything about Africa, my mother's mouth drew a sharp line that shut me up. "What are your plans *now?*" she wanted to know, eliminating the past tense from my vocabulary.

I didn't know. There was no way I would make it till October, the first available surgery in Boston.

Miraculously, Lara, like some enchanted Goddess of the North, came to my rescue. "Come stay with me," she offered. "We've got one of the best sports medicine departments in the country." Her voice on the phone felt like the warmth of the sun after a hard winter. In a flash, all of my memories of Lara's genuine goodness flooded me. She was once again my dream-come-true big sister, the sister I had caught glimpses of throughout my childhood and adolescence. She had always had this guileless quality of caring for the downtrodden, the broken, the forgotten. I basked in her sudden shower of love and concern, and, like so many times before, I simply dismissed the parts of my sister and our past that did not fit this glowing vision.

"I'll talk to the head of the department," she said. "He does all the knees for the UVM ski team. He'll have you back on the slopes in no time." Within a few days, she'd arranged for him to do reconstructive surgery on my knee. She drove down to Schenectady to pick me up.

My parents greeted her like a hero, and I too saw Lara as my savior, amazed at how gentle and generous she was with me. At the time I didn't realize how our family had always depended on this role-playing between us: one daughter in crisis, the other coming to the rescue. For her first twenty years, Lara had been our crisis, and I had been suited up by my parents to help her, to take her hiking or skiing at her bidding. I had always bristled under these expectations, and when I refused the role of rescuer, I was considered deplorably selfish. Now Lara and I had switched roles: I was the calamity that needed saving, and Lara was our knight in shining armor. Perhaps she also felt this was a setup, a trap, but she seemed to assume the role with genuine good nature, as if she were born to it, as indeed she was.

"Thanks for doing this," I said as we zoomed north on I-87 in her Toyota Tercel. "I was going nuts at home!"

She laughed. We were on common ground, and no one understood me better than Lara. When it came to our parents, to their regimented eyes-on-the-prize attitude and their commandeering

311

ownership of us, Lara and I were the only two people on the planet who knew—really *knew*—what it was like to be their daughter. Our bond had been forged ever since I was a toddler in Italy, running after Lara while our parents and Aunt Zosia disappeared into their strange languages, holding their mysterious history close to their chests.

Lara listened good-naturedly as I talked about Lesotho. Before I knew it, two hours had flown by and we were pulling into the gravel driveway of her house a dozen miles outside Burlington. It was set on a hillside, surrounded by woods, with a deck overlooking green rolling hills.

"Wow," I said. "This is nice. But far out."

"Yeah, my roommates and I missed the country," she said. "Working inside all the time, we wanted to be able to get away from town at the end of the day."

She helped me carry in my backpack and sleeping bag, and showed me around. None of her housemates were in. We made a salad and sat down to eat. I told her I didn't know where I would be without her.

And this truth has never changed, throughout the many years and swings in our relationship. Where I am and who I am has always been directly tied to my sister.

That evening, I laid out my sleeping bag on the soft carpet in her dining room, and she introduced me to her roommates—all medical students or residents—who barely lived there, and didn't seem to mind.

The day before I had to report to the hospital for surgery, Lara took me for a walk on a trail in the woods near her house. The trail was gentle, through stands of tall pines and spruce, and the air smelled like freedom, our footsteps silent on the soft floor of pine needles. "You'll be fine," she assured me. "They'll fix your knee, and you'll be as good as new." I hung on her every word. She was the leg I stood on.

nineteen

One morning, at the age of eighty-eight, Uncle walked down the street in Rome as he did every day in his tailored three-piece suit, tie, and matching handkerchief, to get fresh milk and the morning paper at the corner store. On his way back, he was hit by a car that sped off down the narrow street. Uncle was rushed to the hospital and lay in a coma for the next several months. Although Zosia and my mother kept up their daily correspondence, it would be months before Zosia finally let my mother know that Uncle had been in an accident. Zosia had also forbidden Renzo to tell my mother. "I didn't want you to worry," Zosia explained when she finally wrote Mom the news. My mother got on the next flight to Rome. She stayed with Zosia for more than a month, until Uncle died. Then she helped Zosia clean out Uncle's room.

It would be many years before I learned that in cleaning out Uncle's room, Mom and Zosia threw out all the letters and documents and photos of my family's past. Uncle had kept everything, my mother later told me—family mementos that

Zosia had brought from their parents' home in Poland; letters from German and Italian officials during the war, when Uncle managed to save first Zosia, and then my mother. Documents from the Vatican, when my uncle obtained papal dispensation for my parents to marry in Rome in 1946 as Catholics. And hundreds of letters from family and friends in Europe, America, and Israel. Mom and Zosia got rid of all the remaining evidence of our past.

After Mom returned to the States that summer, Zosia suffered a breakdown. For the first time in their lives, Zosia became so angry with Mom that she refused to speak or write to her. When Zosia finally did respond to Mom's repeated pleas for contact, she accused my mother of having betrayed her. "I have no idea why," Mom told me at the time. "I don't know what happened or how to reassure her. Something just broke in her when Uncle died." It would take a year before the two sisters resumed their daily correspondence. Neither mentioned the break again, Mom said, and they continued as if nothing had happened between them.

Lara and I always covered up our rifts the same way—relieved to be back together, we avoided talking about whatever had separated us.

When I woke up, Lara was leaning over me in a goofy shower cap. "You okay?" she said, jiggling my arm. "Hey, Helen, you okay?" I was gulping air and shaking uncontrollably. My right leg, cocooned in a white cast from groin to ankle, felt as if it were being roasted on a spit. "You're in the recovery room," she said. "The surgery went fine."

The betrayal was what hit me first: no one had told me it was going to *hurt* so much. I groaned.

My sister got right on it. "More morphine over here," she said to a nurse. "Her pain threshold is very high."

I was too miserable to argue with Lara about my pain threshold, which was in fact not high in the least. I knew I was a big crybaby, that I would never make it in Auschwitz or Mauthausen or Siberia. Still, it was nice that my sister was looking out for me. The needle went into my thigh, and I passed out.

My mother came to Burlington to supervise my recovery. She swept into my hospital room like a gust of wind, threw open the blinds, and sat on the vinyl chair next to my bed. I was barely conscious when she touched my arm.

"Helen," she said. "What have you eaten today? Have you exercised the leg?"

I lay in a cloud of morphine. "Hurts," I said.

"You can't lie around all day. It isn't good for you."

I closed my eyes.

"I'm going to run out and get a few things for dinner."

She was staying with my sister and came to visit me every day at the hospital. When I was released a week later, she brought me back to Lara's house and began to work on my future. Lara had started her ER rotation and stumbled home every couple of days, stunned by sleeplessness and haunted by visions of catheters falling out of body openings. All three of us were deeply unhappy, in the way that mothers and daughters can be when they want to believe they are helping one another.

"Would you like me to type your résumé?" my mother asked. "You'll need cover letters too."

I closed my eyes and drifted off to the mountains of Lesotho.

"I could do a template for you, and you could fill in the names and addresses of the firms you apply to."

The idea of a legal job depressed me. I was a failure. Only a year earlier, I had made the exhilarating and career-defying decision to work in Africa. I had wanted a life of danger and adventure, but I'd underestimated my need for conversation. And not just conversation, but companionship and love and intimacy and so many other things that I pretended I didn't need.

Now, as I lay in bed, it was starting to dawn on me that my ability to walk—never mind to run or climb mountains—was in question. I would have to rejoin civilization behind an office desk. Trips to the ladies' room and the watercooler would be my only response to the call of the wild. My self-pity knew no bounds.

After two weeks, the surgeon cut my cast open, exposing an emaciated yellow celery stalk of a leg. Angry seams ran up and down either side of my knee, tied off with black, blood-crusted knots. It was breathtakingly repulsive. "In another few weeks you can start PT," he said cheerfully, strapping on a full-length, metal-ribbed leg brace. It had a giant knob and hinge at the knee: Frankenstein in blue Velcro. Gingerly, I swung out of his office, careful not to hook the knob on my crutches.

My mother returned to Schenectady and I lay around my sister's house reading magazines and eating Tylenol laced with codeine. The leg was tender, and voyages to the refrigerator or bathroom required careful planning and mental toughness. Every day or two, my mother called.

"How are you doing with the résumés?"

"Um, I'm working up to it," I said.

"I put a new ribbon in the typewriter before I left."

"Yeah. Thanks."

"Are you eating?"

"Uh-huh."

"What are you eating?"

"Um, chicken. Salads. You know." In fact, I

was following my usual diet of Doritos, M&M's, and ice cream.

"Did you get the check?"

"Oh. Yeah, thanks." My mother was sending me money to cover my household expenses. My active-duty Peace Corps salary had been paid in Lesotho maloti, which did not enjoy a favorable exchange rate with the U.S. dollar. By the end of my service, I had amassed $230 in my savings account. This was another source of shame—I was twenty-five years old, and once again my parents were supporting me. It complicated my anger toward them.

"How's Lara?" Mom asked.

"Okay." Lara and I had exchanged half a dozen words in the last week. She came home exhausted, opened the refrigerator, ate something out of a plastic container, took a shower, and fell asleep until she was due back at the hospital.

Weeks crawled by. My sister was getting the hang of being a doctor, and I was getting the hang of being a wreck. We started swimming together at an outdoor pool when Lara got off work. A standout swimmer in college, she moved through the water like a windup shark. Warily, I removed my Frankenstein brace at the edge of the pool and slipped into the lane beside her. As she powered up and down the pool, I pushed off gingerly and swam next to her, dragging my dead leg behind me. Every twenty seconds I'd choke on the tidal wave of Lara's wake as she crashed past me. We kept this up for an hour or so. It was our quality time together.

By July I had established my rehab routine, paid for by Uncle Sam (I was on workers' comp as a federal employee). Every other day I went to physical therapy, where I cranked out hundreds of reps on the Cybex machine to the soothing voice of a sports medicine man. Then I proceeded to psychotherapy with a psychiatrist in Lara's department. (As a new intern in psychiatry, Lara had offered me a little free professional advice: "Helen, you should really see a shrink.") So at Lara's recommendation, I started seeing a colleague of hers, a funky, frequently distracted young woman who wore long hippie skirts and great earrings.

On alternating days, I started working as a volunteer at the local legal aid office, researching an appeal on a murder case. Despite my resistance to gainful employment, I was attracted to criminal law. Our client had killed his girlfriend after they'd gotten into a drunken argument over whose turn it was to go out for cigarettes. When she refused to budge, he called her a worthless bitch. "Well, why don't you just shoot me?" she'd said. "Not a bad idea," he agreed. He got up, went into the other room for his rifle, and shot her in the head. He immediately called the police in tears. "She's the only woman I ever loved," he kept saying.

I was trying to challenge the admissibility of his confession. We called it the "Not a Bad Idea" Murder Case, and although we had a decent argument, I had the feeling it was not going to be a winner.

One Friday afternoon, Lara came home from work restless. Her weeks of sleepless nights, dealing with psychotic patients and unpredictable emergencies, were wearing her down. She now had the weekend off, and while wolfing down a container of leftover grilled vegetables, she tried to entice me to go home to Schenectady with her. "We can be there in three hours," she said, stabbing a chunk of blackened zucchini.

I would sooner have walked across a desert in high heels than go home to my parents. "No thanks," I said. "You go ahead. I'll hang out here."

"C'mon, Helen, it'll be good. I really need a break."

A feeling of unease slid over me. Lara didn't like to go anywhere alone. She *needed* me to join her.

"You should go, then," I said carefully. "That's a good idea." Even as I said this, I sensed that she couldn't manage to go home without me. Perhaps she didn't want to acknowledge how much she needed Mom to take care of her. Perhaps, like me, she was ashamed of how dependent we were on our parents for comfort and support, even in our midtwenties, when our friends had left home long ago. Her housemates spent their days off with their boyfriends, throwing parties, inviting friends over. How would it look if she went home for the weekend and left me to hop around the house on my own? I didn't know; I only knew that something more was going on here, and it made me nervous.

"We can hit Record Town," she offered. She knew I'd been eyeing the new Eurythmics album. "And we can stop at Ziggy's and get bagels."

I shook my head. "I just can't handle a weekend with Mom and Dad right now. They'll drive me crazy."

Lara's face clouded over. I recognized that look. The hairs on the back of my neck stood up, and I could feel the familiar panic seep through me.

"I'm really not up for it," I said as gently as I could. "You go ahead."

Something flashed in her eyes, and in an instant, I knew I was in trouble. She flung the food container across the room. "You're coming to Schenectady!" she said.

I was up on my crutches in an instant. She lunged at me, fists clenched. "You're coming with me!"

I ducked and spun away from her. My mind

raced. I had to grab whatever I could of my belongings and get out of the house. I'd sleep in the woods if I had to. Frantically, I crutched into the dining room where my sleeping bag was stuffed into its sack in the corner. I scooped it up with one hand, managed to grab my wallet and shove it into the pocket of my shorts. In my haste, I slammed my leg into the dining room table. The pain took my breath away, but I kept going.

Lara was bearing down on me. "We're going to Schenectady!" She grabbed my shoulder and slammed me against the wall. I tried to keep my balance and protect my leg, holding the crutches in front of me to keep her at bay.

"I don't want to! Leave me alone!"

She grabbed the sleeping bag and used it to bat my crutches aside, shoving me into the wall. She was breathing hard now, her face red with fury. She was the Lara of my childhood, and we were once again alone with her rage, in a house in the middle of nowhere. I tried to protect my face with the crutches, but she kicked my leg instead. I let out a shriek, twisted free, and hopped across the room to the foyer. Her fingers clawed at my back. I reached the front door, threw it open, and hopped out to the landing. The sleeping bag flew out after me, hitting me in the back of the head. "Fuck you!" she yelled, and slammed the door.

My arms were shaking as I leaned over and picked up the sleeping bag. It was nearly six in the evening, and the sky was steel gray. I side-stepped puddles from earlier showers, and made my way down the driveway onto the country road. The highway was visible in the distance. I began crutching the half mile or so toward it. I had just cashed a check that week, and I had eighty dollars in my wallet. It began to sprinkle lightly, and I realized I was crying. Tears streamed down my face, and the rain felt good. My arms were getting tired, but I didn't dare slow down. I had to hitch a ride into Burlington. Once there, I could find a place to stay for the night. Tomorrow I'd go to the university and look for a cheap room. My clothes and belongings were in Lara's house, but I had my down bag and my wallet, and that was enough.

By the time I neared the entrance ramp to the highway, my armpits were burning. A solid drizzle pasted my hair to my forehead. I stood on the shoulder of the two-lane road propped on my crutches, holding my thumb out. My leg brace absorbed the rain like a sponge—it felt as if a baby whale had attached itself to my thigh. I knew I looked deranged. There was almost no traffic, but the few cars that passed me swung out in a cautious loop, and I could see the drivers and passengers peering out at me as if I were an axe murderer on crutches.

Nearly an hour went by. I was soaked and chilled. I considered hopping up the ramp and onto the highway itself but I didn't want to get stopped by a trooper. So I stayed on the road near the ramp and waited. Surely someone would be heading to a grocery store in town. Finally a car appeared in the distance, coming slowly toward me. It was taking its sweet time, and I thought my chances might be good—maybe a local farmer or his wife. When it was a few hundred feet away, I realized it was Lara's dark-blue Tercel. I began crutching down the road like a maniac. Within seconds, she was upon me. I cut across the road, reversed direction, and hopped wildly, hoping another car would come by. Now I had to get to that ramp, get up to the highway, where I would be able to head against traffic so she couldn't reach me. I no longer cared about state troopers. I was running for my life.

Lara had turned the car around and rolled up beside me, the passenger window down. "Come on, Helen," she said in a tired voice. "Get in the car." I wheeled around and darted back across the road.

"I brought our swimsuits and goggles," she said. "Let's go for a swim." Her voice was empty of emotion. She turned the car again and the engine purred as she crawled up beside me.

"Leave me alone!" I shouted.

She pulled the car over and got out. I started shrieking as if I were being torn apart by hyenas. "DON'T TOUCH ME!" I started leaping through the crutches, taking a running hop between swings. My knee was on fire. I heard her get back in the car and slam the door. She crawled up beside me again.

"I'm not going to hurt you," she said quietly. "Just get in the car, and let's go for a swim."

I was exhausted now, and my arms were worn out. I stopped and stood on the side of the road, leaning over my crutches, shaking with sobs. I knew how crazy I looked, how hysterical, compared to Lara, who had calmed down. And this sudden flip of my reality, from having been attacked by her to being rescued by her, made me even more unhinged. I felt the repetition of my entire history with Lara, my impotent rage when she suddenly reverted to being the calm, rational older sister, as if nothing had happened at all.

She waited behind the steering wheel for me to calm down. Then she leaned across the front seat and flipped the door open. A minute or two went by, while I tried to come to terms with my anger and defeat.

"I'm moving out," I said. "I am not going home with you."

She took a deep breath. "We can talk about that later. You need a swim. A swim will do you good."

"I can't live with you," I said. "I mean it."

"You're upset now," she said patiently. "You'll feel better after a swim." She held up the gym bag with our towels, suits, and goggles. "We'll just go to Sand Hill, go swimming, and then you can do anything you want."

Humiliated, I inched toward the passenger door, took baby hops to ease myself into the car, and sank into the front seat next to her. I dragged my crutches and sleeping bag in after me and yanked the door closed. My leg was throbbing, a monster with its own beating heart. Lara drove up the ramp onto the highway. Sitting as far from her as I could, I stared out my window, crying.

At the pool I changed into my suit, removed my leg brace, and examined the damage. My armpits were raw; they burned when I eased myself into the water. The rain was coming down hard now, in thick sheets, so we had the entire fifty-meter pool to ourselves. I swam with the fury and frustration of the past year, of the past twenty years, of my miserable future as a cripple. My goggles filled with tears, and I kept swimming. An hour went by, maybe more. I lost count of my laps, I lost track of Lara, and just swam without stopping, wishing I could swim all the way back to Africa.

Someone was shouting. "Hey! HEY!" It was the lifeguard. He was leaning over my lane at the shallow end, screaming at me. "We're CLOSED. Get out of the water."

I went to the showers. My teeth chattered and my lips were blue, and I toweled dry, replaced my brace and wet clothes. I let Lara drive me back to her place. "I'm moving out tomorrow," I told her, and crawled into my sleeping bag.

The next morning, I packed my backpack with shirts, jeans, a toothbrush, and my sleeping bag, and waited by the car for her to drive me into the city.

She came out to the front stoop. "Helen, you don't need to do this," she said, annoyed at my stubbornness. "You can stay here."

I stared at the ground and moved a stone with the tip of my crutch. "I'm not living with you anymore."

"Oh, come on, Helen. You're being ridiculous."

I shook my head. "Just give me a ride to town, and I'll find my own place."

She let out a sigh and rolled her eyes. We drove in silence into the city, and she dropped me off at the medical center. I felt nothing but relief when she drove off.

I studied the bulletin board at a nearby coffee shop, and a notice caught my eye: a battered women's shelter on Stanford Road offered safe rooms, a common kitchen, and group therapy for $26.50 a week. I didn't think of myself as a battered woman, but I did need a cheap, short-term place to stay, and this seemed perfect. I made a phone call and took the city bus across town. I completed the intake interview with the program director, an MSW more or less my age. I was her first lawyer. She accepted me into the program, and although I was assigned my weekly chores (cleaning the kitchen, vacuuming and dusting the lounge and rec room), she said I didn't have to participate in group therapy, since I was already getting physical therapy and psychotherapy at the medical center. Her name was Adrianna, but everyone called her Andi. We became friends. We almost became more, but she was married, and her days with women were over, she said. And mine had not yet begun.

That evening I called my parents from the pay phone at the shelter to let them know how to reach me, and to tell them everything was fine.

"Lara told us you moved out," my mother said. I could hear the exasperation in her voice. "What has gotten into you?"

I knew better than to try to explain myself. Mom never considered Lara's behavior a reason for me to leave. "I just can't live with Lara," I said. "And I found a great place! It's super cheap, a county-funded housing program."

The next day, my mother left a message for me to call her. In the meantime, she and Lara had talked, and Lara had recognized the name of my housing program. She and my parents were horrified that I'd chosen to go to a *battered women's shelter.* What was I thinking? Why didn't I just go home to Lara? She was my sister! Just because we had a fight, my mother said, I didn't need to make such a big deal out of it.

I was a little ashamed myself. The other women at the shelter looked truly needy—empty-eyed, beaten down by life. Most were African American, and many had children who tugged at them as they did load after load of laundry in the coin-operated machines. I felt so much luckier than these women; I worried that I might be taking advantage of the system. Yet there were plenty of beds available, and I needed the housing. And although I didn't want to admit it, I actually had a lot in common with my housemates. I was disabled and unemployed; I had been assaulted by a family member, and didn't feel safe at home. So I was legit—a bona fide battered woman, by the county's own definition. I told myself I was giving back by volunteering at the legal aid center downtown.

"She's my closest friend," I told my shrink in Burlington. "I just can't live with her." I was always talking about Lara—Lara my hero, Lara my tormentor—always swinging from one extreme to the other within the blink of an eye. Once I moved out of her house, I felt much safer. Of course, I still had to live with myself, someone I didn't know very well, someone who careened into eating binges and pockets of depression without warning. Even so, I genuinely liked living on my own, getting around on the city buses, doing my own shopping and laundry.

My shrink nodded thoughtfully. The phone rang, and she held up a finger. "I'm sorry," she said. "I have to take this." I waited while she gave instructions to admit someone to the hospital. Here was a real emergency, I thought. It made me feel marginally better. I was not *that* wretched. There were people who had it a lot worse.

"I'm really sorry," she said, gathering her purse. "I'm the only one covering." She glanced at her watch, a thick-banded contraption with multicolored beads. "We'll talk next time, okay? I have to go."

I wanted to impress her with my composure and maturity. "No problem." I collected my crutches and hopped out the door. It occurred to me then that perhaps she didn't believe my story that Lara had actually attacked me. I must sound like a hysteric. After all, Lara and my shrink were colleagues in the same department. For all I knew, it could have been Lara on the other end of the phone, alerting my shrink to an emergency they had on their hands. My therapist probably felt for Lara, for having to put up with such a wack-job sister as me.

Lara and I never spoke about that summer, and now I wonder what her version would be.

Memory is unreliable, a beam of light with which we bend the past to suit our needs. In the end, I finally learned, all I can do is lay claim to my own memories.

twenty

1983

My first job as a lawyer was at the Office of Bar Counsel in Boston, steps from the courthouse in Pemberton Square. To my surprise, I actually liked the work. My office of ten attorneys was responsible for overseeing the professional conduct of every lawyer in the state, funded entirely by bar dues (including our own). It was an efficient way to make attorneys pay for the brooms and detergents necessary to clean up their own messes. We were sort of the janitors of the profession.

We prosecuted complaints of attorneys stealing their clients' money; attorneys sleeping with their clients' wives; attorneys snorting coke; attorneys who didn't answer their phones or their mail—in short, attorneys who were pretty much just like everyone else in the world. I started at $18,000 with full benefits, and the first thing I did was go shopping for a shrink. Paul Russell, the psychiatrist who had freed me from group therapy, medication, and law school two years earlier, now referred me to a former student of his in her own private practice.

Her name was Lisa. I sent her a letter before meeting her. *My sister,* I wrote, *is borderline, and also my closest friend.* Years later, when Lisa showed me the letter, I was shocked to see that I'd used that term—*borderline.* Had I really already known this back then? I realized that Lara herself had told me this; she had come up with the diagnosis, and discussed it with her own shrink. For years, I would refuse to believe it; I would pretend it wasn't true, I'd pretend it didn't matter. Each time I landed on this word as an explanation for my relationship with Lara, I would evade or minimize it.

So she had a borderline personality disorder, I would think—but hey, who didn't?

So did I, so did you, so did everyone I knew. Borderline or not, Lara was the only person in the world who understood me, who shared my history, who knew in her bones the strange warp and woof of the war my parents had survived and carried to America with them to wrap around our shoulders.

1984

Like most medical residents, Lara was saving lives on little sleep, while I spent my days chasing lawyers whose clients' funds somehow wound up in their own bank accounts. She called me a few times in the spring, moody and depressed. "Helen, this sucks," she said. "I mean, I like psychiatry and all, but . . . I don't know."

"Can you get out to the mountains for a break?" I was still on crutches from a second knee operation in January. The surgery in Burlington eight months earlier hadn't worked.

"Helen, I get, like, six hours between crazy-long shifts."

As usual, we never mentioned our last crisis—the time she'd attacked me when I was on crutches the previous summer. It was uncomfortable to acknowledge these violent rifts in our relationship, and so, by unspoken agreement, we pretended they had never happened.

We commiserated over our limitations, and compared shrinks. "Lisa is all I think about when I'm not working," I said. "She's amazing."

Lara too had finally found a therapist she liked a lot, but her shrink was young and pregnant and about to take a maternity leave, which made Lara anxious. We talked about how inconvenient it was to be in love with your shrink. How crazy it seemed to have to respect all those rules and roadblocks—the fifty-minute session; the lopsided conversation focused on you, you, you; the supposed blank slate of the shrink, when she was sitting right there, with her legs and arms and breasts and lips and . . .

"I know," Lara said. "I understand the need

for boundaries, but . . ." She sighed. "It can get ridiculous sometimes. You know?"

"Yeah. It's not like I'd want Lisa to go on a date with me," I said. "I mean, that would completely freak me out. But at the same time, I think I would just like to marry her. You know? We could just live together."

Lara laughed. It felt good to know she felt the same about her shrink as I did about mine.

Within moments of having met Lisa, I was smitten. I was in love with her soft lilting voice, I was in love with her asymmetrical smile, I was even in love with her nose, which was perhaps a bit longer than absolutely necessary. She moved with a feline grace, tantalizing and mysterious, but it was the quality of her attention that tipped me off balance and removed my free will. She gazed at me with warmth and interest and intelligence, drawing me into her confidence as easily as a wave pulling me onto the beach.

I could never keep straight what color her eyes were—blue? gray-blue?—they were somewhere in there, a mountain stream. She was quiet but fierce, and I had the feeling she could fight with surprising verbal strength if she had to. I felt sure she'd had to—but then again, I didn't really know anything about her.

I once called her in the evening, because she'd urged me to call if I felt depressed. When she answered, I heard classical music in the background, and I became so overwhelmed by her voice in my ear and the violins in the background that I had trouble remembering what I said or what she said, or why I had called in the first place. It was her presence, her voice, her *self* that held me transfixed; and although I tried very hard to hold on to the actual words she spoke, the substance of our talk fell away, leaving me adhered to her sublime Lisa-ness.

She didn't look the least bit dykey—I was pretty sure she wasn't queer, and that was fine for a while. I told her that I thought I probably was, though I hadn't dated any women yet.

Unlike Dr. Flak, Lisa was highly professional, which posed a number of problems for me. The hour started right on time (this was good), but it ended promptly fifty minutes later, which was difficult to accept. Fifty minutes was a pathetic little serving of love. It seemed absurd for me to be expected to walk out of her office twice a week and resume my life, which was clearly not all that it could be.

I started bringing her carefully selected gifts to make her love me more: a small beaded witch-doctor doll from Lesotho; a smooth stone I found at the beach; a book of photographs by André Kertész, whom I worshipped; a mix tape I compiled of my favorite garage rock, opera, and jazz tunes. We had to analyze all of these gifts, why I liked them, why I wanted her to have them, why, why, why. It was an exercise in delay of gratification. I don't think I ever said precisely that I wanted her to love me more than anyone else in the world, and that each gift was calculated to make her do so. Overall, they did not accomplish the intended objective. But it was obvious that some were better than others. Poems were good. I brought her poems from various books I was reading, until a couple of those backfired. To a poem by Ai about the moon and knives and severed heads, Lisa remarked drily, "All this drama." I defended the poem as art; Lisa dismissed it as sensationalism. She tried to get me to talk about me.

"I *am* telling you about me," I said. "This poem is about me."

She looked skeptical, an eyebrow up. "The moon as a severed head. That's you?"

"Never mind. Forget it."

"Why don't you tell me what you're feeling right now?"

I looked behind her shoulder at a small statue on her bookcase. I wondered what she'd done with the rock from the beach I'd given her. What was I even doing here? I was sick of myself, irritated with my inability to snap out of it, to stop being such a loser. It was my habit of self-loathing that got me down. I found myself boring and hopeless and, well, angry.

"Are you angry?"

The clock above my head ticked quietly. *What a waste of time,* I thought. At least this was covered by health insurance. I didn't have to pay a penny out of pocket in those days.

"I'm depressed," I said eventually. *Would it kill you to be a little nicer?* I thought.

We argued about why I was depressed, but I held my ground about not being angry. I don't know why this was such a point of pride for me, but obviously a patient must put her foot down somewhere. Over the next few weeks, I admitted to being "frustrated," "upset," and "annoyed," but never angry.

Lara was the angry one in our family. Not me.

Of course I wanted to get fixed—I was suffering from mind-reeling bouts of depression and occasional periods of bingeing, and obviously, whether I could admit it or not, plain old-fashioned rage. But it seemed that my first order of business was making Lisa fall in love with me. I wanted to seem worldly and intelligent, a person of substance. I was an elitist, just like my parents, and I had a great deal of disdain for popular culture, which caused problems for me because I was completely and utterly a creature of popular culture, right down to my passion for football and punk rock and popcorn. I wanted to be the sort of person who played classical music and sipped Courvoisier, but instead I played

"Sympathy for the Devil" and guzzled Diet Coke.

I don't know what she really thought of me. She listened as if everything I said was of enormous import, as if my feelings mattered, which I had trouble believing myself. I fell in love with her just by listening to myself talk to her. It would take a long time—years—before I realized that she was teaching me something I didn't even know I needed: to look at myself with the same openness and curiosity that she offered, to trust my own truth.

The call came in early April. I was alone in the apartment—my roommates were all out for the evening—and I was standing on crutches in the kitchen trying to solve dinner. The phone rang, and I hopped over to answer it. It was my mother, calling to let me know that Lara was in the hospital. I could hear the strain in her voice as she fought to compose herself.

"It's all right, she's going to be okay." My mother took a deep breath, and I realized I had been holding mine. "She tried to kill herself."

My stomach lurched. I felt like one of those cartoon characters that get knocked down and have stars and squiggly marks around their heads. "What . . . I mean, how—"

"It's my fault!" my mother cried. "I gave her permission—remember when she broke down during medical school?"

She was talking about the summer three years earlier, when I was working as a law clerk in Troy and my parents told me I couldn't call home because Lara was so angry at me.

"Mom, it's not your fault."

"I gave her permission that summer," my mother said. "I told her that she could. She begged me and I—"

My face was wet with tears. I was sitting on the floor now, crutches by my side, staring at the scratches and scuff marks on the pale-yellow kitchen cabinets. I'd never noticed them before. Time seemed to collapse and expand. Four years ago my mother had called to tell me that Lara had cut herself up with a razor. But now, instead of demanding that I come home, Mom was blaming herself for Lara's self-destruction.

"She was so desperately unhappy." Mom was saying. "And she begged me."

"Mom, there's nothing you—"

My mother talked over me. "And I realized then that I couldn't help her out of her pain. I couldn't do anything anymore. I told her it was all right. That she had my permission."

My face felt hot. Now I'd managed to crawl under the kitchen table and held my good knee to my chest and rocked.

"Mom, that was years ago. That doesn't have—"

"She's in the ICU now. We're very lucky. Tanya found her and got her to the hospital."

Tanya was Lara's closest friend, a surgical resident.

"She's going to be all right," Mom said. Her words sounded hollow. "She just needs to rest. They'll keep her there for a while."

After Mom hung up, I stayed under the table, crying. I was scared. My sister had nearly done it. She was really sick. I needed to wake up.

Lara was transferred to the psych ward of a community hospital outside town so she wouldn't be treated in the same hospital with her patients. After a few weeks, she called and invited me to visit her for Easter. I could take her out to a restaurant. I was so eager to see her, I splurged on a plane ticket and rented a car at the airport. I was no longer on crutches, but my knee was still swollen, and it ached as I drove out to pick her up at the psych ward. Lara looked surprisingly good—thinner than when I'd seen her at Christmas, but her face was pink and fresh and she was in good spirits. We hugged, and I nearly burst into tears with relief to see her.

"I took a bunch of pills," she said over brunch. "I was just in a really bad mood. Really pissed off."

I was grinning idiotically, just happy that she was alive. She looked positively radiant. Although she was telling me about one of the worst days of her life, she spoke easily, almost with wonder, like an adventurer to the North Pole who had survived a terrible storm.

"And I guess I . . . um, I had a bottle of vodka, and I drank some of that. . . ."

It was so good to have my sister alive and sitting across the table from me. I didn't think about how this had affected me or my parents yet. All that mattered was that she was here.

"So I got pretty fucked-up, you know. And I guess . . . I must have called Tanya at some point." She paused and looked at her hands. They were remarkably smooth, free of the usual dried skin and torn cuticles. "I don't really remember." Her voice drifted off. Around us, families were helping themselves to seconds at the buffet, and the smell of scrambled eggs and roasted chicken filled the room. "Tanya told me about it later," Lara said. "She was working a shift at the hospital, and I guess she got really worried. So she managed to get off duty and drove out to the house. But there was some huge traffic jam, and she got tied up."

I tried to picture Tanya in her little VW, stuck in a snarl of traffic. They had been friends since their first year of medical school, and Tanya must have been freaking out. I sympathized with Tanya in a way that I couldn't yet feel for my parents or myself.

"She said by the time she found me, I had no pulse," Lara said. "I'd stopped breathing." Lara seemed amazed and a little impressed by this fact. As if she were talking about someone else entirely.

"Jesus, Lara." My scalp prickled.

"She did CPR, and called nine-one-one, and they brought me to the ER. I don't remember that part."

I took a gulp of my wine spritzer and nearly choked on the bubbles. Tanya had saved her life. If she'd arrived a minute later . . . If she weren't a surgical resident, if she hadn't known CPR . . .

"I didn't mean to kill myself," Lara said, rolling her eyes, as if this should have been obvious to anyone. "I just didn't realize I'd taken that much." She shook her head with disgust. "They didn't have to make such a big deal out of it."

"Well, it is a big deal," I said, suddenly annoyed. I clamped my mouth shut so I wouldn't say something I'd regret. What a nightmare for Tanya. Lara's cavalier attitude was maddening. She'd scared the shit out of everyone.

"But you know what pisses me off?" Lara said. "At the ER, they cut up my beautiful blue ski sweater—you know, the one Zosia gave me?"

I knew exactly which one she meant. Zosia had given me one too, but I had outgrown mine years ago.

"I'm still really mad about that." She shook her head. "I mean, they didn't need to cut my clothes off me! Jesus! That was a good sweater!"

I looked down at my plate, unable to meet Lara's eyes. I didn't want her to see how angry I was. It was inconvenient, this anger of mine; it didn't seem to belong here, at this nice meal we were having, this joyous reunion after a terrible scare. I was so happy she was alive. But it pissed me off that she seemed more concerned about her sweater than anything else. Didn't she get it, that she'd nearly died? She didn't seem to realize that she'd put her best friend in the position of having to save her life. What if Tanya hadn't gotten there in time? What if Lara had died despite her efforts?

All I managed to say was, "Lara, this is serious. You nearly died."

She shrugged. "So how are you? How's the knee?"

By the time she was released from the hospital after a month, Lara had fallen in love. Maybe that explained her good mood when I'd visited over Easter. Jess was a psych nurse in the hospital, and it was complicated. But eventually Jess managed to disentangle herself from a bad marriage, and moved in with Lara.

I visited them over the summer, and I liked Jess immediately. She was sweet, she was smart, and she loved my sister. Lara seemed to glow in her presence.

And something else happened. Now that Lara

was living with Jess, Lara and I magically got along better than ever before. Jess's presence in Lara's life seemed to smooth out all the waves in our relationship—as if Jess served as a buffer for Lara's rages, for her demands on me and her anger at me for failing her. These seemed to melt away. Lara listened to Jess. She wanted to keep Jess. And she would, for the next twenty-five years or so.

Eventually Lara returned and completed her psych residency, passed her boards, and became a psychiatrist at the same hospital where she had trained. She seemed pretty happy. She began to live her life. Our sisterhood blossomed. I came to rely on her for advice, for solace, for friendship. We were a team.

It's strange to think about that time now, thirty years later, after I've been disowned by my parents—after they've unequivocally declared Lara their only child. Because back in 1984, I came pretty close to being my parents' only child. It's as if there was only room for one daughter, and Lara and I played Russian roulette with each other all our lives. As if one of us could actually win at the game.

Despite the fact that death—murder, suicide—was such a big topic of discussion among us, none of us ever succeeded in actually killing ourselves or each other in person; I got killed off on paper. Being disowned is violent and shocking, and although you can still move your arms and legs, it's a permanent display of murderous rage, and it gets you thinking. How do you go from being the most treasured creature in the universe, the embodiment of your mother's and father's hopes and dreams, to being wiped out by them? What had I done?

twenty-one

The years after Lara's near-suicide and hospitalization in 1984—before we found out we were Jewish, long before the publication of my book about our discovery—were a sort of golden age for my relationship with Lara. We emulated the perfect sisterhood of our mother and Zosia, who had taught us that the bond between sisters was sacrosanct. Husbands were nonessential family members, compared to sisters. You tended a husband more or less like a shrub: he needed to be fed and trimmed, but then you left him out in the rain. Sisters came inside with you.

But like many of my mother's lessons, what had enabled her to survive the war did not always translate well into living in America in the late twentieth century.

One evening in the fall of 1991, Lara called me in tears. I was in my living room in Cambridge, watching a football game when the phone rang. "There's something I have to tell you," she said. Her voice teetered, as if the words were strung across a high wire. "Oh God, what am I going to do?"

I muted the television. "What happened?"

"I . . . I'm starting to remember things. About Dad. When I was really little."

Something recoiled inside me. On TV, a running back plowed into a wall of bodies in breathtaking silence.

"It's . . . This is really going to freak you out." Lara choked back tears. The men disentangled themselves and trudged back to their huddle. "Look, I'm sorry to tell you like this, but . . ."

"What? Just say it."

She drew in her breath. "I'm having recovered memories. I remember Dad raping me as a baby."

A silence opened up in me, like a dark lake under a ceiling of stars. I stood and walked in a small semicircle, twisting the phone cord around me.

"I know it sounds crazy, Helen. Just listen. I've been having these memories, and they're hard to make out. I've been working on it in therapy. It's been completely overwhelming, and—"

I felt a little queasy and placed the palm of my hand on my forehead. Lara had always had a gift for the dramatic, but I didn't know what to do with this revelation. In my bones I knew it wasn't true, but I wanted to be supportive. "It's okay," I said, though I was pretty sure that nothing was okay, and nothing had ever been okay in our family.

"The images that come back to me are just horrible," Lara said. "It's been really, really hard.

And—it also involves you, Helen. I remember him doing the same thing to you."

"*What?*"

"Dad raped you too, Helen."

I froze.

"When we were infants. Toddlers. Before we could even speak."

On TV, Jerry Rice leapt five feet in the air and caught a pass one-handed over the heads of two defenders. I stared at him, as if he could help me make sense of what my sister was saying.

"Helen, you there?"

"Yeah. But I don't think—"

"I've been reading the literature, and it's terrifying. I guess this is pretty common with trauma victims. Especially when it happens when you're so young, as we were. The only way to survive the trauma is to repress it, split it off. . . ."

Her voice galloped on, but I had trouble following her. Was she confusing her patients' memories with her own? My fingers hurt, and I realized I'd been gripping the phone so hard my hand was white. *My sister's crazy.* I tossed sibling loyalty out the window.

"Are you there, Helen?"

"Yeah, sorry."

"Look, I'm sorry to dump all this on you, but I think you need to know. I mean, it's bound to come up for you too. And I just want to warn you, it's really hard going. You might find that—"

Her words swept past me now like a strong current. The more confused I felt, the more self-assured she sounded.

"You've got to believe me, Helen. Do you believe me?"

"I guess . . . I don't know. I mean, I gotta think about it."

"I always knew something was wrong with Dad," she continued. "He's really, really sadistic. You know? He's very disturbed. He's a monster."

I closed my eyes.

"With my therapist," she said, "I've come to see so much. Dad's a paranoid schizophrenic. When you start looking at our past, it's really obvious. Everything is starting to fall into place."

Everything was falling apart. Nothing made sense. Allegiance had always been so confusing in our family. Either you supported each other, heart and soul, or you were archenemies. My sister and I had been pitted against each other throughout our childhood, and I couldn't afford to lose her now. But I wasn't prepared to give up my father for her. Sex abuse? It was ludicrous, it couldn't be true. Our father could barely bring himself to touch us; how could he have had sex with us?

"I don't know, Lara." I tried to remain calm.

"I need you, Helen."

The trouble was, I couldn't find what she needed anywhere in my house or in my mind or in my experience. A dark line fell between us, like a crack in the earth, and it grew deeper and more impossible to cross. I wanted her to go out for a run and come back to her senses and realize it was all a mirage, a strange, scary mix of memory and imagination that had created a bogeyman out of nothing.

"Maybe you should talk more with your therapist," I suggested.

I could hear her crying softly. The gap between us opened wider, and I couldn't find the words to close it. I held on to the receiver as if holding her hand. The silence grew uncomfortable.

"Helen, don't you remember it?" Her voice was soft, clear, chilling.

I bit my tongue. "I don't know," I finally said. "I just—I don't think so."

"You should think about it," Lara said. "You should try to face it. But go slowly. It's really, really hard. It's the hardest thing I've ever had to do. The urge to repress it is huge. It's classic PTSD." She had regained her confidence now, and was explaining it from her expertise as a shrink.

I pictured my father, the hard line of his jaw, the pale blue of his eyes. I'd just been home a few weeks ago, and as usual, he had sat in the living room, reading a medical journal, listening to Dvorak on the hi-fi. He was mildly interested in hearing about my work as a public "offender" as he liked to call it, but we didn't say much; we were happy simply hanging out together. It seemed impossible to think of him as raping anyone, much less me and Lara as little kids.

"It explains so much," Lara said. "I mean, look at us—we're both lesbians. We're so much alike. I think that stuff is deep-rooted. It goes back to what Dad did to us."

The following day I reported the news to my shrink, who cast a fishy eye and found it just a little alarming how much recovered memory of child rape and incest was going around these days. She reminded me that my sister was doing a fellowship in child psychiatry, and had been treating youngsters who had been sexually abused. Perhaps the power of suggestion had led her to make similar associations in her own life?

I called Lara back that evening, but she was adamant. "I know what happened to us," she said. "And at some point, Helen, you'll remember too."

Over the next few days, Lara's words followed me wherever I went: to the swimming pool for my early morning laps; on the T downtown to work; back home where I vacuumed and did the laundry. The more I thought about it, the more impossible it seemed. Dad had been our family doctor since before we were born. He had brusquely steered us through mumps, chicken pox, scraped knees, sprained ankles, fevers, the flu. "Say 'ahhhh,'" was one of his more endearing remarks. His examinations were quick and precise. "Okay," he'd say, with a perfunctory pat on the head. "You'll live." He had always seemed about as interested in my body as in a banana peel.

It was curvy blondes he found attractive, women with large breasts, narrow waists, and swishing hips. Like his first love before the war, a blond Polish girl who'd accompanied him on the piano when he played violin.

I also knew something about sex offenders from my work. A few years earlier, as a trial lawyer, I had defended men charged with rape. Child rapists tend to be unable to stop preying on children until someone *forces* them to stop. (Lara claimed our father abused us when we were babies, but never afterward.) I had once cross-examined a six-year-old child who believed he had been raped at a day-care center by one of my clients. I'd called an expert psychiatrist who testified to the lack of credibility of such recovered memories. "A child's mind is highly susceptible to suggestion," he'd said. "A kaleido-scope of factors can influence the reconstruction of false memories." Like all criminal defense attorneys, I worshipped the god of reasonable doubt; I believed in the possibility of mistake.

But what if Lara was right, and I was repressing everything? After all, I was hardly the picture of mental health myself. So I tried to remember. All night I lay awake in bed, picturing my father coming into my room when I was a child. It's true, he did have a creepy way of suddenly materializing in a room without warning. He used to slink around the house, appearing now in the kitchen, now in the hallway, his size-twelve shoes soundless on the shag carpet. I tried to conjure images of my father leaning over me at night, and I managed to freak myself out. I have a wonderful imagination. But it was hard to ascribe these shadowy images of my father to memory. They were inventions, suggestions. In my clear moments, I saw that they were born of a desire to be like Lara, to have no barriers between us. Sexual abuse at the hands of our father would bind us together like nothing else. Her hand was extended across this terrifying new land; I just needed to remember what my father had done to me.

But I couldn't. And because my memory was different from hers, our alignment as sisters was threatened.

"I got ahold of Dad's journals," Lara told me later that fall. She was calling regularly to see if I had finally recovered my own memories. "Last weekend, you know, when I went home.

After Mom and Dad were asleep, I searched the basement. They were sealed shut in cardboard boxes labeled with your name on them. Among boxes of your childhood stuff."

"You went through my stuff?" The old rage welled up in me, calling up the times Lara had broken into my room and read my diaries. I used to go wild—it was as if she'd broken into my mind.

"They're *his* diaries. I didn't take any of your stuff."

"He was going to give them to me! He told me so!"

"Helen, listen, you won't believe what he's written in here. I took them to Kinko's for photocopies—there's a million pages."

"How could you—?"

"Don't worry. I put the originals back—no one will know. Besides, it's not like he confessed to anything in writing."

I'd known about my father's journals for years—he'd shown them to me one night in his office the summer after my first year of college. We were holed up there while my sister was rampaging through our house on one of her marathon tantrums. We'd spent many hours like that, my father and I, joined in our helplessness and anger. His office was quiet and free of my sister, and we'd feel like temporary deserters from a long and dirty war.

It was on one such evening that my father had taken out several big loose-leaf binders from a locked cabinet. He opened them for me and paged through them. They were impressive for the sheer quantity of words, miles of ink running across the pages. "One day these will be yours," he said. "I am writing them for you." I felt honored by my father's confidence. He was tight-lipped and did not divulge much. But he had poured himself onto these pages, and he had written them for me.

"You had no right!" I told Lara.

"What do you mean? After what he did to us? He's the one who violated *us!* We were *babies!*"

"I don't care," I said. "It doesn't give you the right to go through his private journals."

"Jesus, Helen, how can you defend him? Why are you protecting him?"

"Look, he's my father too! I mean, I'm trying to be open-minded, Lara, but I don't know. You're asking me to believe that he raped us when we were babies, and—"

"I'm not asking you anything! I'm *telling* you. It happened. He did it. I remember it. I was there, and so were you. You don't have to like it, but you can't deny it forever." She hung up.

How do you choose between members of your family? Lara and I had swung from one extreme to another, and in our family, you always had to pick sides. The stakes were too high, the feelings too intense, the accusations too violent. You couldn't just float above the crisis. One way or another, you were going to be dragged into battle—as if opposition was the only way we could show our love for one another.

twenty-two

My loyalty to Lara was instantly restored a few months later. Apparently in the midst of her crisis over her recovered memories, Lara had been sending inquiries to various international organizations, hoping to learn more about our family. Now in March 1992, she received a bombshell: a packet of documents from a rabbi at Yad Vashem in Israel proving that we were Jewish and that we had dozens of family members who had been killed in fields, ghettos, and camps in Eastern Europe. This discovery knocked the wheels out from under us, and Lara's allegations of child abuse now took a back seat to the Holocaust. Although her recovered memories would haunt her for decades, she stopped trying to convince me that I had shared her experience.

Instead, for the next year Lara and I spent hours on the phone, trying to understand the enormity of the secret that our parents and aunt had kept from us all our lives. In August, we traveled to our parents' hometowns in Eastern Europe and found witnesses who led us to the sites of mass shootings in the woods outside their villages; we went to Israel to meet with the rabbi who had sent us the pages of testimony. The story that emerged was overwhelming, and I wanted to write a book about it.

But given my parents' and aunt's insistence on silence, writing about my family was complicated. I spent the next few years agonizing over whether I even had the right to tell their story. By 1996, four years into the project, I was finally on a roll, which meant that I could string together two or three sentences before having to stop, play a dozen games of solitaire on the computer, and worry about my mother's likely reaction to what I'd just written. I figured my father would be okay with it (I'd shown him sections, and he said he didn't care whether people knew he was Jewish), but I was pretty sure that my mother would flip out. It was Zosia who insisted on keeping the secret, and my mother was terrified of doing anything against her sister's will. Just as I was now terrified of doing anything against my mother's will.

I had been living with my partner, Donna, for two years by then, and she was supportive of the project. But it was my sister who really championed my writing of the book. "You can't worry about what Mom and Dad think," Lara said. "They've lied to us our whole lives. You're thirty-eight years old! You have a right to your own voice—your own truth."

In what was shaping up to be a battle between

the old generation and the new, I felt lucky to have Lara, the star psychiatrist, on my side. She was even more zealous than I. Not only did I have the *right* to write my memoir, she insisted, I also had the *historical obligation* to do so. "Your book will be a testament to the lives of our grandparents and aunts and uncles and cousins!" she said. "It's kind of ironic, don't you think, that by denying their own past, Mom and Dad are actually participating in covering up the Holocaust?"

I enjoyed this brief tour of grandiosity provided by my sister—it was a welcome respite from my usual state of drowning in guilt over my project. I needed Lara. I'd even given her a copy of my very rough manuscript for safekeeping. Now, instead of blaming each other for our little-shop-of-horrors history, Lara and I could finally join together in blaming Hitler for our shattered parents' lies.

That spring, I was invited to give a short reading with friends at a fund-raiser in Boston for a small press. I was nervous—still afraid of my mother's wrath if she were to find out I was writing about our Jewish identity.

"Don't worry, you'll be great," Lara said over the phone. "What section of the manuscript are you going to read?"

"I don't know, Lara. It's just a mess of rough

draft pages, and I'm scared. I don't want to read anything about Mom and Dad or being Jewish. I don't think I'm ready to put that out there."

"Then just read the few pages about us as kids," she said. "You know, the part about how crazy we were, and our fights, and going to family therapy and all."

So I polished up the section and read it at the fund-raiser, and I thought, *Well, that wasn't so bad.* I told Lara all about it the next morning, during our debriefing.

"Way to go!" she said. We high-fived over the phone. She asked me to send her a copy, so I popped the seven pages in the mail.

A few days later she called me up excitedly. "Helen, this is fantastic! You have to publish it!" I was thrilled, of course, that she liked my writing. But I still didn't feel ready to publish anything. I was having enough trouble just writing the damn thing.

Lara, however, had already thought it through. She'd even found a publisher for me—a professor at her university was putting together an anthology of essays by adult children of Holocaust survivors. "Your piece is perfect, Helen—don't change a word, just stick it in an envelope and send it to him."

It took me another week to work up the nerve to send my seven-page essay to the professor. The day after I dropped it in the mail, Lara called. I could tell from her voice that something bad had happened, and I knew immediately it was about my writing.

"Listen, Helen, um . . . I've been thinking. You know that piece you wrote about us when we were kids? Well, you gotta change some things in it. I mean . . . I'm a psychiatrist here, and . . . I have a reputation and all—"

Oh shit, I thought. *Here we go.* It was as if some part of me had been expecting it. All these years that I'd been relying on Lara's support of my writing, I seemed to have forgotten this—her tendency to flip. I kept doing that, forgetting the parts of my sister that she and I both needed to forget, in order to fuse our relationship. It's what my family had always done—just sweep the bad parts under the rug, and *poof!* return to Happy Family. Rinse and repeat.

"Helen, you've got to take out that part about me hearing voices as a little kid. I mean, that's psychotic, and that would really hurt my career."

"Okay," I said carefully, "I could take that out."

"And you also have to take out the part about me being anorexic. That's really loaded; that could ruin my reputation. And also about my nighttime checking—the whole OCD thing."

I tried to sound calm, but I could hear my heart banging in my ears. "Lara, you *told* me to send it out without changing a word!"

"I know," she said, "but I've had a chance to think about it some more. And you have to take that stuff out."

"But all that happened ages ago! We were just little kids!"

"It doesn't matter, Helen. This is my career!"

How could this hurt her career any more than her near-fatal suicide attempt seven years ago? She'd been a resident at the same hospital where she now worked as a psychiatrist; she'd overdosed on Tranxene and vodka and landed in the ER. Certainly *that* could have put a crimp in her career, yet her teaching hospital had welcomed her back with open arms. She'd risen through the ranks as a beloved and respected colleague ever since.

"Lara, the whole point is that our family was a disaster!" I said. "The Holocaust didn't just affect Mom and Dad; it affected all of us. I mean, if we were a perfectly happy family, we wouldn't have wound up in family therapy in the first place. It wouldn't make any sense! I have to show that this family has serious problems, to get us into that room with the shrink."

"Well, you could make me bulimic," she said. "But not anorexic."

Seriously? I thought. *Bulimia is okay, but anorexia isn't?* I said nothing. *Okay,* I thought, *I can work with bulimia.*

"Well, how about this," Lara said. "Why don't

you be the sick one? Why not just write yourself as the one with all the childhood problems?"

I actually considered it. After all, who really cared? I wanted to please Lara. "I guess I could do that," I said.

But then I realized it would pose narrative problems. "I can't have Character A grow up to be Character B," I said. "I don't think that's going to work." Besides, I explained, it would blow the whole purpose of memoir—if I made stuff up, then it would no longer be memoir, but fiction. I'd lived my whole life in my parents' fiction, governed by lies and secrets and half-truths. I needed to write something that was my own truth.

"Well," Lara said, "I'm just telling you that you can't put that stuff in about me."

Less than a week later, I received a letter from my father. *We heard from Lara about your intention to go ahead and publish our life story very soon. . . .* He went on to accuse me of destroying my family for my own personal glory. Exposing my parents as Jews would undo them. My mother would flee to Rome, he wrote, and since he hated Italy, he would have to relocate to another state. In effect, I would be forcing my parents to separate and leave their home, their state, and their country. What I was doing was immoral, he said; my conscience would never forgive me.

And then, in his final sentence, he suggested that perhaps if I changed their names, all might be well.

I sank to the sofa. I had feared that my writing would somehow kill my mother—irrational as that seemed—but here it was, irrationality confirmed. I was condemned by the two people I worshipped most, and I hadn't even published anything yet.

And then my rage rumbled in—not at my parents, but at Lara, who had called them into the fray. I burst into tears and showed the letter to Donna. She looked shell-shocked as she read it. "What did Lara tell them?" she said, sitting next to me on the sofa.

"Who the fuck knows?"

Donna held me and said everything would be okay. She was firmly on my side, and I needed her. Once I calmed down, I immediately wrote my parents back, reassuring them that of course I would change their names and protect their privacy, and in any event, the manuscript was nowhere near completion; the possibility of publication was even more remote. This was true: the book would take another three years to complete. And since I'd never published a book before in my life, the chances of getting the thing published were about as likely as my mother marching in the Gay Pride Parade.

I also immediately wrote the professor and

withdrew my submission, explaining that my family was having a meltdown over it. He called and asked me to reconsider, but I was so shaken, I couldn't imagine letting him publish the piece. I wasn't yet strong enough to defy my parents. Even though I was almost forty years old, I still saw things through their eyes, and had trouble relying on my own.

And then there was the timing of all this.

In two weeks, Donna and I were getting married. It wasn't legal in those days, and we'd invited a total of ten guests, including Lara and her partner, Jess. I'd told my parents about our plans in an awkward phone conversation months earlier, and they'd met the news with dead silence. They liked Donna, but they could barely bring themselves to pronounce the word *homo-sexual,* much less congratulate me or ask for details. To spare us all the discomfort, I didn't invite them, and they never said a word about it.

Now Donna and I were running around, cleaning the house, planning the meal—so many last-minute details to attend to—when Lara called again. "By the way," she said darkly, "I'm *not* coming to your wedding." She slammed down the receiver.

"Thank God," Donna said.

I called Lara back and got her answering machine. "I think you're right," I said. "I think it's *not* a good idea for you to come."

But over the next few days, Lara called and left half a dozen messages begging to attend our wedding: *"I really want to be there, Helen. Why are you being so mean to me?"* She followed with a postcard, a letter. *Please, please, please. Why won't you let me come?* It amazed me that she could not acknowledge what she'd just done.

Perhaps even more surprising was that I had trusted her in the first place. How many times had she and I repeated this pattern? How old was I?

She had not changed, I realized; *I* had. After all, Lara had always been like this—one moment my closest ally, the next my worst enemy. In her mind, she'd done nothing wrong; I was overreacting.

She continued calling, so I stopped answering the phone. This gave me a sense of safety, a bit of breathing room, although I still had nightmares of Lara showing up at our door, or breaking into our apartment and stealing my writing and journals. I did not return her telephone messages. I did not respond to her cards either. I was afraid of the slightest contact with her, lest I be sucked back into the vortex, like an alcoholic's first mesmerizing sip of whiskey after a long separation. In that sublime unity with Lara, I would forget the other side of her, the parts that we both preferred to ignore as if they'd never existed.

So what was different this time?

For one thing, there was no time. I was getting married in two weeks. Donna was my beloved, the one in whom I placed my troth and trust and faith. Maybe this was precisely part of the problem for Lara: she was losing me.

And then, of course, there was the problem of my book. I was trying, however ineptly, to feed it, to protect it, to nurture it into existence. This fledgling manuscript, scruffy and malnourished, was the voice within me that would not compromise. I could finally stick up for it. And I had Donna to help me.

Wedding, May 1996

Our spontaneity surprised us. Months earlier, on an evening in January 1996, when gay marriage was still completely illegal in all fifty states of America, Donna was cooking Country Chicken—a double-barreled cholesterol bonanza with bacon, cream, and black pepper—and I was sitting on the stool in our kitchen, yakking about nothing in particular. She held out the wooden spoon for me to taste. It was so amazingly good, I asked her to marry me. She tilted her head, a sly smile forming. "Okay," she said.

"Really?" I jumped off the stool.

"Yeah." She threw her arms around my neck, spoon still in hand.

• • •

Donna's foster brother, Frank, was a heretic Presbyterian minister in Kentucky, and she called him first. "That's wonderful!" he said, and agreed to be our minister. He gave us some dates he could be in Boston, and we picked Cinco de Mayo.

Neither of us wanted anything big. We figured we'd just invite some close friends, and have a sit-down wedding at home. If we emptied the living room of furniture and stacked it all in the bedroom and on the little deck, we could stretch out the dining table and fit everyone in. Donna planned the meal: she'd make four thousand hors d'oeuvres to start things off. Champagne, and sparkling cider for the folks in recovery. Next she found a recipe for an appetizer of boiled cabbage and lox, in honor of my shtetl roots. Main course: beef tenderloin (everyone we knew ate red meat back then) and potatoes au gratin with haricots verts, in honor of Donna's French grandmother. I was responsible for the words—writing vows for us to say over the main course, and choosing various friends' poetry and prose to recite at other points during the meal. Donna would make my mother's mocha torte (a recipe she'd gotten from an Auschwitz survivor friend), and I'd bake a flourless boule that registered eleven on the chocolate Richter scale.

Donna was in charge of dress selection, which

she accomplished in less than a week: we both wore white linen, though mine was a little tunic-thing you might find on a schoolgirl in the British colonies, while Donna's was longer, graceful and flowing. We had our rings custom-made by a metalsmith with Paul Bunyan fingers, whose shop was in the belfry tower of a church overlooking Copley Square. Donna wore flip-flops for the wedding, or maybe she went bare-foot—I forget.

It was easy to come up with a guest list: at the top were my sister and Jess; Donna's brother, the minister; Victor, our opera singer friend who had set us up two years ago; my young Italian cousin Nina—Renzo's daughter—who had just come out as lesbian; and a handful of close friends in the area. As it turned out, a few guests canceled: Donna's colleague from work backed out because she couldn't hack the whole gay thing. And my sister and Jess were last-minute casualties of Lara's mood swing over my writing.

Considering everything else that was going on that spring, our wedding went really well. The food was out of this world; our friends made us feel special; our vows actually meant a lot to us (including our promises to be patient, to seek help when we needed it, and to take the dog out even when we didn't feel like it). Lara's absence was palpable, but not devastating. I was beginning to see that I could survive without her.

twenty-three

I didn't speak to Lara again for two and a half years. It was my mother who begged me to reconcile with Lara, and I finally agreed to go home for the weekend after Christmas in 1998. By then, my book had been sold and was scheduled to be published in February.

Lara and Jess were already at my parents' house when Donna and I arrived the day after Christmas. The house was mercifully filled with golden retrievers—my parents' dogs, my sister's, and now ours—and their wriggling, happy bodies relieved much of the tension. After a mandatory cup of tea and piece of linzer torte, Lara and I decided to take the dogs for a romp on the golf course, leaving Jess and Donna to themselves.

We took two cars so we could fit all the dogs in, and I followed Lara's Toyota hatchback down Natchaug Road, the same route we used to run twenty years ago when we were both home from college. New houses had popped up where small farms and woods used to be. There was a new traffic light at the corner of Cromwell, where I had once hitched a ride with Suzanne Murphy in the seventh grade, certain that we would be raped and murdered, but in fact we'd been safely dropped off at her house half a mile away. I turned right at the light and followed Lara's Toyota up the hill. It was comforting to see Lara's car ahead of me, as if I were behind her on skis, following her tracks without having to think. We parked at the golf course, and as we opened the car doors, the dogs hurled themselves out into the icy air, overjoyed to be galloping across the snowfields. My sister and I both smiled—the automatic pleasure in seeing our dogs running with wild abandon. My dog had pulled a tree branch from the nearby woods and was now proudly prancing around with it, chest out, head high, tail wagging like a flag. Lara and I started walking side by side along the perimeter of the course.

"You look good," I told her.

"You too."

The dogs raced back and forth across the fields, circling back every so often to make sure we were okay. We threw sticks for them to fetch. As usual after a period of absence from Lara, she was friendly and fun to be with, and I felt foolish for having been so afraid to talk with her for the past two years. And also as usual, we did not say a word about what had caused our rift in the first place. Instead, we talked easily about our day-to-day lives, work, friends, activities. To my surprise, Lara already knew that my memoir was due to come out six weeks later. A friend of hers ran an independent bookstore, and kept Lara posted.

"When are you going to tell Mom and Dad?" she asked as we walked back to our cars.

"Once I get the advance copy in my hands," I said. "It doesn't seem real yet."

She pumped me for more details, but I told her I'd rather not talk about it, and she let it go. When we returned home, we found Donna and Jess talking in the TV room. Years earlier, when I'd left Donna and Jess together, Jess had told her the story about Dad sexually abusing Lara. "I wouldn't leave your *dog* alone with him," Jess had warned her.

"Your family is scary," Donna had told me afterward. I'd smiled, as if this were a point of pride; if you were going to have a crazy family, you might as well go for broke.

Of course, you would never have known it, to see Lara and Dad together that evening as we sat around the fireplace. She and my father talked about medicine, music, science, you name it. The strange thing about our family was that we didn't just love each other; we genuinely *liked* each other. We liked being together. If you'd looked at the four of us—Dad, Mom, Lara, and me—that holiday weekend, you'd have thought, *What a happy, loving family.*

After my book came out in February, I did not hear from my mother or sister again for nearly three years.

My dad was the only one who seemed to be okay with my having revealed that our family was Jewish, and that our parents had survived the Holocaust. I'd sent my parents an advance copy of *After Long Silence* as soon as I received it from my publisher after Christmas. I'd attached a note to my parents saying that I loved them, that the book was written out of love, and without any intention of hurting them. I told them that they need not read it, but that I simply wanted them to know that it would be published soon and I did not want them to feel hurt.

A week later, I received a letter from my father. *I do hurt,* he wrote, and chastised me for writing about private matters that were *not intended for public consumption.* His next paragraph began, *So much for ethical squabbling.* He went on to praise the book and my writing. He pointed out some misspellings of Polish words. He told me it was a good book, and that he was proud of me and loved me.

My mother did not respond. I imagine it was then, in early 1999, that my mother's world must have crashed around her, when she must have decided I was dead to her. It would be another few years before she made it official with the help of an inexpensive lawyer, but it was when the book was first published, I think, that she killed me off in her head.

All I knew at the time was that she returned the Mother's Day gift and card I sent her that spring. I knew she had to be out of her mind with rage, because she didn't simply refuse delivery of my package; she made a special trip to the post office and paid the postage to send it back to me unopened. And to do that—to get in the car and drive to the post office; to write out a new label in her own handwriting with my name and address on it; to bring it to the postal clerk and not care that the clerk would see that a package addressed from Helen Fremont to "Mom" for Mother's Day was being returned to the daughter unopened—my mother must have been so angry, she would have been unrecognizable even to herself. Mom had always been very big on appearances, on what other people thought. And my book—however filled with my admiration and love for her—had ripped open her façade. At this point, Mom didn't care what anyone thought about her relationship with her daughter Helen. She even spent the $5.95 for Priority postage to make sure that the package I sent her—a nightgown and letter, all unopened—would be returned to my door.

I understood, of course, the humiliation of

having one's secrets exposed. I understood the sense of betrayal. But I hadn't grasped the degree of her distress, or what was at stake for her. By the time I'd finished writing *After Long Silence*, Mom had already had seven years to come to terms with our discovery of our Jewish identity. During that time, she knew I was writing the book. She knew that I'd agreed to change their names to protect their privacy. She also knew that, with Lara's encouragement, I had already revealed our discovery to Zosia and Renzo.

So why, seven years later, in 1999, when my mother was eighty and Lara and I were already in our forties, did Mom have such a violent reaction to the long-delayed publication of my book? What was still so important to her that she killed me off in her mind, after we were all adults? Who *cared* whether we were Jewish or Catholic?

That's when I began to wonder whether there might be more to my mother's and Zosia's story that I hadn't yet grasped. I don't think my father knew the whole story either. Uncle Giulio, I suspected, had played a bigger role than I'd thought. After his death in a hit-and-run accident in 1988, my mother and aunt had destroyed all of his personal belongings, documents, and photos, but now I tried to reconstruct what I remembered about him.

The Count

I had always adored Uncle; he was gentle and charming, and whenever I visited Zosia in Italy, he seemed to live with us like a very sweet, very polite housemate, his movements small and delicate, quiet as a well-dressed mouse. Zosia ignored him, for the most part, or dismissed him with an irritated flick of her wrist if he got too close to her. He cooked his own meals, ate at his own hours, took a siesta by himself, and spent his days poring over the mountains of legal and heraldic documents in his bedroom that doubled as his office.

While Zosia spent her summers with my mother, either in the States or in Europe, Giulio spent every August at his favorite spa in Tuscany with his friends. My aunt scoffed at his careful attention to his diet, his digestion, and his grooming. We joked that Uncle was the only true lady in our family, attending to his toilette with greater attention than any woman we knew. Dad dismissed him as a weakling and "unmanly." Mom treasured him and always said he was born in the wrong century. He was a romantic, she said, and although he was born in 1900, he was better suited to the Renaissance. He was proud of his heritage as a count from a long line of nobility, but Uncle Giulio had been estranged from his aristocratic family for reasons that no one ever spoke of.

One winter while I was staying with Zosia in Rome, I asked her whether she and Giulio had ever wanted to have more children after Renzo. She looked startled. "Oh yes," she said. "Yes, of course."

"So why didn't you?"

"There wasn't enough room," she said, gesturing to indicate the penthouse apartment in which we were seated, where she had lived with Giulio since the war. The apartment was enormous, extending across half of the apartment building, with two roof-deck terraces, three bedrooms, an enormous living and dining room area, and a separate room for a live-in maid. I said nothing, and she quickly changed the subject.

It never occurred to me in those days that Uncle might be queer. One didn't talk about sexuality in our family. Many years later, after Uncle had died and I was in my thirties, I finally came out to my aunt as gay. She smiled thoughtfully and said, "You know, Giulio was like that; he would have understood."

twenty-four

November 2001

My sister called to let me know my father had died. She and I hadn't spoken since that Christmas of 1998 when we'd gotten together in Schenectady, six weeks before the publication of my book. "There's going to be a funeral service in Schenectady," she said. Her voice was cold, a hint of frost. "Are you going to want to be there?"

I was standing in the living room of our apartment in Boston. My hand on the telephone felt strangely foreign to me. "I don't know," I said slowly. "I may have to process this in my own way."

"Well, I'll let you know when I find out more details."

"You don't have to," I said. What did it matter? My father was gone.

"I'll let you know," she said in a kinder voice.

We hung up, and I waited to feel something. My father was eighty-six. When I'd last seen him three years earlier, he was already quite wasted from Parkinson's; he'd had trouble speaking and moving. We'd cut his food for him, but it was hard for him to get it to his mouth. And he had shrunk to a fraction of his size, the Olympic decathlete decreased to a hunched figure of skin and bones.

Over the years since that Christmas, my father and I had continued to correspond, his handwriting becoming more jittery and illegible with each letter. My mother was caring for him at home, and I was not welcome to visit since the publication of my book. Despite my repeated efforts to reach out to her, the last time I'd heard from Mom was in May 1999, when she'd returned my Mother's Day card and gift. Other cards and letters I sent her went unanswered. I clung to my connection with my father, yet it was my mother whose love I craved, my mother whose anger I couldn't bear to face. I kept hoping that at some point she would relent, respond to me, invite me back in. But as the months and years went by, I resigned myself to the fact that as long as he depended on Mom for his care, it was unlikely I would ever see my father alive again.

Why didn't I just drive to Schenectady and show up at their door? I could have forced my way in, demanded to see my father, whether Mom liked it or not. But in truth, I didn't have the stomach to stage such a confrontation. It was hard enough to take my mother's rage from a distance. I didn't think I could bear to have her slam the door in my face.

So it could be said that in this way I collaborated in receiving my family's rejection by legal instrument, delivered via the cool remove of the U.S. Postal Service six weeks after my father's death. It was I who had chosen to avoid a face-to-face confrontation in our home. Clashing swords was Lara's style; that's what she had done all our lives. I was different. I was a writer. I gave and took my blows on the page.

And in some way, I accepted estrangement from my mother as punishment for having published a book I knew she would object to. Of course, I had waited for her to come around, but over the six years it had taken me to write *After Long Silence*, I had finally reached the decision to put my book out in the world and just hope for the best. I was, in effect, throwing down the gauntlet, standing up on my hind legs and saying, *I can't remain silent any longer. The secrets are crippling me. Choose me over the secrets.*

It was a risky gamble, and I miscalculated. I lost my mother. And in the package deal, I lost my father too.

But was it really a miscalculation? I had, in fact, considered the possibility of losing my mother forever. I had hoped that she would rise to my challenge, but I was determined to speak my truth even if she couldn't join me. Perhaps, painful as my excommunication from my parents was, it was the only way to be free.

I was no longer an appendage of my parents, no longer an apparatchik of the family enterprise. Terrifying as it was, I was finally my own person.

So when Lara called to tell me that my father had died, I was not surprised. I was not filled with grief or sadness or rage or relief or remorse or any of the things I should be feeling. All I felt was nothing.

Donna tried to reassure me. "It's so complicated," she said. "It's like your father has been held hostage by your mother for years. You don't get to have a simple reaction to his death."

I went to work the next day and didn't tell anyone my father had died, because I was ashamed of my lack of feeling. Here it was, I thought, incontrovertible proof of my psychopathology. All day I observed myself at work. I went to meetings, laughed with colleagues, drafted memos, investigated complaints. I had to remind myself, *My father died*—to see if anything had changed in me. I called a friend. "It's okay," she said. "Give it time. At some point, we should do some kind of ceremony or something—just a gathering of friends here in Boston, something to help you process it."

I had trouble imagining a ceremony. Wouldn't that be awkward? We'd sit around and talk. About what? How could I begin to describe my father, to explain how trapped he was in our family? How trapped I was?

Six months earlier, Donna and I had flown to Atlanta for her mother's funeral; Lucy had died suddenly of a heart attack. At the time, Donna was also quite sick—she had endured six months of chemotherapy after a recurrence of cancer, and it had seemed that death was everywhere. Thinking back on Lucy's death, I was grateful that Donna's family accepted me as one of their own. But it was disturbing to realize that I had been more welcome at Lucy's funeral than I would be at my own father's.

I returned from work the following evening and found a phone message from my mother on the answering machine. Hearing her voice for the first time in nearly three years knocked the wind out of me. Her accent was thicker than I'd remembered, but it was Mom, and her tone was warm and wistful, and I could hear the tears in her voice. *"Helen, it's Mom. We are having a service for Dad on Monday."* Then her voice cracked: *"I know that Dad would have loved for you to be there."* She paused, and I could hear her collecting herself. *"And so would I."*

And so would I. I'd been waiting to hear words like this from my mother for what seemed like forever. Now, finally, with the death of my father, Mom wanted me. She wanted to see me, she wanted me there. I burst into tears.

I called her back, and she picked up on the first ring.

"Mom! It's Helen." The words came easily to me, as if I knew what to say to my mother after such a long time. "I just got your message . . . about Dad's funeral. And I want to—"

"Who is this?" my mother asked.

"Helen," I said louder. "Mom, it's me, HELEN."

"Who?"

"I'm Helen," I said. A chill crept down my spine. "Your *daughter.* Mom, it's *Helen.*"

Silence.

"Mom, you called me about Dad's service, and—"

I heard my mother break into a sob. "Helen? Can it be . . . Helen? Is it you?"

"Yes, Mom, I just got your message." She had called me only an hour or two earlier.

"Oh, I'm so glad you called!" she said. "Dad's service is on Monday. I hope you can attend." Suddenly she was all business.

She gave me the address of the funeral home, I promised to be there, and we hung up.

I couldn't know it at the time, but four years later, my mother would be diagnosed with dementia. In retrospect, it is likely that she was already suffering from the beginning stages of the disease in 2001. Her inability to recognize my voice on the phone alarmed me, but in other respects, her brusque response to my call was not so different from how she had always been.

It wasn't a funeral. It wasn't a memorial service. It was at some random funeral home in downtown Schenectady. Lara and my mother had arranged it, but my father wasn't even there. He was in a box of ashes in the basement at home. The funeral home provided a large room where people could show up, express their condolences, and either hang out or leave. My father had always said he didn't want any kind of service or ceremony—no hoopla, nothing that would draw attention or cost money. Just burn him and be done with him. But this place seemed about as far as one could get from my parents' taste. It was like a mobster's idea of swank. The wall-to-wall carpet was busy with burgundy and white doohickeys reminiscent of fleurs-de-lis; the wallpaper was striped with garish hints of silver and gold. A few love seats in an aggressive shade of pink or green sat back-to-back, and an end table offered a small glass bowl of peppermint pinwheel candies. It took me a while to notice two cloth-covered consoles along the wall. My father's old leather medical bag and stethoscope were displayed on one table, next to two issues of the *Harvard Review* in which his personal essays about the Gulag had been published. They'd also laid out his violin in its velvet-lined case—a sort of miniature open casket with his bow leaning against it. On another table rested an intricately carved rectangular wooden box that he had made for my mother in Rome as a surprise for her twenty-eighth birthday in 1947. It was large enough to fit documents and letters, photos and knickknacks. The lid had warped with age, and the delicate trim he'd carved out of ebony had started to break off. The broken pieces were loose inside the empty box that would no longer close.

Donna and I had driven the Mass Pike from Boston earlier that afternoon, and arrived at the funeral home at dusk. My anxiety was through the roof—I was afraid to see my mother after such a long and painful silence. She was the one person whose love I still longed for. Would she be gracious or cold? Would she pretend nothing had happened, or would she pretend not to recognize me at all?

The prospect of seeing Lara also made me nervous. Ever since her flip in 1996 over my writing, I had ceased to trust her—or rather, I'd ceased to trust myself around her; I was afraid I'd be lulled back in by her charm. I missed her terribly, and my longing for her scared me.

When Donna and I entered the funeral home, a clutch of people I didn't know were milling about on that hideous carpet. My eyes landed on a beautiful woman in an elegant black wool dress that made her look like she belonged on Fifth Avenue. Cultivated, sophisticated, a commanding woman of good taste: my mother. Her hair was swept up in a wild burst of silver and white with some darker notes, like a very rich, very lush black-and-white photograph.

Mom walked briskly toward me, saying, "Oh, here she is," as if I had just stepped out for a cup of coffee. Before I could say a word, she linked my arm in hers, and off we went. My sister, I realized, was on her other arm; I could feel Lara's eyes assessing me. We said nothing. Mom was steering us around the room as if we were the prow of a ship, the three of us, aligned and intertwined, moving as one.

Donna had simply disappeared. I don't know how it happened. One minute I was walking into the funeral home with her at my side, and the next minute my mother—how radiant she looked!—collected me as if I were a package she had been expecting. She didn't even pause to greet or thank the delivery person—Donna, my wife. And I was too caught up in the world that is my mother to notice that my wife had fallen by the wayside. I was pulled into the world I knew by heart, that I knew in my bones: Planet Mom.

My mother was introducing Lara and me now to Mr. So-and-So, who had been a patient of Dad's, and to his wife, whose parents and even *grandparents* had also been his patients.

I smiled and nodded, and on the opposite side of my mother, Lara did the same. Off we went to greet someone else. I let myself be paraded. It was surreal, my hopes through the roof. Just like that, I seemed to be welcomed back into the fold as if nothing had happened. A wonderful relief, a giddy sense of possibility, and also that unreal quality that I recognized so well: the whiplash of going from three years of estrangement to instant intimacy, without passing Go, without a moment's pause. Like an alternate universe we had all just stepped into, over an invisible threshold.

Hours later, when the room emptied, Donna materialized, together with our Italian cousin Nina—Renzo's daughter—who now worked on Wall Street. Nina's girlfriend, Claudia, and Lara's partner, Jess, had both stayed back at Mom's house with Jess's kids, aged five and two. My mother turned to me. "Are you coming home?" she asked. "We'll have dinner—there's plenty for everyone."

Donna and I agreed, and we drove back to the house. I hadn't been there in years. It was strange to enter now—the dark brick floors of my childhood, the majestic Oriental rugs, the immense fire in the fireplace. Nothing had changed. Everything had changed. *I* had changed.

By the time Donna and I arrived, the house was

already full of lesbians. We were everywhere—cooking a giant pot of pasta in the kitchen, setting the table, finding extra chairs, playing with Lara and Jess's kids. For the first time, I met Claudia, and marveled at how young and sharp she and Nina looked together. Earlier at the funeral home, Mom had made sure that none of our partners were present or came near us. She'd introduced only Lara and me to the guests; occasionally she might introduce our cousin Nina. I was used to playing it straight around my mother. But now in the privacy of our home, Mom seemed perfectly happy to be the matriarch of a family of six lesbians and two little girls conceived with the help of an anonymous donor. Dad's death had left the family completely free of testosterone.

Dinner was boisterous and good-humored. Wine helped. I started to relax a little, enjoy myself. We laughed and told stories—some involving Dad's battles with squirrels and snow and peanut shells; others about our own foibles. Although Lara couldn't meet my gaze, I felt relieved to be welcome at home. We seemed to draw closer with each story, each peal of laughter. As if we were a family again.

"How long are you staying?" my mother asked at the end of the evening.

"Just overnight," I said. "We're staying at a motel on State Street."

"So come for breakfast!" she said.

Donna and I exchanged glances. I was quietly elated that my mother had invited us, but I also wondered whether perhaps we should quit while we were ahead. I tried to assess how Donna was holding up, whether she could take any more of this. She was doing the same with me. Optimism won out, and we exchanged an *oh, what the hell* shrug.

By the time we got to the house at nine the next morning, everyone but Mom and Lara had already left. Jess had driven the two kids back to Burlington; Nina and her girlfriend had taken the train to New York. Mom made us a fresh pot of coffee. Her homemade babka, sprinkled with powdered sugar, rose proudly from a platter of crumbs, half of it already ravaged.

"Sit, sit!" my mother commanded, and rushed around, pouring coffee, cutting giant slabs of babka onto plates. Lara hesitated before sitting across from me. She seemed uneasy in my presence and shifted sideways in the chair, facing Donna, who sat next to me.

Donna smiled at her. "So, how are you doing?" she asked Lara. Donna had always liked my sister, but had been jolted by Lara's outburst five years earlier, when she had called in a rage, backed out of our wedding, and slammed down the phone. It was the first time Donna had seen that side of Lara for herself.

Lara shook her head. "It's really rough," she said. "But you know, it's also sort of bittersweet. Dad was so debilitated—this past year, it's been really touch-and-go. So in a way, it's almost a relief. But still . . . I don't know . . . have you ever lost someone close?"

Donna nodded. "My mother died in March."

Lara's eyes went wide, and she looked as if she'd been sucker-punched. I was pleased. It didn't seem to have occurred to her that our lives might not have gone swimmingly this past year either.

"Oh, wow," Lara said. "I'm sorry. Um . . . how did . . . ?"

"It was very sudden," Donna said. "She had a heart attack."

"Oh," Lara said. "So you've been through all this. . . ." She looked uncomfortable.

My mother said nothing.

Lara slouched lower in her chair. She had avoided eye contact with me ever since I'd arrived yesterday, and now that we were sitting directly across from each other, her discomfort was even more evident. I studied her closely, interested in how she would handle my presence, and surprised by her obvious difficulty in playing the part of friendly sister set for us by our mother. Instead, Lara stared at her hands, picked at her cuticles, and turned to face Donna. "So how are you doing now?" Lara asked.

Donna shrugged. "Well, I just finished chemo. I had a recurrence of cancer, and surgery last year. So I was still on chemo when my mother died. I had to interrupt treatment for a week to go to Atlanta." Donna didn't mention that after surgery, six out of the eight lymph nodes had tested positive for cancer.

I enjoyed seeing Lara's reaction. It seemed to take the wind out of her sails. I dared Lara to look at me, but she kept her head down. She even had trouble looking at Donna now.

My mother remained silent, but I could see that she had been following the conversation closely. Her face was attentive, but she said nothing.

"Oh," Lara mumbled. "I'm sorry."

Donna changed the subject. "The babka is delicious!" she said.

My mother beamed. "Would you like another piece? Another cup of coffee? Helen?"

We shook our heads.

I realized that I was hoping for something like sympathy from my mother. At least some acknowledgment that Donna and I had been through our own nightmare during the past year. But Mom seemed utterly unaffected by our news.

"I was afraid I would lose her," I said to my mother. "It's a very aggressive cancer."

My mother's eyes flashed. "This was my *husband!*" she said.

I felt as if I'd been slapped. I kept quiet.

Lara abruptly pushed away from the table. "I'm going to do some work outside," she said. She had been fidgety all morning, and she was already halfway across the room before my mother called her back.

"Wait, Lara! Wait, before you go—bring me one of your cards, would you? You know, your new business card."

Lara rolled her eyes. "Mom—"

"It won't take a moment—just bring the card. Please, darling?"

Lara sighed and left the room.

"Wait till you see it!" my mother said excitedly. "I am so proud of her! You know, she was just wonderful to Dad over these past years. . . . I don't know where I would be without her. She helped with everything—the doctors, the medication, the paperwork. . . . It's her thought-fulness, you know—she is so generous, so loving and devoted."

I found my throat tightening with hatred for my sister and irritation with my mother. *She's just lost her husband,* I reminded myself. *I have no right to expect anything from her. I'm lucky she's even invited me into the house.* Still, it grated on my nerves, her going on and on about what a fucking hero Lara was.

My mother smiled. "You know, whenever Dad asked, Lara would drive home to be with him. He wanted her all to himself, so she would come alone, without Jess, without the kids. I think this was a very important time for them—they repaired their relationship, you know."

I said nothing, but thought acidly, *Wow, it must have taken quite a while to repair Lara's memories of Dad repeatedly raping her as an infant.*

"Oh! Here it is!" My mother jumped up when Lara came back with her wallet. "Look at this!" Mom said, holding Lara's business card out to me. "Just look at this!" My hackles went up, the old jealousy. At forty-four, I was still angered by my mother's rapture over my older sister.

Lara dropped her head, apparently uncomfortable herself under the circumstances. I almost felt sorry for her. She tried to slip out of the room, but Mom called her back.

"She's a professor! Do you see?" Mom said. "Here, look—take it, read it! You see? She's a professor, chair of the department at the medical school!"

I pretended to look at the card—I noted the university's seal in red and black ink—okay, so she'd rated a card with color. Big deal. I used to have a business card with two colors too, till Massachusetts suffered budget cuts and everything went back to black and white. Mom motioned for me to pass the card to Donna. "Imagine! Chair of the department! A professor!"

Lara managed to escape out the back door

and started attacking the yard with what looked like some kind of giant machete. My mother sat down, still beaming, staring at the card. "You see," she said in a more solemn tone. "It was all worth it." She nodded thoughtfully. "All those years . . . We had some hard times. . . . But it was all worth it."

I was too stunned to say anything. On the one hand, I was relieved that Mom acknowledged those "hard times." That was not like Mom. Usually she swept anything unpleasant out of memory, and certainly out of mention. She edited the story of her life over and over, as one might crop a photograph in a darkroom, so that she could bear to see the image of herself reflected back at her. I hung on to this tendril of validation from my mother, and choked back my rage. Lara's career achievement made it "all worth it"? Thank God Donna was here, I thought. I needed a witness. I needed someone to tell me that I hadn't made all this up.

My mother poured herself more coffee and began talking animatedly about the last year with my father, how crippled he was from Parkinson's, how she'd insisted on taking him outside on forced marches to keep him moving, holding on to him with a thick leather belt she tied around his waist so he wouldn't fall over.

I could picture her doing this, my eighty-two-year-old mother marching Dad up and down the long driveway, feeding him when he could no longer hold a spoon, cleaning him, nursing him with her matter-of-fact love. She told us about the times he passed out at breakfast, the times his heart stopped and she had to call an ambulance, the times she'd followed in her car, and then taken him home once they'd brought him back to life. She had been through such a hard year, I thought. Yet she was not complaining; on the contrary, she spoke about these ordeals as if they had been a series of challenges and accomplishments. She even joked about how she had felt like Dad's personal trainer, proudly dragging him around when he could barely move. She was nothing if not a survivor. The two of them, tough, stubborn fighters.

Outside the window now, I could see my sister hacking up giant tree branches, hauling them across the yard, and raking up the smaller branches as if she might rip the tree's roots right out of the earth.

My mother kept talking vivaciously, filling us in on every detail of the past few years. Donna listened quietly, while I jumped in now and then with a comment or a question or a laugh. It felt so good to be talking and catching up like this, to feel the warmth in Mom's voice, the evident pleasure we took in each other. She said nothing at all about my book, nor the cause of our break in communication for three years. But she did mention the "deal" she had made with my father.

"What we agreed on, Dad and I, is that he would have a separate relationship with you. Of course, his Parkinson's was very bad, you know, he could barely hold a pen. But I agreed that as long as he could still address the envelopes to you, I was willing to attach the stamp and put his letters in the mailbox." She leaned toward me, smiling warmly. "But I was so relieved," she said, with a confidential nod, "when he finally forgot your birthday this year, so I wouldn't have to post the card to you."

Strangely, the content of Mom's words slid right past me and Donna; we were both enchanted by the tone of her voice, the sweetness in her face. It wasn't until we were driving back to Boston that afternoon that we began to make sense of what Mom had actually said, the meaning of the words she had spoken.

"Did she really say that?" I asked.

Donna nodded.

"Wow. That's pretty wild." And yet, it was so like Mom. She had always seemed so comfortable with contradictory feelings. Had I challenged her, I'm sure she would have thought nothing of it. Of course she loved me, she would have said blithely, but surely I could share her relief when Dad forgot my birthday?

We stopped on the way home for Donna to call her father from a phone booth. She had been calling him regularly since Lucy's death; today was her parents' anniversary. "I think Helen and her mother are finally reconciling," she told her father. Afterward she told me that he was genuinely relieved. I smiled, my grief at having lost my dad now mixed with gratitude for the reawakening of my relationship with my mother.

Later during our drive, Donna told me what Lara had said to her as we were getting into our car to leave. I was hugging my mother good-bye, while Donna was talking with Lara. "You've certainly been a saint through all this," Donna told her.

Lara looked at the ground. "You wouldn't say that," she said, "if you knew what I've done."

Six weeks later we would learn what she was talking about.

If madness reflects an inability to cope with reality, then in the context of my family, I had always been the "normal" daughter as a child, and it was Lara who had been crazy. But years later, Lara emerged as the true-blue, stable, and devoted daughter of our parents, and it was I who had gone off the rails; I was the one who no longer fit the family norm.

Did Lara have a real mental illness? She wasn't schizophrenic or bipolar or diagnosed with multiple personality disorder. The only word ever mentioned consistently was *borderline*. But I think it's more accurate to say that she is imbued with the madness that comes with being the loyal daughter in a family of secrets and trauma.

The envelope arrived Christmas Eve. It was bulky, so I assumed my mother had sent me an article from a magazine that she thought I'd find interesting. But when I opened the envelope my mother's short note fell out—*It is a sad and difficult time for all of us.* The cover letter addressed to her from her attorney unsettled me, but I felt relieved when I skimmed through the ten pages of my father's will dividing every-thing equally between me and my sister. And then I reached the last page, the codicil. A list of numbered paragraphs, each starting with the words *Delete HELEN FREMONT* and ending with the word *predeceased.* The blow felt visceral, and I collapsed to the couch, unable to breathe. The papers fell to the floor at my feet.

Donna was in the kitchen, finishing up her rice casserole which we were going to bring to our friends in Sudbury, as we did every Christmas Eve. I had already made the dessert, a flourless chocolate torte with raspberry coulis. "What is it?" Donna said, stepping out of the kitchen.

I looked at her, but no words came. She rushed over to me. "What happened?"

"I'm . . . dead," I finally said.

"What?"

"My mother sent my father's will."

Donna picked up the pieces of paper at my feet, trying to understand what had happened.

And then a sound escaped me, a long-drawn-out howl of rage that sounded utterly foreign, a sound so loud and strange, it seemed to have issued from somewhere else altogether. It didn't sound human. It alarmed me, and it must have scared Donna too, because she started crying. She was sitting next to me now, and had thrown her arms around me, and we started rocking back and forth, and I was crying, hot tears that streamed down my face. I tried to speak, but no words would emerge, just that terrible scream, that gut-wrenching wail.

I don't know how long we stayed like that, holding each other and crying. I finally calmed down enough to speak. "He signed a codicil and killed me off."

Donna shook her head. "Oh, Helen," she said.

The following weeks were a blur. I did not contact my mother or sister, and I did not hear from them. I managed to stumble through my days at work, but kept my head down and my door closed and avoided conversation. My shrink wrote me a scrip for an anxiolytic that helped me get some sleep, but I still found myself awake in the middle of the night, shaking with rage. I wrote in my journal and tried to pass the time until the gym opened at five, when I could work out for a couple of hours.

Later that winter, I hired a lawyer and drove to Schenectady to meet with him. He helped me find out more about the codicil: my mother had driven my father to the small-time lawyer who preyed on the elderly—*Don't let Uncle Sam take your hard-earned money!*—and Dad had signed the codicil removing me from the family four months before he died. My mother signed an identical codicil to her own will that day, though I wouldn't find out until I received hers in the mail after she died twelve years later, at the age of ninety-four.

Contesting a will is rarely successful, my lawyer told me. But when he saw the name of the attorney my family had chosen, he blanched. Apparently their attorney was not known for his scruples. If you were going to contest a will, my lawyer said, you had a chance of finding something wrong with a will written by the attorney my parents had hired. I suppose I had a slight case, if I wanted to fight. My father had been suffering from Parkinson's for fifteen years by the time he signed the codicil. Although he had been a ferociously willful man in his prime, it's fair to say that he was under my mother's and sister's influence at the end.

"Just be aware," my lawyer advised, "if you contest the will, it will mean war."

That seemed fitting. Fifty-six years after my parents had survived one war, I could start a new one in a court of law.

I drove home and mulled it over for the next few days. The days turned to weeks, and then the weeks became months. I tried to imagine what it would be like to take my mother and sister to court. I tried to picture Lara and Mom driving to their attorney's office and spending money to defend themselves from me. It seemed like a colossal waste of time and money, and besides, what good would it do? Even though my parents had squirreled away hefty savings, I didn't really care about their money. I cared about their killing me off.

My new status as "predeceased" occupied my life now. I became a sort of Dead Helen Walking, defined by that piece of paper, and compelled to tell everyone about it. Being disowned seemed to fit naturally into even the most casual conversations with colleagues and friends. For a dead person, I certainly inhabited the role with great gusto.

But despite my rage, I couldn't generate the desire to fight my mother and sister. Contesting the will would only keep me more closely bound to them: we would be engaged, literally, in a battle of wills, and we would become even more entrenched in our outrage at each other.

So I decided not to contest the will, and not to sign it either. I had spent four decades wrapped tightly around the open wound of my family's past, and now I'd been sliced free. It was a violent separation, to be sure, but there were no bloody limbs, and I had Scotch-taped together a new family for myself: I had Donna; I had the dog and a cat and two fish and an apartment in Boston and a job and a small but solid group of friends.

And I had a lot to think about.

twenty-five

O ver the following years, I continued to try to make sense of what had happened to my family. It's instinctive to search for meaning, to arrange and rearrange the pieces of the puzzle in such a way that they fit, that there is a satisfying snap of recognition, a sense of truth, of something resonating deeply.

As I discovered in 1999, soon after the publication of *After Long Silence*, my family's Jewish identity wasn't such a big secret after all. Although my parents had hidden it from Lara and me, and from their postwar friends and colleagues, it turned out that dozens of *other family members* (of whom Lara and I had been unaware) knew all about us. My mother had sworn them to secrecy.

It was only after my book came out that these cousins of my mother's—living in the States, in Canada, in Europe—contacted me and invited me into their homes, where they showed me decades' worth of correspondence from my mother, dating back even to before the war, when Mom had still been in high school. The cousins explained that in 1961, when I turned four, my mother told them never to contact me or Lara again; Mom was afraid we would remember them and realize we were family.

For the next forty years, unbeknownst to Lara and me, Mom and Dad had continued to get together with these relatives for bar mitzvahs and weddings and other celebrations. Here was a photo of my father in a yarmulke, standing in a synagogue in New York at my American cousin's bar mitzvah. There was a picture of my mother smiling with the bar mitzvah boy, her own cousin's son. My mother continued to send her cousins photos of Lara and me in grade school, junior high, and high school each year, together with news of our lives. There I was, in a red jumper in the first grade with my front tooth missing; here was Lara in her blouse buttoned up to the collar. My mother's handwriting on the pictures identified our grades and ages.

Ultimately whatever secrets Zosia and my mother were keeping played a hand in defining my relationship with my own sister. Our family was built on a construction of lies that rattled our very foundation and held us in a state of madness. But even in writing *After Long Silence*, I didn't understand the extent of the secrets. It would take another decade before I could see more clearly what had eluded me for most of my life.

The first lie was simple and obvious: like

thousands of other Jews during the war, my mother and aunt denied their Jewish identity and pretended to be Catholic in order to survive. In 1945, after the war was over, most survivors let go of this pretense and reclaimed their heritage. But my mother and aunt couldn't do that. They both owed their lives to Uncle Giulio, the only real Catholic in our family. By marrying Zosia during the war, Giulio not only provided her with a Catholic identity, but he also elevated her to the status of countess. She was safely above suspicion during the wartime roundups of Jews in Rome. Their marriage was convenient for my uncle as well, I think, since it provided Giulio—who I believe was gay—legitimate cover as a family man.

Giulio also used his influence as a prominent lawyer and government official to rescue my mother when she was arrested at the Italian border in 1942 after escaping from Poland. As the (presumably) Catholic sister of Giulio's wife, Mom was later spared the Nazi deportation of Jews in Italy.

In short, neither my mother nor my aunt could expose their benefactor. To reveal that he had married a Jew—even after the war was over—would have destroyed Giulio, both financially and socially.

And then there was Renzo.

"I wouldn't be surprised," Renzo told Lara

and me years ago, "if, in fact, I'm your mother's son." Lara nodded; she'd already done the math. Nine months after Mom escaped from Poland with Luigi, the Italian officer who saved her life, Renzo was born. Mom's arrival at Zosia and Uncle's apartment in Rome in 1943 coincides with Renzo's birth.

At the time Renzo suggested this, I have to admit I was skeptical. This was 1993, fifty years after Mom's escape and Renzo's birth, and I was still struggling to understand the implications of our sudden discovery that Mom, Dad, and Zosia were all Jewish Holocaust survivors. By comparison, the question of whether my cousin was really my half brother seemed less pressing.

It's only now, after so much else has unraveled in our family, that I find myself returning to this conjecture, turning it over in my mind, examining it from every angle. The stories that my mother told me of her escape and imprisonment came in small snippets over decades. Now, piecing them together, the narrative emerges more clearly.

Mom told Lara and me that Luigi, the Italian officer stationed in her hometown of Lvov, had risked his life to help her escape Nazi-occupied Poland in October 1942 by providing her with false papers and an Italian soldier's uniform. At the age of twenty-three, she posed as a soldier under his command, and Luigi brought her with him on furlough to Italy. But the two were arrested at the Italian border, and Mom, presumed to be a spy, was held for execution by a firing squad. Uncle Giulio sent a lawyer to the border who explained to the Italian officials that Mom was not a spy, but the Italian officer's *girlfriend.* Luigi had a wife and children in Bologna; he needed to keep the story of his Polish girlfriend a secret. The Italian officials had a soft spot for romance, and with the help of Uncle's bribe, they released my mother.

From there, Mom said she was transported to an Italian concentration camp in the south of Italy, where she and the other inmates (all women) were treated surprisingly well, and allowed to spend their days knitting and reading.

"Really?" I asked her when I was in college. "They let you knit and read in a *concentration camp?*"

My mother had smiled. "Yes," she said, adding in a whisper, "Many of them were *prostitutes.*"

"But prostitution was legal in Italy," I said. "Why were they in a concentration camp?"

My mother shrugged. "It was the war," she said.

I kept quiet.

"We had it easy," she continued. "We were fed reasonably well and didn't have to work." She smiled mischievously, admitting that in the concentration camp, she had more food than most people in Italy had during the war.

So why was she released nine months later in June 1943, when the war was still raging?

"Oh, the warden let me go," Mom said, waving her hand as if this were a silly question. "Zosia came to visit and buttered him up with her baked goods."

So according to Mom, she was released from the concentration camp on the whim of the warden, who became good friends with Zosia. Mom arrived in Rome that summer and lived with her sister and my uncle Giulio, and the newborn Renzo. "I was *fat* then," Mom told me years later. She said she'd destroyed all the photos taken of her during that time because she hated how "chubby" she looked when she first got to Rome.

I never questioned Mom about it, but now I wonder. She'd always told us how hungry everyone in Italy was during the war; there was never enough food to go around. She and Zosia and Giulio had had to sell their clothes and belongings for food; Mom often skipped meals, so that Zosia and Giulio would have something to eat.

In retrospect, it seems less likely that Mom could have gotten fat as a prisoner in an Italian concentration camp during those nine months of the war, than that she had grown large with child at a home for unwed mothers in southern Italy.

I'm guessing that when Mom and her newborn infant came to live with Zosia and Giulio in Rome, all three pretended that Renzo was my aunt and uncle's son. They baptized Renzo and raised him as a Roman Catholic count, the legitimate heir to his father, Giulio, and mother, Zosia. He was exempt from the Nazi roundups of Jews in Rome a few months later. In the privacy of their home, I imagine that my mother nursed Renzo and raised him as her own. Renzo was three years old when my father—Mom's long-lost fiancé from before the war—miraculously escaped from the Gulag and turned up at my mother's doorstep in Rome.

My father's survival was inconceivable. "No one came back from Siberia!" Mom told me. Since learning of his deportation by the Soviets in 1940, she'd heard nothing further. People simply disappeared in Siberia. Until he showed up in November 1946, my mother and aunt and uncle had pretty much solved the problems of genocide and homophobia and illegitimacy. They had outwitted Hitler and Mussolini and proper society. The sisters had come under Uncle's skirts; he had taken them in and covered them all with his Catholic nobility. He sired a son—it was a perfect story. It worked. They had forged a family of four, just like that. It was brilliant.

My father's appearance a year and a half after the war ended threatened to blow the lid off that story. They had to scramble to incorporate him into it, but this is where the lies became corrosive. This is where the secrets began to do real psychic harm, I think. My father had made it out of the Gulag, and into the arms of a plot so twisted that he was trapped and frustrated by it for the rest of his life.

Within days of my father's arrival in Rome, Zosia and Uncle had arranged for Dad and Mom to be married during my mother's lunch break from work. Dad agreed to pretend to be Catholic; he couldn't have married her otherwise. After six years in Siberia, he told me, he no longer cared what religion he was. Time was short; he wanted a family.

What was more difficult for him to accept, he told me, was the "unnaturally close" attachment between three-year-old Renzo and Mom—my father's new wife. Renzo had always slept in Mom's room, and now the child threw a fit at the prospect of being moved into Zosia's room when my father showed up. "We were newlyweds!" my father told me. "But Mom wouldn't part from the boy, so the child slept in the same room with us. I was very hurt by that." My father would resent Renzo for the rest of his life. Years later when he told me about Mom's overriding attachment to the child, he was still angry. Why wasn't she happy to be reunited with him, her long-lost fiancé? Why did she only care about her *sister's* child?

It wasn't until five years later—when Renzo was eight years old—that my mother finally left Renzo behind with Zosia and Uncle, and emigrated to the States with my father. The parting at the Rome train station was so traumatic, my mother told me, that she couldn't bear to leave the boy. "Renzo was in hysterics," she said, her eyes tearing up forty years after the fact. "It was devastating." Heartbroken, she traveled with Dad north to Hamburg, the port from which their ship would take them to America. But my mother was so distraught by the separation, she left my father the next day and returned to Rome, in order to spend one last day with the child. The following day, she rejoined my father just in time to board the ship for America.

As Mom tells the story, my father was also hurt that she had refused to have children right away. "I put him off," my mother told me. "I wasn't like the other women who survived the war. They couldn't *wait* to have babies! The DP camps were filled with screaming infants, and Dad was desperate to start a family. But I didn't want to have a child until I was settled down."

My mother managed to postpone for three more years, until Dad finally put out his shingle in Evans Mills, and Mom ran out of excuses. In 1954, Lara was born. This is when my mother collapsed in an all-consuming depression that lasted years.

If my conjecture is true—if Renzo is actually my mother's son, fathered by Luigi, the Italian officer who saved her life—then the baby embodied all that my mother had lost and left behind: her parents who were murdered soon after her escape; her friends and other family members who were gassed, shot, and starved; her hometown and community that were destroyed. She escaped with nothing but the seed of this child growing inside her. Years later, to be ripped apart from Renzo must have been cataclysmic for her.

How does someone survive what she went through? How could Mom endure the weight of her secrets and losses? At least she and my father could share the secret of their Jewish identity with each other and with a handful of her other surviving relatives in the U.S. But I imagine Mom was utterly alone with the anguish of her separation from Renzo. Only Zosia and Uncle knew the truth. No wonder she depended so desperately on her sister. Their bond was built on a lie so difficult and painful and protective, Mom would have lost her mind without Zosia. As for Lara and me—we were the malleable offspring, living receptacles of a contorted reality of which we were unaware.

That's madness. Maybe that's why we had no

diagnosis when we went to family therapy in the 1960s. Our madness was an ill-fitting story that chafed against the reality of who we were and whom we loved and why. We weren't in the *Diagnostic and Statistical Manual.* We were just what people look like who are suffering a mistaken identity, people who are forced to live in a plot they don't understand and cannot make sense of.

In 1992, after Lara and I discovered we were Jewish and learned of our parents' experiences during the Holocaust, I asked my mother why she had hidden this from us. After all, many of their Jewish friends had posed as Catholic during the war, but dropped the façade afterward. "But I couldn't do that," my mother said. "Don't you see?"

"Why not?"

"Because—" She stopped abruptly, and a look of despair crossed her face. "I would lose Zosia."

"What do you mean?"

Mom shook her head. "Zosia wouldn't have allowed me to continue to be her sister," she said. "And Renzo—" She choked up. "I could have visited only as a friend, but never as family." Then she looked away, and I couldn't bear to press her further. She changed the subject, and I let it go.

My father survived the war on his own wits,

with luck and minimal outside help. But my mother and her sister—their story would have ended in the war. Without Uncle, they would be statistics, folded into the six million. I would not be here to figure this out and write about it.

There's irony for you—so I am predeceased, after all. By exposing the truth, I have revealed the fact that I shouldn't even be here in the first place, that I'm alive only thanks to the lies that Uncle, Zosia, and Mom made up in order to survive the war in Fascist Italy in the 1940s. If not for my father's arrival in 1946, I have no doubt that my mother, Zosia, and Giulio would have raised Renzo together and lived in Rome for the rest of their lives. Mom always told me that by the time she got to Rome, she had no interest in men or marriage, and she flatly refused all the men who asked her out. But my father's miraculous survival messed up the arrangement. He wanted a family—his own children—and my mother's attachment to her son nearly broke her in two.

It was this broken mother, stripped of her own son, who became my father's wife, and my sister's mother and my mother, on a new continent, across the sea from her firstborn. My mother raised me and Lara in a state of loss that she could not admit even to her own husband.

The Jewish thing—that was just the loose thread hanging out. That's the piece that had been dangling in our faces all our lives, but Lara and I didn't realize it till we were in our thirties. That's the string we pulled, and look what fell out!

It must have thrown Mom into a panic. You pull on that string, and it's only a matter of time before the entire delicate weave of stories unravels. Mom and Zosia made it to the finish line. They protected my father from finding out, but only by cutting me off and away. They could not risk losing their story in order to keep me. That's the bargain I made them choose: me or the story. They chose the story they had made, the fictions they had spun, the others who depended on those lies for their lives.

And Lara? Like me, she is collateral damage of the war. She too suffered the loss of sense and the loss of her sister in the fallout of our family. Lara and I tried to make up for our parents' losses, but more often than not, we reenacted them. Our bond is strong; we are tied together in our estrangement.

epilogue

My sister and I are now in our sixties. She's a good person. Following my mother's death at the age of ninety-four (twelve years after my father's death), Lara offered to share what was left of my parents' finances, and I accepted. It was all arranged through lawyers and bankers. She has never acknowledged her role in disowning me, and despite her efforts to reconnect, I feel safer keeping my distance. It's not clear whom I trust less with our relationship—my sister or myself. I have learned to be more realistic about the limitations of repair.

For decades I tried to figure out what was wrong with our family, whether Lara was actually mentally ill or whether her behavior—and mine—was simply the result of living in the contorted reality of a history that was hidden from us. I can't put a name to what was wrong with my sister, or what was wrong with me. She and I are survivors of a family of secrets, and perhaps that's the most accurate diagnosis of our condition. We represent two sisters' different expressions of a similar past.

I've also wondered whether scientific evidence

could prove that Renzo is my mother's biological son, rather than Zosia and Uncle's child. But having been disowned and declared dead by my family, I'm in no position to obtain DNA samples from them. As a lawyer, I'd like that kind of proof. But as a writer, I need something more important—to understand who my mother was and how she managed to survive with the lifelong debt she felt to her sister, the love she felt for Renzo, and the obligation she felt to us. And I need to understand how my father managed to carry on, feeling that he had married a "deranged" woman, but unable (and perhaps unwilling) to know the details of the six years during the war in which they had been separated. And finally, of course, I need to understand my own relationship with my sister, to have compassion for the children we were and the adults we became, and to come to peace with how we managed to live under the burden of so many secrets and lies.

Even with scientific proof, I would still need this narrative to help me make sense of my family, to understand the crazy logic in the decisions we made and learned to live with. After the war, Zosia forced Mom to make a choice: either be true to her own identity, and lose her sister and Renzo; or choose to live a lie, but remain sisters with Zosia. Fifty years later, I faced a similar dilemma—I could either continue to live a lie, and remain in my family; or I could lose my sister and family, but speak my own truth. Unlike my mother, I chose my truth, and in so doing, I lost Lara and my family.

Families are proof that love and loss go hand in hand. My family is gone; my family is everywhere. They live inside me, and we're finally learning to get along with one another. Or at least to accept what is, and love what can be loved. After all, there is an awful lot of love in our stories. It would be a mistake to think otherwise.

acknowledgments

I am ridiculously lucky to have had so many people help me with this book. My *bashert* editor, Jackie Cantor, and agent, Gail Hochman, form the greatest dynamic duo of superheroes in the galaxy. Jackie, your smarts, enthusiasm, zany sense of humor, and friendship mean the world to me, not to mention the freakish amount of time and hard work you've put in on my behalf. And Gail, you are at once fairy godmother and magician, having managed to tease a manuscript out of the 400 pounds of alphabet soup I kept sending you. Thank you for your tireless encouragement, savvy, and pizazz.

I'm bowled over by the extraordinary talent and dedication of the whole team at Gallery Books and Simon & Schuster. Special shout outs to John Paul Jones, Joal Hetherington, and Lisa Rivlin for making this book so much better than it was before it reached your nimble minds. I am equally indebted to Jennifer Bergstrom, Sally Marvin, Lisa Litwack, and Sara Quaranta for your support and expertise—dreamboats all.

Elise and Arnold Goodman, thank you for your unwavering support and energetic work for over

421

two decades. I don't know where I'd be without you. I'm also grateful to Sam Gelfman and Kirsten Wolf, whose thoughtfulness and advice were invaluable. Deanne Urmy, a bouquet of thanks for your generosity and for offering me a way forward.

Helen Epstein was the instigator and overseer of this project for nearly twenty years, providing meticulous editorial and writerly advice, psychological counseling, excellent meals, and friendship. Helen, I would probably still be frozen before a blank screen if not for you.

Heartfelt thanks to Lisa Rubinstein for listening to me for the past thirty-six years, for nevertheless believing in me, and for patiently teaching me to believe in myself.

I have subjected a number of dear friends to countless awful drafts of this book, and their patience, insight, and friendship made it possible for me to continue. Special Gladiator gratitude to Mari Coates, Susan Sterling, Tracy Winn, and Stan Yarbro. Additional shipping containers of thanks to Jim Ayers, Joanne Barker, Charlie Baxter, Michael Collins, Nancy Gist, Cynthia Gunadi, Trish Hampl, Ehud Havazelet, Richard Hoffman, Marjorie Hudson, Madeline Klyne, Geoff Kronik, Maria Lane, Guillaume Leahy, Sumita Mukherji, Bob Oldshue, Lisa McElaney, Kevin McIlvoy, Peg Alford Pursell, Mary Elsie Robertson, and Robin Romm for providing help and support along the way. For those of you not listed here (you know who you are), thank you.

I am grateful for the generosity and support of Henry Ferrini and the Gloucester Writer's Center and to the Warren Wilson MFA Program for Writers and its merry band of alumni who have sustained me all these years.

Finally, thanks to Donna, my first and most faithful reader, accomplice, and soul mate. This is not the only line she's fixed in this book.

Center Point Large Print
600 Brooks Road / PO Box 1
Thorndike, ME 04986-0001 USA

(207) 568-3717

US & Canada:
1 800 929-9108
www.centerpointlargeprint.com